Touched by Magic

The Tommy Bolin Story

By Greg Prato

Printed and distributed by Greg Prato
Published by Greg Prato
Front cover photo by Jim Summaria [www.jimsummariaphoto.com],
back cover photo by Richard Galbraith [www.myspace.com/richardgalbraith],
and dedication photo by Marvin Rinnig [www.musikfoto.com]
Book design and layout by Linda Krieg
Copyright © 2008, Greg Prato. All Rights Reserved.
First Edition, December 2008

ISBN: 978-0-578-00317-7

Contents

Foreword

After reading 'Touched by Magic,' it seemed to me every interview 'takes you there' for the moment. Being three years younger than Tommy, it walked me through my teen years; when I used to visit Karen and Tommy in Boulder, listen to Zephyr live at 15, and growing up following his career/playing music together, and eventually, joining the Tommy Bolin Band. One of the many things being said in this book is how kind and loving Tommy was, and what a beautiful soul Tommy had. Yes, he did have a serious drug problem, but we all have our problems, and deal with them in different ways. He chose his path because he truly was going to be a star, whatever it took. He had very loving parents, two brothers, and a very religious upbringing. My mom was truly a saint, and it showed in all of us. Enjoy the book—I give 105 stars to Greg!

Thanks,
Johnnie Bolin (Iowa, October 2008)

Introduction

Let's think back to the late '80s/early '90s—before Nirvana dropped—shall we? Perhaps more so than any other time in history, within the realm of rock guitar, most guitarists played exactly the same (speed demon city), and looked like a bunch of dorks (spandex, hairsprayed mile-high hairdos, pointy guitars, etc.). Remember? This was exactly the time in my life that I got serious about playing guitar, and during my first year of college, I was always on the lookout for bands and guitarists that stood out from all the same-sounding foolers. This is when I first came across the music of Tommy Bolin.

It was around this same time that a double disc box set of Tommy's had been released, 'The Ultimate,' which I had read about in all the guitar mags. But since I wasn't familiar with any of his music, I was hesitant to take the plunge . . . that is, until I saw it in a 'bargain bin' at my favorite local record shop for a price I couldn't pass up. Flipping through the box set's booklet, I was pretty taken by the fact that Tommy looked totally different from most guitar heroes past and present—in fact, with his multi-colored hair, leopard fur platform boots, and silver lamé suits, he was so flamboyant that he probably even made Freddie Mercury blush.

Then came the good part—listening to the music. The first few songs had some tasty bluesy licks, but nothing really extraordinary. But about midway through the first disc, when a little song named "Alexis" came on, it all seemed to come into focus. For most of the remainder of the set, I was pretty darn blown away—here was a guitarist that technically could hold his own with all the guitar heroes you could think of, and also, could handle just about any imaginable musical style. And for the most part, the quality of songwriting seemed to be the most important thing to Tommy. In other words, it was not all about mere fretboard blazing.

But there was only one catch . . . Tommy was not a modern day guitarist. In fact, he had been dead for nearly a decade and a half by this point. Never the less, I began trying to turn on as many friends as I could to his music, and purchased a healthy amount of Tommy-related recordings. Although I never went on to do much as a guitarist, my love for Tommy's music remained very much intact. And even when my musical tastes would shift throughout the years, I would continue to go through sporadic 'Tommy listening phases,' which is a testament to how great and enduring Tommy's music is.

As some of you may be aware, I eventually became a writer for a bunch of music sites and magazines, and in 2005, I convinced my editor at Classic Rock Magazine to let me do a feature on Tommy's career. It was through doing interviews for that subsequent article (which ran in November of that year), that I became friendly with two gentlemen—Tommy's brother, Johnnie Bolin, and producer Greg Hampton, who was working on what became the 'Whips and Roses' releases. After doing quite a few interviews for the article, and with everyone happy with how the article came out, I realized that I had a pretty good head start for a book. After consulting with Johnnie and getting his blessing, I was eventually off and running with putting a book together.

It still baffles me that Tommy Bolin remains as underrated and overlooked as he is. Of course, dying before he had truly 'made it' certainly didn't help matters. But he still has a large and diehard cult following—take a look at the large amount of posthumous Tommy releases and Tommy-related sites on the internet. There is no reason why Tommy Bolin shouldn't be mentioned in the same breath as Jimi Hendrix, Jimmy Page, Jeff Beck, Eddie Van Halen, etc. If this book in any way helps heighten awareness of Tommy's music—and accomplishes telling his equally triumphant and tragic life story—then I'll be more than happy.

Enjoy!
Greg Prato (New York, October 2008)

p.s. Have questions or comments? Email me at gregprato@yahoo.com.

Cast of Characters

Carmine Appice [Vanilla Fudge/Cactus/Beck Bogert and Appice/Rod Stewart drummer, played on 'Teaser' and 'Private Eyes']
Martin Barre [Jethro Tull guitarist]
John Bartle [Friend of Tommy's]
Bobby Berge [Zephyr drummer, played drums on 'Teaser' and 'Private Eyes,' and for part of the Tommy Bolin Band's 1976 tour]
Ritchie Blackmore [Deep Purple/Rainbow/Blackmore's Night guitarist]
Barbara Bolin [Tommy's mother]
Johnnie Bolin [Tommy's middle brother, played drums for part of the Tommy Bolin Band's 1976 tour, vice president of the Tommy Bolin Archives, Black Oak Arkansas drummer]
Richard Bolin [Tommy's father]
Rick 'Pudge' Bolin [Tommy's youngest brother]
Tommy Bolin [Zephyr/Energy/James Gang/Deep Purple guitarist, session guitarist, solo artist, singer]
G. Brown [Former rock journalist/KCUV D.J.]
Charlie Brusco [The Outlaws' manager]
Max Carl [Energy singer, keyboardist for part of the Tommy Bolin Band's 1976 tour, solo artist, .38 Special/Grand Funk Railroad singer]
L.C. Clayton [Tommy's security guard for part of the Tommy Bolin Band's 1976 tour]
Jeff Cook [American Standard/Energy singer, Tommy's lyricist]
David Coverdale [Deep Purple/Whitesnake/Coverdale-Page singer]
Tom Dowd [James Gang producer]
Mike Drumm [President of the Tommy Bolin Archives]
Robert Ferbrache [Employee of Ebbet's Field and Feyline Management, sound engineer, photographer]
Barry Fey [Tommy's manager for most of his career, concert promoter]
Harold Fielden [Legendary 4-Nikators drummer]

Mike Finnigan [Keyboardist/singer, solo artist]
Jim Fox [James Gang drummer]
David Givens [Zephyr bassist, ex-husband of Zephyr singer Candy Givens]
Bill Graham [Concert promoter]
Jan Hammer [Jeremy Steig/Mahavishnu Orchestra/Billy Cobham/Jeff Beck keyboardist, played on 'Teaser']
Greg Hampton [Producer of 'Whips and Roses I & II,' Science Faxtion singer/guitarist]
Jimmy Haslip [Bassist for part of the Tommy Bolin Band's 1976 tour, Yellowjackets bassist]
Glenn Hughes [Trapeze/Deep Purple/Tony Iommi singer/bassist, Black Sabbath singer, solo artist]
Earl Johnson [Moxy guitarist]
Eddie Kramer [Jimi Hendrix/Led Zeppelin engineer, producer/engineer of Zephyr's 'Going Back to Colorado' album and Jeremy Steig's demos that Tommy played on]
George Larvick [The Patch of Blue bassist]
Jake E. Lee [Ozzy Osbourne/Badlands guitarist]
Jon Levicke [Photographer]
Reggie McBride [Session bassist, bassist on 'Private Eyes,' and for part of the Tommy Bolin Band's 1976 tour]
Alphonse Mouzon [Session drummer, Weather Report drummer, solo artist, Tommy played on Alphonse's 'Mind Transplant' album]
Jeff Ocheltree [Stage manager and drum tech for 'Private Eyes' tour, John Bonham's drum tech]
Kenny Passarelli [Energy/Barnstorm/Joe Walsh/Elton John bassist]
Henry Paul [The Outlaws singer/guitarist]
Gene Perla [Session bassist, Jeremy Steig bassist]
Dale Peters [James Gang bassist]
Phillip Polimeni [Friend of Tommy's, owner of Glen Holly Studios]
Prairie Prince [The Tubes drummer, played on 'Teaser']
Elliot Rubinson [C.E.O. of Dean Guitars]
Stanley Sheldon [Energy/Peter Frampton bassist]
Nicholas Simmons [Artist, designer of Dean's Tommy Bolin 'Teaser' tribute guitar]

Nikki Sixx [Mötley Crüe bassist]

Mark Stein [Vanilla Fudge singer/keyboardist, keyboardist on 'Private Eyes,' and for part of the Tommy Bolin Band's 1976 tour]

Tom Stephenson [Energy/Joe Walsh/Gary Wright keyboardist]

Otis Taylor [Harmonica player/guitarist/singer, solo artist, friend of Tommy's]

John Tesar [Tommy's lyricist]

Karen Ulibarri [Tommy's girlfriend]

Steve Vai [Frank Zappa/Alcatrazz/David Lee Roth/Whitesnake guitarist, solo artist]

Narada Michael Walden [Songwriter/producer/drummer, drummer on 'Teaser' and 'Private Eyes,' and for part of the Tommy Bolin Band's 1976 tour, solo artist]

Joe Walsh [James Gang/Barnstorm/The Eagles guitarist/singer, solo artist]

Gary Wilson [Energy singer]

Dedicated to the memory and music of Thomas Richard Bolin
August 1, 1951-December 4, 1976

Early Years/Iowa

Johnnie Bolin: My mom was born in Nebraska, and my dad was born here in Iowa—outside Sioux City. When they first met, my dad was in the service and my mom was manufacturing cookies—in a factory. They had met at the base or something like that, and eventually married. He was full-blooded Swede and she was full-blooded Syrian. Our name wasn't Bolin; it was Erickson when my grandparents came from Sweden. But there was too many Erickson's—so they changed their last name. Bolin's a German name. My dad worked at a packing plant—he was a beef de-boner. My mom, her brother owned a grocery store, so she did that as a family business. She did that a lot of her life, and my dad, it's good money in the Midwest to be working in a packinghouse. It's really hard work—he was only going to do it for eight months, but wound up working there for 38 years. That's when they had Tommy.

Tommy was born in Sioux City on August 1, 1951, I was born on August 17, 1954, and my brother Rick was born on January 24, 1957. My mom's birthday was January 24th—she had him as a birthday present [laughs]. My dad's was February 25th. I got pretty close to Tommy—I got to know Tommy a lot easier than it was for Rick, because he was six years younger. I had another brother that died—he was born in '53. His name was Bobby. He died at birth—it was a malpractice deal, but they didn't have that back then. The doctor was drunk or something. He's got a little baby grave out there in the cemetery. He would have been one year older than me and Tommy would have been two years older than him.

This is my grandfather's house I live in now—when my mom and dad got married, they all lived here. It was handed down from my grandfather to my uncle, to my aunt, and eventually, it was willed to my mom. Now I have it. At one point, one uncle and four of my mom's sisters were living here—it's a six-bedroom house. My mom, dad, and Tommy briefly lived upstairs when Tommy was young—his bedroom was upstairs, next to my mom and dad's bedroom. Most of Tommy's baby pictures were taken here. But my family and me didn't always live in this house. When they had me, we moved downtown, by the river—by South Bottoms. It's at the bottom of the hill, by the Missouri River. Me, Tommy, my mom, and dad lived down there until my younger brother, Pudge—which is what we called Rick—was born. Moved from there, and got a three bedroom house on the north side. We grew up there, went to school right around here, and then we moved on the other side of town completely. We went to Catholic School—I think Tommy went 'til eighth grade, I went 'til sixth grade, and my younger brother went 'til fifth or sixth. Then, on to public school.

Richard Bolin: I told him, "You've got to be the best. You're going to be the best at something." He tried boxing, and he'd seen someone getting his nose [bloodied], and he gave that up. Football, a guy broke his leg, and he gave that up.

Johnnie Bolin: My dad was a huge fan of Elvis. He didn't play any instruments at all—I mean, he played the harmonica . . . doesn't everybody? And my mom wasn't really musically inclined, but very caring—both heavily behind us. He bought us all instruments.

Tommy Bolin: I used to watch this show on T.V. called 'Caravan of Stars.' I saw Elvis, Johnny Cash, Carl Perkins. After seeing them perform, I knew that was what I wanted to do.

Richard Bolin: I took [Tommy] to see Elvis at the auditorium, and he thought to himself, "Well, I want to be on that stage." He liked that, being on the stage, and I said, "Yeah, you'll get to be on a stage." He got so enthused about Elvis. I got albums, and he started . . . the one he got down pat was "Heartbreak Hotel," so I had him do that, and he pantomimed that. He did it over at 'Kids Corner' [a local T.V. talent show], and they thought he was so good they had him back three days later. There was so many phone calls that came in, and I thought if he's that good, I'll bring him up to the lakes [Lake Okoboji]—they had a deal up there, an amateur show. About a hundred kids tried out for it, and he got to be one of them to get to do the program, and he said, "I know dad—I'm going to win." He came in second to a tap dancer from a little town there that won, and he felt kind of bad about that. But I said, "Well, about half the town was there applauding for her, so that's what they went by, the applause." Then he says he's going to start up his own band. So I got him a guitar from Sears, I bought one for 65 dollars, an amplifier, and the whole works. He kept beatin' on that, and said, "Dad, I'm going to be the best at something."

Tommy Bolin: I actually started on drums when I was thirteen, and played them for two years.

Johnnie Bolin: Drumming can help your guitar playing out, and guitar playing can help your drumming out. Tommy's rhythms came from him messing around on the drums.

Tommy Bolin: Then I went to guitar for a year, played keyboards for a year and a half, and went back to guitar. It was just the right instrument. You're in direct contact with the music you're making by having the strings under your fingers. It's not mechanical like a piano.

Johnnie Bolin: He knew he wanted to play guitar.

Tommy Bolin: I started off on Hawaiian steel. I didn't want to, but for some reason, the guy said to start on Hawaiian steel. Mr. Flood was his name. He tuned the guitar to the E-ninth, which is real Hawaiian, but I would never play it. I'd always stand in front of the mirror at home and put on the records and pretend I was playing rock. Mr. Flood didn't know Elvis—he liked Hawaiian music. So I left that and started taking lessons from this lady, Mrs. Sullivan, who had an unbelievable collection of guitars. She had tons of them. And she was very 'country and western.' I started off reading, and the first song I learned how to read was "On Top of Ol' Smokey," but I thought, "This isn't it either." So then I went to another place, the music store where all the bands hung out—all my local heroes—but what they taught me wasn't it, either.

Johnnie Bolin: Tommy got his first electric guitar when the Ventures came out—he liked all that surf music. Got to the Beatles, and my dad knew I was interested. He really wanted us to play—it was our idea, but it was more his idea getting the equipment. It was a priority to him to get us good instruments at a young age, and get us playing as soon as he could. I mean, after the first two weeks I had my drums, I was playing at a bar—I was only twelve. About a year after Tommy had the Sears guitar, he got a Gretsch guitar—a Country Gentleman—which was about $800. He had a Telecaster—I guess that's where the Telecaster neck came in later. He and I had a Mosrite, which was about $500. My first set of drums was $400—a nice pink champagne set of Ludwig's with cases and cymbals. And eventually, my younger brother got a guitar—Rick had a really good voice, but he was kind of unsure of what he wanted to play. He always had a guitar, but it didn't come real natural. I can play guitar a little bit—drums are my gig. But with Pudge, he jumped in and out of playing guitar and singing. Tommy was sensational.

Richard Bolin: He'd practice and practice and practice. In fact, he'd walk clear out to Morningside Peters Park [about five miles]—there's a musical store out there, and he went out there a dozen times a week, and he'd beat on a guitar, and he just kept beating on it day and night. He'd go to bed with a radio in his ear, and wake up with one.

John Bartle: He and I met in this local music store in Sioux City—United Teachers of Music. We were both twelve or thirteen. We started meeting there every Saturday, and learned how to play. He was special right off the bat—everybody knew it. I went to West Junior, and he went to North Junior. Then we ended up going to Central High School together.

Tommy Bolin: It was a waste. I was getting into guitar and wanted to take a music theory course. Well, I found out that they only offered it in alternate years. Where's that at? Do they teach English every other year?

George Larvick: I had started a band called the Triumphs, which included some of the members that eventually played in Denny and the Triumphs. The members were Denny Foote, I, my brother Brad, Steve Newhouse, and Dave Stokes, who was the singer. We played for a while, then we made a change with Steve Newhouse to a couple of other players—Danny Owens. That went along for a while, I then went with a band called the Mustangs, for about six months. In that period of time, the band had changed—they got Steve Bridenbaugh, Brad Miller, and then Brad brought along Tommy. When the Mustangs wanted to go a different route, the guitar player in that band, Steve Fleck, wanted to play bass. That meant that I had to leave, because I was the bass player. At that time, I talked to the old guys I played with, and we were really interested in doing the band again and letting some members go. So I had come up with the name 'Patch of Blue'—I had gone to the Sidney Poitier movie, 'A Patch of Blue.' That day, we got all the guys together, let Denny Foote go, I became the new bass player, and changed the name to Patch of Blue. It was '65.

There was a real nice melting pot of music to play at that time. That was another issue—Patch of Blue didn't just play songs by the Kinks. We played the top songs on the bill at the time, and on top of that, we'd jam "Call Me," "Girl From Ipanema," a lot of jazz things. That's what became [Tommy's] style—it was so much different than a lot of other people, because we jammed all day long on "Stormy Monday Blues," and we'd do stuff like "It's Not Unusual" by Tom Jones. He liked that music just as much as playing something by Cream or Jimi Hendrix. He was very spunky. He knew always what he wanted to do—play music. He was very energetic in the music way of wanting to learn and play. He loved playing jazz-rock things and he loved anything with a non-standard beat—he liked to develop different things. We played a lot of R n' B in those days too—stuff like the Four Tops, or older stuff by the Impressions or the Temptations. And at the same time, you might play something by B.J. Thomas. So we had every kind of style you could think of in our line-up. But Tommy was outgoing, and he liked to be a bit of a showboat. That was part of his charisma, and that's why he became who he was—you have to have that part of him.

John Bartle: He liked Wes Montgomery—that's how we both learned to play octaves. We used to listen to the Blues Project, he liked Michael Bloomfield. Hendrix was a major influence on all guitar players. A friend of ours, Legs Diamond—his name was Stan Sowienski—was in Denver. He was older than us, and he brought back Frank Zappa [a single that included the song "Why Dont'cha Do Me Right"] and [Jimi Hendrix's] "Purple Haze." It was certainly the first time I heard it, so I think it was pretty close to when Tommy heard it. And we all wigged out. Stan brought back the single, but then immediately, everybody started getting the 'Are You Experienced?' record.

Tommy Bolin: Well, Django Reinhardt and Carl Perkins. But, really, anything I heard I was influenced by. There wasn't any particular person, outside of Hendrix. In high school bands, we used to play anything and everything—"96 Tears," "Gloria," "Hang on Sloopy," whatever. I used to listen a lot to Rolling Stones records and play along with them when I was first starting. I'd just experiment around the I-IV-V progression. It's a good way to learn, jamming around basic music; and the Rolling Stones' first albums were pretty basic.

George Larvick: When we had the Patch of Blue, I went out to a music store in Sioux City and bought a 215 blue Kustom head with reverb in it, and two cabinets. And then [Tommy] traded in his Bandmaster, and went to a blue Kustom head, and a blue/green 215 cabinet. Then he couldn't get enough treble out of the Kustom, so he bought a VOX treble booster, and he amplified the guitar with that. For about a year, he played that.

John Bartle: At that time, we had a couple of different amps—Super Beatle, a Kustom, and then we both went to twin reverb Fenders. We used to do some trading.

George Larvick: There could be a band every two or three blocks, and there were a lot of barrooms to play in. In those days, you had Y.M.C.A. dances and sweetheart dances everywhere. Every junior high had a dance, and every high school had dances. Our band—because we had opened up for other bands that were a little older than us—had grown two crowds. We had a crowd that was used to the older bands, and a crowd for the schools. We worked for two agencies in the area—Eddie Skeets, and C&M Booking Agency, which was Dick Matousek. We had a lot of bookings, because the band looked really good—we had nice clothes. The band was real responsible and on time. Our parents were there and very supportive—we had a school bus converted and painted, with the name on it. Because we were responsible and looked nice—at that particular point, we were all alcohol and drug free—that made us reliable. The other part of it was we sounded good. We could play the music as good as the actual original players, or even better. We played with several bands, like the Beach Boys, Herman's Hermits, the Animals, Paul Revere & the Raiders. Eddie Skeets had us open up for a lot of the bands that came into this area—because we were affordable and had a following of 2,000 kids from schools. He knew he was going to have a crowd—through the kids and through the bands.

Johnnie Bolin: My father was really behind what we were doing, as far as this music thing. He'd drive the bus for Tommy—they had a school bus, and the dads took turns driving the bus. I was three years behind Tommy, so whatever he did for Tommy, he did for me three years later—he was also our bus driver. It was great having your parents behind you. Allowed us to stay out. We weren't really troubled kids, but sometimes going to play these gigs out of town, we didn't get home until 2:00 in the morning. And when you're fourteen years old, you've got to kind of wonder. But they took real good care and offered guidance—they knew exactly what was going on with us.

Richard Bolin: I had to get up and go to work at 5:00, and that was about the time I got in and got everything situated. There wasn't much sleep, but I sacrificed, and it was worth it.

John Bartle: He had a terrific relationship with [his parents]—they dotted on the boys. Everything that his parents did was for their [sons'] benefit. They were totally selfless, really.

Phillip Polimeni: I was about 14/15 years old, and I was in a band in Sioux City. There was an Air Force base there, and my dad was in the Air Force. I was playing in Sioux City, and on the side of the stage, I saw this kid with long hair. He walked up to me, and goes, "Where did you get those clothes?" I said, "They're from New York—my cousin owns a clothes store, and he sends me clothes." We started talking, and just hit if off. He was one of those guys that knew mod stuff right away—the stuff was from Jumpin' Jack Flash in New York. Sioux City didn't have those kind of clothes, and he was tripping—it was stuff that the Cream was wearing. He right away identified with the clothes, and then we started with the music. We became friends—he would come out to the house and jam. I remember him coming to the house in a snowstorm with his guitar. My dad walked in the room, listened for a minute, called me over, and said, "That fucking kid is good! He's going to make it." You knew as soon as he picked up a guitar, he was amazing. He could play anything—"Misty" or any rock n' roll song. He had that versatility that he could play jazz, Brazilian. And he couldn't read music.

Tommy Bolin: A lot of times I wish I would have learned to read [music]. But I'm very impatient. I used to try and take things in leaps and bounds. Now I've realized it's got to be step by step.

George Larvick: I don't want to say that Tommy wasn't a good player, but when he started in the band, he was adequate to do the job. You could see that he had talent. He was a year and a half younger than me, so if I was 15, he would be 13½, and he was very surprising at 13½. What he had that really made him good was his desire to want to learn and play. He cared about music all the way—he didn't want to do school or any of that stuff. He was totally enthralled in the music—and so were we at the time. We practiced from the time we got home at 3:15/3:30 until 10:00 at night if we could—every night of the week. And then we'd play on the weekends. His desire was so good, and he played 24/7. By us being established, playing all those jobs, and rehearsing all the time, he soon got to the stage where we were. The ability has to be there, and it was for him. He was six or seven inches shorter than me, but as time went on, we were about the same height.

Johnnie Bolin: When we used to watch him rehearse, at first, we couldn't even go downstairs. And then eventually, we could sneak down and sit on the landing so they couldn't see us. Eventually, we could go down to the landing where they could see us . . . but we couldn't go down in the basement [laughs].

Bobby Berge: I'm here in Sioux Falls, South Dakota, and Tommy lived in Sioux City. I was playing with a group called the Velairs—that was about

'65/'66. We used to play five, six nights a week. All the young guys kind of looked up to us—they used to come see us play and come to rehearsals. And Tommy was one of them. When I first met him, it took a little while to know what was going on there. I started jamming with him and some of the local guys. See, the Velairs was an oldies-type band. Then the psychedelic and English stuff started happening, and these young guys were into it. So I started loving that, and started jamming with him on the side. The first time I saw him play was with the Patch of Blue—I saw him at the Rooftop Ballroom. They were a horn band, and did R n' B and stuff. But what struck me was they were doing Tom Jones' "It's Not Unusual," and then Tommy did a solo. It really struck me—"Damn, this kid is good!" I played in town there for the next couple of years, then [Tommy got into] Hendrix and Eric Clapton. Then me and him got together more—he could play the Hendrix stuff, so we used to jam down at a club called the Patio, in Sioux City. He could do all that stuff, and I loved it, because that's what I wanted to play.

John Bartle: When we were fourteen, we played in a lot of bands together. We were playing in a band in Vermillion, South Dakota, called the Chateaux. It was a cover band. We bought a '37 Plymouth together—we didn't even have licenses. We paid $7.50 a piece. It was 30 miles to practice, so we used to drive that to practice, and then take turns taking it home and parking it around the corner from our folks' house [laughs]. Finally, the police pulled us over, and made us sell it because we were too young.

Johnnie Bolin: It didn't have any seats, so they put a couch in the front seat! Tommy drove a little bit back then, but then he never drove again. He never wanted to drive—that was it.

George Larvick: See, when he decided to play with the Chateaux, that was a full-time college touring band. That band was three-pieces for a lot of the time—they would add a piece now and then—but Tommy really had to learn to play a lot of things there. He had to be 'the fill man' as well as the lead player in that band, and they were full-time, so he was playing a lot more college venues than teen dances. He grew a lot right there.

John Bartle: Tommy had an M3 Hammond organ at the time—we'd switch off playing guitar and organ, back and forth. We'd do stuff like "Here Comes My Baby" by the Tremeloes, "Higher and Higher" by Jackie Wilson, "To Love Somebody" by the Bee Gees. And the standards of rhythm and blues back then—"Midnight Hour," etc. Jimmy Smith was the rage and [Tommy] had always been a jazz nut. He learned how to play in the key of C, so everything we played, we had to transpose to the key of C. Eventually, that's how I learned, too. So, we'd trade off back and forth on the organ and guitars, and two guitars sometimes. But Jimmy Smith, like "The Cat" and those songs, was a big influence. He was real jazzy. Again, he managed to come up with a way to play some riffs that were really totally legitimate. But as far as being accomplished? No. He knew straight triad chords.

John Tesar: I was in Vermillion, seeing a friend at the University of South Dakota. He was a keyboard player, and he played in the kind of bands that the radio station played, KLMA. That was an A.M. station that people in the Midwest listened to—and he played a Hammond B3 organ, with soul bands. Jaime Kibben was his name—he ended up being a soundman for N.P.R. [National Public Radio] and a filmmaker. He recently died. Anyway, he and I were about 18, and were talking about music. He knew that I had been writing lyrics for about a year or more—without knowing exactly where they were going to end up. He said, "Hey, there's this 15-year-old kid that just came out of locking himself in a basement somewhere, teaching himself how to play a Hammond organ. Since I know how hard it would be to play at the level he's playing, I think we ought to go over and hear what he's done. When I heard him yesterday, I couldn't believe it." So we just went over there to kill some time and see what this guy sounded like. But as you can imagine, 18-year-olds don't take 15-year-olds all that seriously. Until we heard him. Then we said, "Oh . . . a young rock n' roll Mozart!" So in the conversation, Tommy knew who Jaime was, because Tommy was playing guitar in these same kinds of bands, and knew that Jaime had been on stage and touring already. He looked up to him like a more senior member, although he was only 18. The three of us started talking.

Bobby Berge: He took the time to send me a letter in Sioux Falls. All I remember was in the middle of the letter, in big letters, was "I LOVE JAZZ." He underlined it. He was so influenced by Hendrix, and got that big, fat, thick, sustaining sound . . . technically, I can't explain it. He was into jazz from the get-go, and blues, funk, R n' B, and rock, and that's what set him apart from everybody else. He could play it all.

Tommy Bolin: My first joint I smoked on the stage of a place in Sioux Falls, South Dakota. I smoked my first joint live. The band was smoking it right on stage in this club, no one knew what it was.

George Larvick: Tommy was a lot of fun to be with. He was kind of cocky. You could tell it in his playing—he could be wild.

Johnnie Bolin: We grew up together—he did tell me to stay home and don't hang around with him downtown [laughs].

Tommy Bolin: When you come from the Midwest, you have a more open mind than if you come from the West Coast or the East Coast. At that time, you had vagrants, rich kids, and everything.

John Bartle: [Tommy dated] nobody steady. I used to see him at night sometimes—there was a girl that he'd see quite a bit, that lived three doors down from me.

Tommy Bolin: The first time I got laid was with this chick whose mother used to work at night. She says, "Come on over." I think it was her first time too. Her dad was home, I had to sneak through the window. I was fourteen. I didn't use a rubber. I never used rubbers. I found one once, used, and the looks grossed me out too much, that I thought, "*No.*"

John Bartle: When we were kids, we used to stay over each other's house a lot. We used to pick pot down at the creek—these great big things of wild ditch weed—and we took a big batch to his house one day. Poured a bunch of Chianti on it, and put it in the oven to dry it. His dad walked in, and he goes, "What the hell is that smell?" And we said, "We were cooking a pizza . . . and we burnt it!" We tried to smoke it, got big headaches, and threw it out [laughs].

Johnnie Bolin: They were all pretty good—#1 band in town. But you could tell Tommy was growing fast as a player. I remember the time that Patch of Blue fired him, they came over the house. They went to his bedroom for about 15 minutes, came out, and left. Then Tommy came out about five minutes later, and goes, "Well, they fired me. I play too loud." But y'know, he couldn't hang here very much longer.

Colorado

Tommy Bolin: The turning point probably came when I was kicked out of high school in my hometown, for having long hair.

Barbara Bolin: One day, [the school] called and said, "Come and get him." I went, and he said, "They told me to cut my hair." The rule of the school was to cut it just to the collar. And we did. He went back to school, and they said, "No, go back home and cut it above your ears." He said, "Never. If you can't accept me, then I can't accept you. I followed all your rules, and they aren't good enough." But we tried—we went to the superintendent of schools to see what we could do, because he did want to finish school. And he said, "I can't see anything against it. I've got George Washington here on my desk, and I don't see anything wrong with him." But he said, "I guess a rule is a rule." I said, "But it isn't a rule—to cut it above his ears." He said, "Well, there's nothing I can do." So we went home, and the next day, they came from his school, and said, "You're doing wrong by not making him come back." And I said, "No. I have faith in him, and I know him—I'm his mother. It's like he said, if you can't accept this, then that's the way it is."

Tommy Bolin: I got kicked out of school when I was 15, just approaching 16, for my hair. I said, "Who's complaining, which teacher?" And he goes, "The teachers aren't complaining, the kids are." I said, "O.K., here's what I'll do—before each class, I'll stand up in front of the room, and if one person objects, I'll cut my hair." But he said they didn't do it that way. I remember the seniors cutting everybody's hair but mine, because I would always hang out with the seniors. The leader of the pack was a guy named Stan. Stan and Dan, twins. One was a hardcore 'can't-wait-to-get-into-the-army' guy. That was Dan. Stan was like a freak, a real freak, and a really good bass player.

Johnnie Bolin: My mom and dad were behind him 100%. I mean, to let a kid go hitchhike at 15 . . . it's not like they didn't care, but he said, "That's what I really want to do." And my mom didn't like the fact that they kept throwing him out of school.

Tommy Bolin: After they kicked me out of school, there wasn't anything else for me to do back there. I can't do anything but play guitar. So I moved to Denver and started a band there.

John Bartle: I'd say that last three to six months, he was talking about it a lot. Then, before he left, that's all he talked about—"I've got to get out of here." The next thing I know, "Hey John, here's a postcard."

Johnnie Bolin: A couple of his buddies moved to Colorado. He had a place to stay for a little while. Actually, a guy out of the Patch of Blue moved out there—he was two years older, so he was 17. So Tommy thought, "That's the closest, coolest place." Denver had a scene.

Barbara Bolin: I went and talked to the Carmelite Nuns, and asked them to pray so he wouldn't go. And they said, "No, we'll pray so that if he goes, that was the right move." And then I felt right about it. We missed him, but we knew he was doing what he wanted to do, and we had faith in him.

Jeff Cook: I first met Tommy when I had a band called Crosstown Bus, and we were rehearsing in the basement of a dress shop in downtown Denver. We were playing away, and we kept hearing this rattling upstairs. We went upstairs, and standing at the door was this kid. There was a blinding snowstorm—it was the dead of winter—and there was a kid with a guitar in his hand. He said, "Hey man, can I jam with you? I heard the music." We wanted to blow him off because he was a couple of years younger than we were. But he was so persistent—we let him come in, set up, and play. Needless to say, we fired our guitar player the next day and Tommy joined our band right there. He had a really great spirit. He was very full of life and pretty fearless for somebody of his tender age. But he played with a confidence and skill level that was far beyond his years. Very funny, very impish. Always in search of a good time—no question about it. The music industry was a giant ticket out of whatever lives we were leading—we were becoming successful doing it, and it was a tremendous experience. After that band broke up, we formed a band called

American Standard, which was a trio with me as the lead singer, and our first gig was at a love-in or a bee-in. It was a hippie gathering/lightshow kind of a thing, and our performance caused a riot—it was unbelievable. We knew we had something then.

Otis Taylor: I met him at the Denver Folklore Center. We were like in the same 'Denver Folklore Center Classroom.' It was a great store—a lot of people learned a lot of things. Owned by Harry Tuft. He was hanging out there. [Tommy] was like 15—but I wasn't that much older, either [laughs]. He was there before the Family Dog [a concert venue] opened up in Denver.

John Tesar: Tommy was headed for Boulder, but he needed song lyrics to finish some things he was working on. My friend said, "You ought to talk to John, because he writes well and he's going to Boulder." So we talked a little bit about it. I didn't have an address and he didn't have an address, so, what's the likeliness of anything happening? Well, I got a knock on my door once I got to Boulder a month or two later—it was Tommy! He remembered how to spell my name, called my mother, gotten an address, and found me. So I started feeding him lyrics and being totally amazed at the process—I was still a college student at the time. He was living in a series of apartments.

I would write things on a typewriter and give it to him, and he would critique them and put them to music if he could, or hand it back to me, and say, "This is too long, this is too short. I want this to rhyme down here, and not over there—can you rewrite it?" So we did that throughout our relationship. Normally, I would write alone, and then bring it. In the same way that we would sit down, he would have a whole bunch of chord progressions and some melodies, I'd have some things on paper. So we'd sit down and he'd say, "I've got this chord progression," and at that time, neither one of us would have considered ourselves singers—but we wanted to write. So we would ham it up with this material. Pretty quick we'd say, "This is a really short line, followed by two long lines." We would count where do breath breaks come, and where does he want to change it from voice to instrumental, and where does it seem appropriate in the melodies he was playing. We would talk over things like that and how structure would work. Occasionally, he would say he heard this 'thing,' from any number of places—Cat Stevens or James Brown.

Jeff Cook: I guess you remember the struggling parts more than the triumphs. Because we lived in Denver, we did a lot of playing in the mountain areas. We would hop in a van with bald tires, and drive up in the mountains—crossing ice covered passes to play in Aspen or Steamboat Springs for 75 bucks a night. And that was a great chance to bond—our common struggle. Just being a part of the ride that was associated with being with such an incredible talent. The interesting thing about Tommy—he was very humble about his gift, and he never ever made any of us feel that we weren't as good as he was. And in that environment, we were able to grow, and become better players and people as a result of that.

Otis Taylor: I sat in with them. Everyone saw me play harmonica with them—believe it or not, back in those days, there were no blues harmonica players. So everybody let me sit in and play harmonica. And everybody sat in a lot more back in the old days. Back in those days, you were *supposed* to jam—that was part of the whole thing. Kenny [Passarelli] had a band called the Ducks—they'd play in clubs, and I used to jam with them. It was just part of the atmosphere—that time period.

Kenny Passarelli: I was in the Ducks—right out of high school. And it was the summer of love—the summer of '67. There was a type of a 'love in,' and the band that I was playing in, a guy named Bob, his family owned a restaurant off of I-70 in Denver. The backroom area had a hippie-ish sort of bee-in, and I remember seeing Tommy there. I don't know if he asked to sit in, but I remember this kid with long hair and baggy pants. He was really hip looking for a kid who wasn't living in San Francisco. At some point in the night, he played, and we became friends instantly. During the time, there were a lot of people traveling between Denver and San Francisco, and New York and Denver. Denver was kind of a middle ground spot for the hip—even in the beat generation. On 17th Street, there were coffee shops—Jack Kerouac had come through Denver. There was a beat scene there, and it eventually evolved into a hippie scene. Tommy probably crashed at all these people's houses, playing guitar.

G. Brown: Tommy was kind of 'the new kid on the block' in Boulder back in the late '60s, and I was a few years behind him. My whole writing career was tagging along like a kid brother, rather than having both feet planted in the scene. A young kid coming up to college from a suburb of Denver, landing in Boulder, and seeing this going on. This buzz around Tommy in town, it was kind of the nascent stages of guitar heroes. Certainly, there were some obvious guys—Hendrix and Clapton. And then this whole wave of 'fastest gun in the west' type guitarists were coming down the pike. I think among players, Alvin Lee of Ten Years After got a lot of attention. He was pretty fast, but he was just playing off box chords. And Tommy was just as fast, and he was all over the neck. He was a phenomenal talent. And plus, he started playing with other people. He was just as adept at acoustic stylings and jazz improvisation as he was at playing hard rock.

Otis Taylor: He was a monster guitar player—everybody knew that. Everybody knew he was the best. I learned something about musicians—if they have that 'thing,' they have it when they're really young. I think kids have it at a young age—that special thing—and then they have to develop it. Gary Moore is a friend of mine, and he said he was playing gigs when he was 15. [Tommy] had that thing—he was the real deal. I don't know if Tommy was the most original guitar player, but if you hummed it, he could play it. I think all the truly great lead guitar players are the best rhythm guitar players. People don't pick up on that. I do, because that's my thing—rhythm. Like, Stevie Ray Vaughan was a great rhythm guitar player, Hendrix was a great rhythm guitar player, Gary Moore is a really good rhythm guitar player. Tommy could drive a song rhythmically like a fucking monster. That's where people missed it—they don't understand that.

Johnnie Bolin: They had the Family Dog—the scene in Boulder was getting big.

Barry Fey: It was in 1967, and we had opened the Family Dog. I was lucky—I was in the right place at the right time. I had been promoting since January of '67, and I met Tommy in late September of '67. I think the Dead were playing or rehearsing, and he walked in—he had no shoes on. And went up on the stage and started to jam. And I'll tell you—everybody stopped and looked. He was unbelievable. It was the first and only psychedelic nightclub. I convinced Chet Helms and Bob Cohen from Avalon Productions and the

Avalon Ballroom to open up the Family Dog in Denver. It was a smash, until for some reason, the manager of the club was going to show the Denver Police that he was here to 'make his magic,' and they weren't going to tell him what to do. But my position—as sort of a finder's fee—they let me book the local talent. I mean, I didn't have the ability to book like they did—they had Janis and the Dead just hanging all over them. I was going to get 5% of the gross, and I could also use it for my own shows, because I was a fledgling promoter. And I had booked the Doors—it wasn't even a thought at the time of the Dog. They were going to play D.U. and the University of the Colorado. But I got in touch with the Dog, and said, "We'll play D.U. one night and the Dog the next." The only difference is the D.U. show did not have Captain Beefheart. But otherwise, that was my first show as Feyline—September 30, 1967.

I wanted my company to be called 'Feline,' to be associated with the Dog, because the Dog was all the rage. And Gene Winans—he was my salesman at KIMN radio—took the copy down on a Friday afternoon to the station to make the spot up for my Doors show, and he said, "This guy made a mistake, he left off the 'y'." So the spots went out as 'Feyline Productions,' and that's how it stood. After my September 30th show with the Doors, I didn't like the way things were going. It was shaping up to be a war. The police . . . these fucking hippies from San Francisco weren't going to come to Denver and show them what to do. Canned Heat and the Dead got busted. That week, the Denver police raided the Family Dog—we had the Buffalo Springfield. And that just headed it spiraling the wrong way, because the lawyer who owned the building—who was also the lawyer for the Family Dog people—sued the Denver police! He got an injunction for them coming onto the property, unless they were called in an emergency. And then the Denver parents said, "If the police can't go there, neither can our kids," and it started to die. In February of '68, it went out of business. The lawyer called me and said, "Would you like to do shows in the building?" And I said, "O.K." And I did shows as 'The Dog'—I didn't call it the Family Dog anymore—at the same location. After about the third week, the Dog stopped paying me, because they didn't have the money. But they gave me the right to use the name—that's how we get into Phoenix. The Family Dog on the road, so it was the Family Dog that presented Canned Heat and Tommy, New Year's Eve 1967—[American Standard] played at the Arizona Coliseum with Canned Heat.

Otis Taylor: Tommy played [at the Family Dog] with American Standard. One time I went there and jammed with them—a guy gave me this violin, and I put a fuzztone on it. All I could play was this train rhythm. I couldn't even tune this thing—Tommy tuned it backstage. So I sat in with them, one guy said, "Man, you're the most amazing violin player I've ever heard!" I go, "I better stop doing this, *this is jive*" [laughs]! I jammed with Hendrix at the Family Dog—after the Hendrix show at Regis College. Hendrix was playing bass, Noel Redding was [also] playing bass, and Mitch Mitchell was playing drums. They were doing this Traffic-jam stuff, and I was doing a little harmonica. I think that's where some of those rock guys were getting ready to go—into that jazz/Traffic-jam thing.

Tommy Bolin: One night, someone from another band heard us play, and asked me if I wanted to go to Cincinnati. So I went to Cincinnati. I played with Lonnie Mack. Everyone had a Flying V. It was a neat place. But it got to the point where, let's see, we played a lot in Louisville, Kentucky. I'd always go down a day earlier to see my friends. I went down and got there about 2:00 in the morning, at this restaurant. It was the only place open. I said, "Hey, does anyone know where I can crash?" Some guy goes, "Yeah, up the street," so I went up and walked in the room, and there was about 20 people lying on the floor, crashed out. I was so tired that I crashed out too. It was about 6:00 in the morning, and at 10:15 a.m., a cop with a billy club was beating on the bottom of my feet. I was cold, tired, and scared. I was 16. They checked us all, but found nothing. They arrested me for disturbing the peace. If they want to bust you, they'll bust you. So I was supposed to play that night, but they wouldn't let me make a phone call. Luckily, one of the kids got out and called the club, and this lady who owned the club bailed me out.

John Bartle: He ended up over in Cincinnati, with the Ginger People.

Johnnie Bolin: I think that's when he first met [keyboardist] John Faris—John's from Cincinnati. There's some real short stints he did—he went to Michigan or something with John Faris, trying to get the Ginger People going there. But that was only a month. Like Chuck Berry does, these artists will come in, and whoever backs them up will be their back-up band. I think that was the Cincinnati era—Lonnie Mack was playing around that area. Same with Albert

King, Big Mama Thorton. He did the thing with Lonnie for just a short while, 'cause he needed a band and happened to like those guys. A few scattered dates with him. The drummer for the Ginger People, he died, and they had their equipment there, because that's where they rehearsed. They left the mom and dad alone—they went there like a week later, and the mom had sold all their equipment! Tommy had a Guild 175—they're semi-hollow body and electric. It's kind of a jazz guitar, like a Wes Montgomery/Kenny Burrell kind of deal. He had a nice Les Paul, John had a Hammond. It all went. So he had no equipment at all. Then he hitchhiked back to Sioux City, and had to start all over again—get a guitar. The only time he was ever in jail—he was hitchhiking through Kansas, and the police picked him up for hitchhiking.

Tommy Bolin: I was doing acid one night, and it started to get light out—I was hitchhiking and got as far as Junction City, Kansas. At that time, my hair was down to here and I had a permanent. I guess hitchhiking was against the law in that state. The cop said to show him some I.D. I had eight I.D.'s. This was four days after the other bust. We were sleeping under bridges. So I was down at the station for three days. They wouldn't let me make any phone calls. They took me right to the judge. The judge said 30 days in jail. So I was in jail. You just piss all over the floor. One cop felt sorry for me and called my parents. So they sent me down a bus ticket. At 1:00 the guy goes, "O.K., you can go—your bus is leaving at 4:00." He didn't cut my hair, nothing. So they call me out at 2:00—they knew I was dying to get out of there—and they said the judge said I had to have my hair cut. I said I was leaving, I was leaving their fucking town, and he said it was either that or 30 days. So they cut my hair off for sanitation. They burned my clothes, cut my hair. I'd had a permanent, so I looked like a little poodle.

Johnnie Bolin: We went to pick him up in Omaha—my brother, mom, and dad—and we walked right past him! It wasn't a butch haircut, but it was pretty short. He had to come back here, because he had to be released to a parent—he still wasn't of age. So he stayed for a week or two, and then went back out to Boulder.

Tommy Bolin: I've got arrested for such weird things. When I left Sioux City, for instance, on my first plane ride [returning back to Colorado] ó me and this friend of mine, Rolland, who got kicked out of school the same time for having a pierced ear ó we were sitting on the plane going to Denver, and all of a sudden, all these cop cars pulled up. I said to Rolland, "I don't know why, but I think they're coming for us." What happened was, his mother found a quarter-pound of pot under his bed, but burnt it outside before the cops got there, so they didn't have any evidence. So the stewardess said, "These gentlemen would like to see you." So they handcuffed us, and it was a big, big scene. I was on the third floor and he was on the second of the police station. They asked me what kind of drugs I had, and I said I didn't have any. I didn't know what he was talking about. Then I heard a scream, and I looked out the window, and I saw Rolland running out of the building, down the alley, and nobody was chasing him. He got away, hung around downtown Sioux City for three days, hitchhiked all the way to Seattle, and was there for three months. Then he called me and he goes, "I'm tired of being on the run," so he hitchhiked all the way back, went down and says, "I'm turning myself in." So the guy goes, "I can't find your record, could you come back tomorrow?" Me, they put on probation for the year! They said I didn't break the law of the state. They said I broke the law of society for having my hair over my ears.

Johnnie Bolin: It's about this time that he met Karen Ulibarri—his girlfriend forever. He was 17 and she was 18. I don't know how they met—probably at a gig.

Otis Taylor: I dated her for like two weeks, and he dated her forever.

John Tesar: I knew them from so far back, that I don't remember the story. They say if you remember the '60s, you weren't there!

Kenny Passarelli: The other connection between Tommy and myself—Karen Ulibarri's father was in the jewelry business, and was friends with my dad. When she became Tommy's girlfriend, we had family connections. The Ulibarri sisters—we all knew each other. She was this hip clothing designer, and when she became Tommy's girlfriend, he really blossomed. He had someone to take care of him—all he did really was practice, and Karen made clothes for him. He was on his way to being a star—there was no doubt.

Johnnie Bolin: After he left, and he came back from Denver to see my mom and dad, he asked [a local band] to jam, and blew them all away. He was far more advanced in a couple of years—just being on his own.

Zephyr

Tommy Bolin: Uh, the group Zephyr. A Denver-based group that, uh, I did like right after I left Sioux City when I was fifteen.

David Givens: I grew up in Detroit. I had my first paying gig when I was fourteen. I was originally a singer in a folk group—that would have been '62—then I joined a rock band [as a bassist] when I went to college. I then went to California to see this girl. Got to California, didn't like the girl, and didn't like California [laughs]! I had a friend who was a ski instructor in Jackson Hole, Wyoming—I was 18, and everything I had I could carry. So I got on a plane from L.A. and flew to Denver—thinking that I was going to fly to Jackson Hole. Well, there was no plane that went to Jackson Hole. I always thought I'd like to go to Aspen—I was a skier. So I got on this DC-3, and flew to Aspen. When I got off the plane, I walked into the little terminal, and this guy walks up to me and says, "Do you need a place to live and a job?" So that was that. It was working at a ski lodge—"If we need something done, we'll call you."

It was a small town—off-season in Aspen in those days, the population was about 400 people. Candy was there. She'd been going there for years—she grew up in Colorado. She had actually moved there at this point, and she was singing in a jug band. We bumped into each other at a Thanksgiving dinner. I was living at a house with a bunch of people, and this girl I knew kept telling me about this Candy Ramey, who was her hero. She asked me if I'd go with her to see her sing. When we met, there was a spark, and we'd see each other around town. We sorta 'circled' each other for a while. One night, **we** bumped into each other late—she had finished her gig and I had finished whatever I was doing. She needed a ride home—she was staying at Snowmass, which is a number of miles from Aspen. I borrowed a car from the girl who had introduced us, drove her home, and we were together for pretty much the next 16/17 years [Candy and David would marry on October 23, 1968, in Boulder].

I still remembered how to play bass. So when Candy quit the jug band, we started a band, and I became the bass player. Candy and I were living in Aspen. Tommy came up there with American Standard—they were playing at Galena Street East, the locals' rock n' roll club. This would have been early '68. Maybe our guitar player knew one of the people in their band. We went down and met Tommy, talked to him a little in the club, and Candy jammed with his band very briefly. That fall, Candy and I moved to Boulder with our current band—some guys from San Diego. We had a job at a place called the Buff Room. Kit Thomas and Marty Wolfe, local Boulder promoters, came in and brought Tommy with them—they had seen us play and thought there was potential in getting us all together. Tommy and John—their band was called Ethereal Zephyr. So Kit and Marty brought Tommy in to jam with our band. He sat in and we had a good time—Tommy and Candy hit it off quite well.

When we had met him in Aspen, he was sort of standoffish. He was a good guitar player obviously, but he didn't seem very interested in us, and we weren't particularly interested in him. But when we met at the Buff Room, he was much more engaged. When he felt like it, Tommy could be very personable. We hit it off pretty well—we had a lot of laughs, and we all liked the music—very natural for us to play together. So we decided to get together again, this time outside a nightclub—at a friend of ours' house. We had a drummer who was playing with the Fuch's Hate Band, and John, Tommy, me, and Candy—the five of us—played. It was really good—we all dug it a lot. So the next step was we started negotiating with each other about putting a band together. We wanted to keep our guitar player and have two guitar players. Tommy's position was, "No way is that going to happen." They wanted to keep their drummer, and Candy really didn't like this guy for some reason. So we had to look for a drummer, and that's why we went after Robbie Chamberlin.

George Larvick: Zephyr was like Patch of Blue in a way—Candy and Dave Givens were real grounded. They were professionals in the way of they played music for a living and they traveled. They were nightclub-y, but they weren't your standard suit-and-tie-nightclub-guys. They were *rock n' roll* nightclub guys. [Tommy] played with them for a long time, which is where he expanded a lot of his playing abilities. And he did his things in between, and jammed whenever he could.

David Givens: Candy and I didn't like the 'Ethereal Zephyr' thing too much. Tommy and John didn't seem to care for it very much either. I think their bass player had named the band, and he was gone, so that was it—we were now called simply 'Zephyr.' John's role with Tommy was really interesting—John was Tommy's music teacher. John's a really gifted musician—he played sax and flute in addition to Hammond B3. He was the one who taught Tommy a lot of advanced technical stuff—Tommy was forever asking John for some new chords. The very first time we played at our neighbor's house, we were playing jazz and blues material that came very naturally to all of us, even though we were all pretty young. I think in a lot of ways, it was because of John's influence on Tommy. You would never have thought Tommy was 17. Compared to what I hear nowadays out of 17-year-olds, Tommy was very gifted, very precocious.

The first thing that I remember are the rehearsals that we had. Up until that time, every band that I'd been in, we played almost entirely covers. When we started Zephyr, we were not getting high, and we were writing songs. Most of the songs that were on the first Zephyr album, we wrote within the first month we were together. We all lived in one house—Tommy and his girlfriend Karen, Candy, John Faris and his girlfriend, and a guy named Frank Anton, who was our road guy and helped write some of the material, and myself. We rehearsed every day—we wrote and arranged the songs right there. It was so easy to do. I did a lot of the writing and arranging—all you had to do was hum something, and they'd go, "Oh, *like this?*" People would come by and listen to us rehearsing, and be completely knocked out. Word around town was that there was this band being put together that was going to be really great.

Colorado at that time was a lot of fun. Boulder was not an expensive, rich people's town as it is today. It was a college town—but there was a big I.B.M. facility and a lot of government offices. So there were a lot of educated people, but there were also a lot of people from families that had lived in Colorado for 100 years. You could buy a house for a reasonable amount of money. In fact, it was pretty slow economically. Downtown is now a mall, with upscale galleries and restaurants. At that time, it was just a regular little main street with cars and storefronts—many of them vacant. In fact, we rehearsed for a few months in a vacant storefront owned by Bill Arnold, the local Ford dealer. It was right on Pearl Street.

The first gig we played was on the Hill in Boulder [at the Sink]. It was a tiny little place—a nightclub in the back of the college 'cheeseburger and beer bar.' But they had bands play every now and then. By this time, we had met Barry Fey. Barry and his wife came, and Chuck Morris was the guy who managed the place. [Chuck] was just a kid then—he didn't know Barry. In fact, I contributed to his introduction to Barry later on. He was just this kid that was working for old Herb, who owned the place. We played and everything came off great—the band sounded terrific, people were flipping out. It was a great debut. Then we got seriously involved with Barry. Kit and Marty were the ones who took us to see Barry Fey in the first place. Barry was the big shot of rock n' roll around Colorado. Barry and Tommy already knew each other—Tommy had played at Barry's club, the Family Dog. Sort of 'the Fillmore of Denver.' Barry had a partner, Nate Feld, who ran a number of nightclubs around Denver, and was involved in Barry's promotion business. We went down to one of his clubs—I think it was called the Shapes, on West Colfax Avenue—so Barry could hear us play. So we played, and Barry said to Tommy, "I think you've really got something this time." He tells Candy, "You—you're really something special."

Barry Fey: In January '69, my stage manager says, "You've got to see this band, Zephyr." So they come down and audition, and I was just blown away. They wanted me to manage them, and I said, "Let me do what I can," because I'd never managed anybody. I'd only been in the business thirteen months.

Tommy Bolin: We were like this psychedelic blues band.

G. Brown: Zephyr became the premiere 'boogie band' in Colorado. The interesting thing was the context of the times. Mountain Time Zone—not a lot going on counter-culturally, but Boulder was kind of the outpost for that. Really a wild time. People were hungry for something—they just didn't know what it was. They were reading Rolling Stone and seeing what was going on in the west coast and east coast, but as far as our own backyard, Zephyr was what we had. And Tommy was just a special guitar player. Candy was certainly a galvanizing frontwoman—but I think it was Tommy's guitar that raised the roof. They played all the Boulder and Denver clubs, and college haunts.

Otis Taylor: I played blues guitar, but I never thought of myself as a guitar player, because psychologically, Tommy was always 'the guitar player' and

Candy was always 'the singer.' So I never considered myself anything—I was sort of 'the harmonica player.' It took me a lot of years to decide that I actually *was* a guitar player [laughs]! It was a weird thing, because Tommy was so good, how could you even think you were a guitar player? That's how incredible people thought he was.

David Givens: Candy was 'the girl singer,' and there weren't a lot of girl singers in those days. That's why she got compared to Janis Joplin a lot. The other famous woman singer at the time was Grace Slick—she didn't holler, and Candy did. But if Candy was imitating anybody, she was actually imitating a guy named Bernie Fieldings—he was the lead singer in a band called Black Pearl, a Boston band that had come west to find their fortune. They played around Boulder and Aspen during '67 and '68. Her tricks with the microphone she got from him. And I think her approach as a singer was a synthesis of everything she liked. She was a big Elvis fan, a big Bob Dylan fan, a big Robert Plant fan. All those things popped up. In any band, the singer gets all the attention—that's just the way life goes. And Tommy, as good as he was, was not the focal point. We were really *a group*—it wasn't 'Tommy and the Zephyrs' or 'Candy and the Zephyrs.'

She had two personalities—one when she drank, and one when she didn't. She had a lot of American Indian and Irish in her. Genetically, she was one of these people who processed alcohol into some kind of terrible drug. When I met her, she didn't drink at all. She started to drink a little bit as we went through the Zephyr ascent and then more—much more—later. But, let's ignore the alcoholic personality and talk about who she really was—she was very intelligent, a very direct, up-front person. She didn't play games with people—she was funny, sweet, and compassionate. In general, people really liked her. For example, one time, we were in New Orleans. We went down to the French Quarter, and all the guys were walking into bars to check out the strippers and drink. She disappeared, and I went looking for her. I found her a few blocks away sitting on a street corner with this little crippled guy. He was rolling around on a sort of wide skateboard, begging for money—he didn't have any legs—and she was just sitting there having a conversation with him. This may sound funny—she was a white girl, but she was a lot like a black girl. She was real down-to-earth. Both her mother and father were born in West Virginia to middle class families, and had moved west after World War II. She had been born in Iowa, and raised in Colorado. But her people were 'of the earth.' Her dad was a real intelligent guy—I used to play chess with him, and he was just brilliant. She was like that—real smart. She liked to read. She was an artist, photographer. But above all, a genuinely good woman.

Karen Ulibarri: Sure there was magic—it was very exciting. I mean, here's a girl fronting a band. A lot of people either loved her or were repelled by her. She was very exciting as a performer. And here's a young boy who can play guitar like no one's ever heard. People were responding to them—they were bringing in the throngs. And the fact that they would play anywhere, anytime—they would play for any given situation.

David Givens: [Zephyr lived in a house on] Canyon Boulevard. This place was tiny—if it's 500 square feet, I'd be amazed. It was a little, old ramshackle place—living room, kitchen, bathroom, a back porch. It had been Frank Anton's house. I'm not sure how we all ended up moving in there—I think Tommy and Karen were just getting together. Candy and I had a bedroom, Tommy and Karen had a bedroom, John and his girlfriend, Sheba—real name, Phyllis—had a large closet, and Frank had his room in the back. It had the best water in the world. When we used to go out on tour, the first thing we'd do when we came home was to line up at the sink to get a drink of water, because it was so good coming out of the tap. It used to come from St. Mary's glacier in the mountains above Boulder. Then they built a water treatment plant a few years later and spoiled it. [The house] was right across the street from what is now the jail. A developer had started to build a hotel, and had run out of money. So there were these 'ruins' across the street. Later, the city bought the property and turned it into municipal buildings. But at that time, we had a front porch, [you could see] the Flat Iron Mountains, and this big ruined building. It was a quiet, sleepy little road. A great place for a bunch of kids.

Kenny Passarelli: Karen was in 'the hip scene.' It was San Francisco wannabe time. You had the University of Denver, you had a lot of kids from both coasts who came in that didn't get into the University of Harvard or Yale. You had some kids with some money—usually the kids with the money were the ones that could screw up the most. They were the hip scene. And the Vietnam War . . . things were coming together. There were some really hardass politicos at the University of Denver—I mean, they shut the school down! You've got to remember the times were pretty crazy—Boulder had a big demonstration. So as musicians, we weren't really politicians, but we were in and about that whole scene.

David Givens: At this early stage, Tommy was really happy-go-lucky, and Karen was too. She watched out for him—she mothered him in some ways. But they and Candy and I went out to eat and hung out a fair amount—we laughed a lot. It was real lighthearted, and their relationship was real lighthearted—for the most part. As the years went by, they became very close. Karen made his clothes for him, taught him to wash his face [laughs]. Take care of himself. They were both vegetarians—Tommy ate a lot of cheese sandwiches when we traveled. She tried to make a home for them. After we moved out of the house on Canyon, we moved into an apartment a couple blocks over in Boulder, and Tommy and Karen lived right above us. They had a comfortable apartment—she took great care of it. In the early days, everything really went well.

Kenny Passarelli: There was a very hip store called Cotangent—they were right on the Hill, and I believe Karen was the seamstress for this clothing place. Tommy was a hip kid—he wore hip clothes. Tommy was always dressed to the nines. He didn't care—this was who he was. I remember he colored his hair. Maybe Todd Rundgren or one other person [did it first], and then Tommy colored his hair—way back. He was totally out there. He was one of those kids that always wanted to jam—Tommy would show up and want to sit in. That was the reputation he had—he sat in with everybody. I'd see him on the Hill, I'd see around Boulder, around clubs.

John Tesar: Tommy was working really hard at not only his craftsmanship and his musicianship, but his stage presence. In the early days, he really wanted to come across the right way. So not only was it the clothes and the hair, but especially, *the boots*. It was a funny thing to me, because I was from the Dakotas, so even though I had long hair, I was still in Levi's and cowboy boots. I was completely amused with the notion that rock n' rollers were like modern day cowboys—in the sense that you just wouldn't see cowboys in lace-up shoes or hi-top tennis shoes. All of those guys had their boots. Karen was very fashion conscious. She made her living as a seamstress, and of course, she was making

Tommy's clothes. That's why the boots were important—that was the part that he controlled. She controlled the clothes—his wardrobe. I don't remember how fashion conscious the Zephyr people were—Tommy was for sure, and so was John Faris, But the drummer, David, and Candy, they had a Kurt Cobain/grunge thing going—before grunge. That was 'the look' for them.

Otis Taylor: I used to go over to England, and bring back these platform boots and lizard skin jackets, and sell them to Tommy. He loved that shit. And then Jeff Cook and I went over and brought stuff back. Jeff got his hair colored. Jeff did it first, because Jeff and I were over in England. Tommy saw that, and got his hair colored. Jeff and I were early fashion influences on him, because we brought back all these English clothes. Tommy had bellbottoms—English bellbottoms started higher, and American bellbottoms started at the knees.

David Givens: Karen is Mexican—very beautiful, beautiful skin. Enough Native American in her to look Japanese. Her family was very cultured. All the girls were into Mexican arts and folklore. They were Mexican and proud of it. From what I recall, Karen was a girl that liked guys who played in bands. Her dad, Herman Ulibarri, owned a pawnshop or jewelry shop in Denver. *And he hated Tommy.* He hated all of us, because we were longhaired radicals. He had a bunch of daughters—pretty, nice daughters—and they just loved us. Candy and I had a van—a '69 Ford Van, with no windows in it—to carry equipment. One evening, Candy was driving—it was on 16th Street in Denver—and she ran into the back of a cop car! Got distracted, and it wasn't a big smash-up, it was just a bump. But of course, the cops got out and came over to us, and here's all these hippies in this band. It was right outside Herman's store. He was out on the sidewalk, going, "Get those fucking hippies out of here! Put them in jail!" Tommy's hiding in the back, trying to make sure Herman doesn't see him, and Karen was there—had he found out that she was in the van with Tommy, it would have been the end of the world.

Barry Fey: I called some friends of mine and got them booked [for shows]. I don't know how they ended up in the Fillmore, because that was Bill Graham, but I think two weeks after I saw them, they were with Chuck Berry in the Fillmore. I flew up to see them.

David Givens: Barry calls up, and says, "I can book you at the Fillmore West and the Whiskey in L.A., and I can bring all the record companies to see you guys. All you've got to do is get rid of Kit and Marty." And unfortunately—I think this sealed our fate—we agreed. It really was the wrong thing to do. These guys had put us together, really supported us. But, we all agreed. We could have used some adult supervision on that one.

Kenny Passarelli: When Zephyr really started, [Tommy] had a real gig. I think Barry probably put him on salary—he had a Les Paul, good amplifiers.

David Givens: Once the initial stage of getting Zephyr was done, Barry was behind us, and we were on our 'road to hell,' [roadie] Dave Brown showed up and was with us the whole time. Dave Brown was the closest guy to Tommy—he was like Tommy's 'manservant.' They were extremely close.

Barry Fey: I got them a record deal, but I still didn't have any confidence that I could manage. I was taking ideas on who should manage the group, and Nat Weiss suggested somebody from a guy in New York. He talked to the kids and started managing them.

David Givens: During the summer, before we got involved with Barry, we played at the University of Colorado a number of times, downtown at the park in Boulder, and out in the country on top of the mountains at impromptu parties. We developed a following, and were really having a great time. When Barry became our manager, that all came to an abrupt stop. He said, "I don't want to overexpose you guys." *Big mistake.* We should have played together as much as possible—we didn't really know each other very well. And when the pressure came on, instead of pulling together, we shattered. It was a lot of fun before that happened. But looking at it now, I can see there were things that could have been simply and easily remedied. But that was not to be.

When he got involved, Barry said, "I don't want to be your business manager, I want to be your *personal* manager. I want to help you make decisions. You guys are going to make a lot of money, you're going to have career choices—I want to help you with that stuff. I'll get you a manager that's in the business, that will take care of your business affairs. I'll make sure that business is done properly." And he didn't do any of that. The manager that he came up with—the first one—was Soupy Sales' manager. A guy named Stan Greeson, from New York who had no idea as to what we were about. Frank Anton took his secretary, Roz—with whom Stan was [allegedly] having an affair—and she became Frank's girlfriend and they later married. That was not very smooth. So not only did he not know what to do with us, he didn't like us, either [laughs]. So that was a bad scene. The mismanagement was incredible. I mean, Barry made things happen that were really great. First of all, let me say this—I used to really like hanging out with Barry. We used to spend a lot of time together—the conversations and the time we spent together was really fun. Candy and Barry had a lot of fun together, Tommy and Barry were really quite good friends.

Barry considered me 'the adult' in the group. He used to come to me when things needed to get done. And I was literally the leader of the band—in the union sense and all the other parts of it. We had a good relationship at first, but he kept making these bad decisions, and not doing what he said he was going to do. He made a lot of personal promises—to Candy in particular. "I'm going to take care of you, blah blah blah," and he just didn't do it. He kept coming up with these half-assed things. I'll give you the number one example of that—we recorded a three-song demo in a little studio in Denver, at Summit Studio. Wyndham Hannaway, to whom Barry had introduced us, was an electronics and media guy—he produced it. We went in there—it was one-take/two-takes of the three songs, and we were out of there. But it had a lot of energy in it. In fact, in those days, they had underground radio stations, and there was one called KMYR, in Denver. There was this D.J. on there, Jim Mason was his name as I recall—he was only there at night. You could sometimes hear the station as far away as Boulder. He started playing our demo tape on the radio—they were getting more calls on that than they were getting to hear Led Zeppelin's first album [1969's 'Led Zeppelin'], which had just come out. It was the most-requested thing they'd ever had on the station. We used that demo as an intro to record companies. It created a lot of buzz.

So we went to the west coast, we played at the Avalon Ballroom in San Francisco, and then the next night at the Whiskey A Go Go in Hollywood. All the record companies were there at the Whiskey—Atlantic, Columbia, ABC, A&M, Elektra, and so on. Barry had the connections and they all came out. Unfortunately, at the gig in San Francisco, Candy had to carry the gig on her back—we weren't very good. She had blown out her voice. So she managed to sing one set at the Whiskey fairly well, but she couldn't even come out for the second set. We were down about it, but it turned out that the record companies all made offers. And we all wanted to be on either Atlantic or Warner Brothers—because Joni Mitchell and Jimi Hendrix were on Warner's Reprise, Atlantic had Led Zeppelin, Cream, Buffalo Springfield, and all those English blues bands. We knew that they knew what to do with music like ours. I think Columbia and Atlantic each offered a $30-40,000 signing bonus, which in those days, wasn't all that bad. And the thing that they brought to the table was their expertise and the credibility of being on their label. Unfortunately, ABC, who was trying to start a new, hip label, offered us $130,000. Barry—who didn't know jack shit about making records, but knew how to count—took the big money. Our manager, Stan Greeson, had a friend who was an executive at ABC and there were some kickbacks—it was a bad deal. It was really our death warrant. ABC had no clue as to what to do with us. That was the kind of decision-making Barry was doing. When it came right down to it, there was no love.

Mike Drumm: I was 18 years old—I was a month older than Tommy, and I was a freshman up there. Back then; L.S.D. had become a drug of commonality in those towns that were the more liberal places. That was certainly the case in Boulder. The second time I ever took it, I went to the Glenn Miller Ballroom to see Zephyr. And this was at their peak. The positive side of taking L.S.D. was it did have an ability to open one's consciousness, and enable one to perhaps see things in a way differently than what they'd done before. So here I am, seeing this band that was pushing the envelope with a really great batch of musicians, with a guitar player who is at his most experimental and creative at that time. *It just blew my mind.* That's what happened with those combination of ingredients [laughs]! It changed my whole ability to listen to music in a different way, and started my ability to really appreciate jazz and improvisational music, where you were out of the bounds of a four-minute song. Early the next year, I got a job at a really hip record store, and Tommy used to come in there a lot. That was before they made bootlegs illegal. So we had a lot of Jimi Hendrix bootlegs, and Tommy would come in, listen to them, and take them home. I would always hook him up when he came in. Since he was such a nice guy and down-to-earth—and he had also blown my mind—you just naturally become supportive of that person.

Kenny Passarelli: It was before the dangerous drug laws were passed, and Colorado was a holdout for some reason—they were behind the times. There were meth labs all over Denver and Colorado Springs—I'd say between '67 and '69. There's no doubt in my mind—and I've never seen him do it, but I was told by someone, or it might have been Tommy himself—that he tried [hard drugs] early on. All I know is that the only thing that me and Tommy did together was smoke pot and take L.S.D. I never saw him do hard drugs—it wasn't something that was around us at the time.

Johnnie Bolin: Tommy was really healthy in his younger years. I don't know if he was really into ginseng, but he sure was into orange juice, walking, and no meat. The whole Boulder/hippie vibe. He never ate meat the whole time—he stayed vegetarian.

Bobby Berge: We pretty much got high from the get-go. But it kind of started out back in 'the hippie dippie days'—smoking herb and doing psychedelics. Tommy used to smoke a little herb—in the evening only. I think it helped his creativity and it helped calm him down, because I remember he had a hard time sleeping back in Boulder. His mind was so active.

Barry Fey: I know he didn't sleep at night. He called at all hours of the morning. "Tommy, it's 4:00!"

Johnnie Bolin: I remember he was into Nyquil; he didn't like to drink to get to sleep. He knew Nyquil worked—he took a couple of swigs of that, and you're going to go to sleep.

David Givens: We didn't do a lot of drugs. When we lived on Canyon Boulevard for instance, Tommy really liked T.H.C.—the pill, he didn't like to smoke, and he only got loaded on occasion. He didn't smoke cigarettes, and we all smoked cigarettes—it drove him crazy, he hated it. He didn't like smoking pot—at this time, anyway. We were never high when we played live.

Johnnie Bolin: He didn't smoke cigarettes—he smoked those skinny cigars for looks, I suppose. For pictures, is what it looks like.

David Givens: But you could get T.H.C. in pill form—he loved that. And there was something else, I never even knew what it was—but there was some kind of animal tranquilizer that he liked. I was not into drugs particularly—except for an occasional acid trip. We didn't drink at this time. When we started out, we got high literally off the music. People used to think that we were speed freaks and that we were high all the time. We were not high particularly much at all. As time went by, out on the road, we did get high more often. But we didn't do it a lot.

Johnnie Bolin: It was kind of off and on, I suppose.

G. Brown: It was always a wild college town, so it was more fueled by alcohol than drugs. Drugs were starting to make in-roads, but I remember going to these places, and you had to have a pitcher to get in. Not a pitcher for your party of two or four, but individually! So people 'sardined' in there—everyone grabbing a huge glass pitcher of beer, getting sweaty and soaked, listening to these guys tear it up.

Otis Taylor: Everyone hung out at Tulagi's, the Sink, and the Blind Pig. We didn't have drinking in Boulder for a while—it was just 3-2 beer in Boulder. Then they finally gave liquor licenses to the bars, and the scene changed. It kind of went downtown. [The Sink held] maybe 200—it wasn't too big. Tulagi's was bigger. It was the college bar. It had cover bands, and every once in a while; they'd get John Lee Hooker or Zephyr. One time, I played a concert on the day my father died. That's one of my strong Tulagi memories. It was just a college club—where college kids and hippies hung out. You'd get soul bands like Freddi-Henchi—Tommy would sit in with Freddi-Henchi. Everybody sat in with each other. [It held] maybe 250-300. It was a big room.

David Givens: The same guy [who owned the Sink] owned Tulagi's. When we first started playing there, it was this big, not very nice place. The reason why it was called Tulagi's was because the guy who built the place had fought on Tulagi Island during World War II. He had a mural painted behind the stage of this jungle—the ocean and some islands—and the one weird thing was there was 'a native' in the picture, and the guy looked just like Jimi Hendrix!

There was a band called the Astronauts, which was the big college drinking band. In fact, I think they had an album, 'Live at Tulagi's.' They were sort of Colorado's answer to the Beach Boys. Later, once Chuck [Morris got involved], they renovated Tulagi's and made it a more modern theater-styled venue. But at this time, it was pretty raw—it was a place for drinking for 18-year-olds. But they were really enthusiastic crowds.

Kenny Passarelli: The only place to buy Fender [guitars] in Denver was a music store downtown, called Happy Logan. It had been there forever. Tommy probably bought equipment there. My connection there was I had bought my first Fender bass amplifier and I think my first bass there. I'm a classically trained musician, and when I switched from classical music as a trumpet player to bass, my education helped me become good right away—I had a good ear. Somebody connected with Stephen Stills—we knew Stephen was going to be in Gold Hill, Colorado. I was in the band the Beast, and we signed to ATCO. So I meet Stephen Stills—this is pre-Woodstock. I heard the original acetate of 'Crosby, Stills & Nash'—before it was released. It must have been April of 1969. I went up and jammed with Stephen. He tells me that I have a possibility to play with Crosby, Stills & Nash. The bottom line is I didn't get the gig—I ended up leaving the Beast and joining a three-piece group that worked out of Boulder.

David Givens: At this point in Colorado . . . playing in Zephyr was like playing in a big-time band. We would walk around and people would come and get autographs from us. Everybody wanted to be our friend. The fact that Barry Fey was behind us—to someone like Herman, it started to look legitimate. And that was what he was concerned with. We weren't just some hippies out on the street anymore—we were people who made money and worked for a living. I think at that point, the fact that Tommy could provide a home and put a roof over [Karen's] head, I don't think he was really excited about it, but there was no more acrimony. I don't recall Tommy and Herman ever being really great friends. But Tommy and Karen lived together for a long time, and Karen continued to spend time with her family. There was some tension, but he wasn't showing up with a gun at the house! I never saw Herman and Mrs. Ulibarri ever visit Tommy and Karen, but Karen went to Denver frequently. I think Tommy stayed away, but Karen's relationship with her family seemed fine.

Barry Fey: I was so proud of those kids, they were so good.

David Givens: Barry got us a gig playing in Phoenix—we went down to Phoenix and stayed for three weeks, in April of '69, and rehearsed and whatnot. We were on a show with Steve Miller. I remember Steve talking with Tommy, but he was really Candy's buddy. But I watched Steve Miller watch Tommy play. In fact, he was the first 'rock star' we ever met. And then we also played with Vanilla Fudge, which is where Tommy met Mark Stein and Carmine Appice.

Carmine Appice: I met Tommy—we did some gigs together. I thought he was a really cool, interesting player. He had a good look about him, so we became friends from then on.

Prairie Prince: When I was in high school in Phoenix, we had a band called the Red, White and Blues Band. Zephyr came to Phoenix—they were on tour with Jethro Tull. But our band was the opening band because we were the local act, and we were the number one band in Phoenix at that time—for local boys. Our band opened, and we played at one of the big nightclubs in Phoenix—the Aquarius. I got to see Zephyr play, and I remember being so impressed with Tommy. Just thinking, "My God, who is this guy? He's just incredible!" Incredible looking and everything. It was also the first time I ever saw Jethro Tull.

Martin Barre: I met Tommy when Zephyr was supporting us on one of our early Tull tours in the U.S.A. This was a period when, traditionally, bands were very competitive, mainly trying to outdo each other in audience reaction. This led to a fairly unfriendly atmosphere amongst bands and for a guitarist. New on a large scale touring environment, it was even worse! We had played with many big name acts and had very little personal contact or interaction, so it was a breath of fresh air to meet the musicians from Zephyr. Not only were they completely professional musically, but, they were all incredibly friendly and open. I guess we 'sang' each other's praises, as we definitely enjoyed playing on the same bill. I remember little of the music, yet, lots of the personality of the band. I really got on well with Tommy; he was a very nice person, and accordingly, gave me much confidence in myself and in the nature of our jobs—making working together much more enjoyable. I don't remember seeing Tommy again, although I followed the news of his career with great enthusiasm.

Prairie Prince: As a fan, I came up to him [after the show], and said that I really enjoyed Zephyr and his playing. I think he said he saw us play, too. We had occasions to go out into the desert, take a generator, and jam. I said, "We planned to go out tonight after the concert." I guess it was a Saturday. He said, "That sounds great, I'd like to join you." So he came out. I think we all got in the same van and went out in the desert outside of Phoenix—an area called Carefree, Arizona. We climbed up on the rocks, set up our equipment, and jammed until the sun came up. That was the only time I got to play with him live. I remember playing some Jimi Hendrix tunes, and he *shredded*. I think we played "Stone Free" and "Spanish Castle Magic." And "Voodoo Child"—that was a classic jam song for everybody at that point. And he jammed along with some of our original material, as well. I remember being really taken with him.

Johnnie Bolin: They backed up Zeppelin. Zephyr played, Jimmy Page heard Tommy play, and when Zephyr was done, they went to the dressing room, and Jimmy ran downstairs and couldn't wait to meet Tommy. He heard this guitar player playing his ass off.

David Givens: We were the ones that told Barry Fey about Led Zeppelin. He was the first promoter to hire them, and he hired them because we told him about them. Of course, he doesn't admit that. He claims that it was one of his great coups—that he was the first promoter smart enough to hire Led Zeppelin. Anyway, we played at the Boston Tea Party [May 27-29, 1969]— Led Zeppelin was on their second tour, and we opened the show for them. It was the one gig that we played with a guy named Julie Wilson playing drums. We had played the first set and it was really good. We went back to the dressing room—Jimmy Page came up to me and asked, "Are you the guitar player?!" I said, "No, that's him over there, with the black hair." And he was off like *a shot*—he went over there and was in Tommy's ear. He just could not believe Tommy—he was really tripping. Robert Plant seemed equally interested in Candy. We had a good time getting acquainted and partied with them later at a fancy party in a loft overlooking the Boston Harbor. Years later, when Led Zeppelin were mega-superstars, we'd go to their Colorado gigs—Barry would let us in free, good thing since we didn't have any money—and Robert always remembered her. He really seemed to like her a lot.

Johnnie Bolin: Zephyr and Jimi Hendrix played the same weekend at the Denver Pop Festival [June 27-29, 1969]. I think Jimi was Friday and Tommy was Sunday—something like that. Tommy didn't really say if he met Hendrix.

David Givens: We were backstage—that was the Jimi Hendrix Experience's last gig. Mitch Mitchell and Noel Redding were hanging out in a trailer backstage, and we were back there too. There were a lot of people in there, and I went outside—it was in Bears Stadium, which later became the old Mile High Stadium. This trailer was far from the crowd. I went outside and Hendrix was standing out by the fence. I walked up and said, "Hey," he said, "Hey." We looked at the crowd for a while enjoying the sun, and then later that night, we watched him play. That was it.

I'm sure you heard the story about them gassing the crowd. Well, *we were playing* when they gassed the crowd. We played two nights—this was the first night. It was fairly early—we were unknown, and it was still daylight. But there were still a lot of people there—20-30,000 people. The Denver cops were idiots and they were fighting with some street freaks outside who thought music should be free. There were bottles thrown and whatnot. We're in the middle of "Cross the River," and all of a sudden, there's something wrong with my throat. I open my eyes and the people are pouring out of the stands—it was like water running down the hillside. Running out of the stands down onto the field. It was a bad vibe, very tense. And then Candy took over. We stopped the song and she started talking to the crowd. "You guys, come on down onto the field, sit down. Since we're all crying already, we'll do some blues." She started singing "St. James Infirmary." She really quieted the vibe and she did it with the force of her personality. And saved some severe heartburn for a number of people—Barry Fey included. He bear-hugged her then, but he never proved particularly grateful in the long run. She saved the day.

Zephyr II

David Givens: We recorded [Zephyr's 1969 self-titled debut] at Wally Heider's studio in Los Angeles. We lived at the Hollywood Hawaiian Hotel. It was a place where music people stayed—Miles Davis stayed there while we were there. Real nice, it was sort of this '50's move star place'—swimming pool, apartments with a kitchen. September or October. The guy who was producing was Bill Halverson—he had been the engineer on the Crosby, Stills & Nash and Cream stuff, and a lot of L.A./Tom Jones-kind of stuff. *Didn't have a clue what to do with us.* A real schooled, L.A. musician. We were a bunch of hippies—half of us were teenagers—and didn't know beans about recording. It was a really desperate mismatch. Really bad. We recorded everything we knew the first day, because we were a live band. The basic concept of Zephyr was essentially to be one of the early jazz-fusion bands. We composed songs that were put together the way jazz songs were put together. A melody that you play, then we'd go off into these extended solos that had cues built into them, that said, "O.K., we're going to go to this next section." When Tommy would be done with his solo, he would play something that the rest of us would recognize, and that would cue us so Robbie and I would play some lick that would move us into the next section. And we did a lot of stuff where we would change rhythms. We didn't do too much 'verse-verse-chorus-bridge-out' pop songs. So this guy was like, "I don't know what to do with you guys." He thought we were going to be like Cream. That wasn't what we did either. Another bad mistake. The guy was a pleasant guy, but he was having us do take after take—he was used to working with L.A. studio musicians. But literally, Tommy's solos . . . I remember he had rented this guitar—an S.G., this 'famous' guitar. A beat-up piece of shit, but it was supposed to have 'the hit sound'—it had been the guitar on hit songs. And Tommy literally took 60-something takes to do the solo on one of the songs. That's not Tommy's best playing.

Johnnie Bolin: For the first Zephyr album, he used an S.G. quite a bit. Then he went to a Gold Top.

David Givens: Tommy had written the verses to "Sail On," and it was like a country song. Then I arranged it, and wrote all the instrumental parts in the middle and the tag end on it. We loved playing that. In "Sail On," there is sort of a 'bolero' part in the middle, which we stole directly from Jeff Beck [the song "Beck's Bolero"]. And Tommy took the same approach for each of the various sections of the song. That was one of the things that developed over time. Both Tommy and John in their solos—and Candy playing harp—took the same approach for the various pieces where they soloed. "Cross the River" was the first song that we wrote. It was based on a song that Candy and I had written before we had met Tommy. The solo section was arranged like how I explained—it was specifically, "O.K., here's Tommy's solo, it's going to be like *this*," there were cues that were built into it. Live, that was our opening song. It was really pretty powerful. On a good night, when that thing was rocking, it was a really great song. There were a lot of bands that played with us once, and didn't want to play with us anymore, because we were hard to follow. And that song was one of the reasons.

G. Brown: Zephyr was star-crossed like a lot of bands at that time. If they had gotten with a good engineer and made a good record, that would have been one thing. But it was a primitive recording. People who were fans loved it—it certainly established Tommy as one of the hottest guitarists on the scene. But it really didn't capture that.

David Givens: Tommy first saw an Echoplex being used at the Scene in New York by Rick Derringer, when he was still with the McCoys. This was during our first stay in New York, when we lived in the Village for a few weeks. I had to show him how to use it after he bought it. He was a little 'technologically challenged.'

Johnnie Bolin: I don't know if the Echoplex just came out—Maestro is who made it. He uses it on the first Zephyr album. He probably purchased it a little bit before that, because it sounded like he knew what he was doing. In articles, he said he had a Fuzztone—Sam Ash had made him a Fuzztone, like a personal one. They took a Fuzztone and they jacked it up. Not a lot of pedals—back then, you didn't see a whole lot of pedals. And he loved that Wah-Wah—it was a Cry Baby. Steve Miller used an Echoplex early on. But Steve came out a little bit later, and Joe Walsh went there a little bit. Tommy was playing it in '69—he used it as part of his instrument. For a while, he was playing a steel guitar through an Echoplex.

Prairie Prince: I remember his use of Echoplex and effects early on, that a lot of people hadn't really caught onto yet—electronic stuff. It was mind-blowing—I was hoping he would do a lot more of that. I remember being very impressed by that sound—it was unique. And I never really heard anybody do too much of that besides Tommy.

David Givens: Tommy was remarkably consistent. Tommy could speak music like a language. He wasn't an educated person—he wasn't even a particularly smart person—until it came to music. *He was a genius.* When we went to these cities, he liked to go to music stores. Particularly in New York, we'd go into Manny's, and I'd tell him, "Tommy, you've got to play." I remember one time we went in there, and they had a Flying V, and he hadn't seen one in a long time. He started playing it, and everybody in the store came over and stood around, watching him play—they couldn't believe it. Playing gigs was fun. The other bands that we played with—Led Zeppelin, Santana, and Steve Miller—all became fans. When we played in San Francisco or New York, they would all come out and see us. Carlos Santana is the only person I've ever seen who brought a television to the gig! He sat backstage and watched T.V. The drummer, Michael Shrieve, and Candy were really good friends. The bass player, Dave Brown, Tommy, and I, were friends. It was nice being Zephyr. We never had a huge commercial success, but amongst other musicians, we had a good reputation, and we were pretty well respected. All of us could play, and the stuff we did was really different from what other people were doing. We thought of ourselves as 'artists'—it sounds a little pretentious now, but we were genuine about it.

John Tesar: David was trying pretty hard to be 'adult supervision' for the band, and John Faris was a character. Candy was really impressive.

David Givens: Candy really was *a singer.* Some kid from the internet sent me a DVD a month ago, and it had a promo movie that we made, and also clips of us playing somewhere. They didn't have the sound for this movie, so they had taken some bootleg tape and used it as the soundtrack. There's a version of "Sun's A Risin'," and she and Tommy sound fantastic. She's singing blues, she's not screaming. I was there at all these shows, and in the reviews following the shows, she was the center of attention—not Tommy. Tommy would get mentioned, no doubt, but the other three of us would get mentioned somewhere further down [laughs]. It was always Candy first. She was the one talking to the people, she was the vocalist—thereby, the centerpiece. She and Tommy had a pretty nice relationship for the majority of the time we were together. They did what Robert Plant and Jimmy Page did—trade licks—and they were pretty good at it. And Candy played harp—she was a really good harp player. She played with a lot of the blues guys that came to town. She played with John Lee Hooker, and she and Willie Dixon were really good friends. She was well respected as a harmonica player.

I understand why people don't like her if all they ever heard was that first record, or even 'Going Back to Colorado.' Early on—and particularly the first record, because they're all 'take 500'—she sounds really stupid and over-amped. She was in some ways 'the female equivalent of Robert Plant' in the beginning. If you listen to 'Sunset Ride'—the Zephyr album that we made after Tommy—you can hear that she can actually sing beautifully. Later on, John, Tommy, Candy, and I started a band called the Legendary 4-Nikators with our friends Mick and Harold from Flash Cadillac and the Continental Kids, doing covers—Motown stuff, R n' B, 50's, the Shirelles, British Invasion. And I mean, she *sang* that stuff . . . it was knocked out. Before we were in Zephyr, in Brown Sugar, we did Aretha Franklin songs, Gladys Knight and the Pips songs. She was required to actually sing. The Zephyr stuff, she did a lot of howling—it was such a shame. And we all talked to her. Steve Miller really liked her, and he was forever going, "Would you quit yelling? You have a nice voice, just sing!" Recently, I found an acetate that we made—it was early versions of some of the songs that went on the first album, and they're far better than the versions that got on the album. You can tell the difference—the singing is rhythmic, it's got nuance. There's more to it than just howling at the microphone. It was such a disappointment for all of us that it came out that way.

Zephyr toured pretty thoroughly. There were a few places we missed, but we hit all the high spots—Chicago, Detroit, San Francisco, Dallas, New Orleans, Philadelphia, Cleveland, Phoenix, Salt Lake City, Des Moines, Seattle, Portland, Vancouver, L.A. We were really popular all over Texas, and in the

Midwest. We did really well in New York—we played at the Fillmore East and the Central Park Summer Music Festival. Canada is as far as we got outside the United States. We were supposed to go to Japan at one point—a Mount Fuji Pop Festival or something—but that fell through. Barry 'threatened' to send us to Europe a number of times, but it never happened. Just the U.S. and Canada. I found out recently that our records sold well in South America and Mexico, but we never went.

Johnnie Bolin: Robbie Chamberlin—Tommy never did like him. He got rid of him, and that's when he got Bobby Berge.

David Givens: Tommy said, "I know this guy from South Dakota, Bobby Berge." So we brought Bobby out. Bobby was this really weird, un-hip, backward guy. He had a really domineering wife. He was really a sweet guy, but we picked on him. He was really not like us—we were in this sort of 'hip community' in Boulder. We were into the arts and foreign movies, we read a lot, and we didn't watch television. We were sort of snotty hippies—he didn't fit in real well socially. Originally, I loved playing with him, because he played dance music—after playing with Robbie, he was a rock. His meter was great, he hit the drums really hard almost all the time, he picked up on enough of Robbie's licks—he really admired Robbie and he liked our first record a lot. So he learned those first album songs really well, and didn't change them significantly. Robbie was jazzier and smarter, but he was just too temperamental. Robbie was hard for everybody to get along with. I saw him about ten years ago, and he was O.K.—much more pleasant than when he was young. But he was a smug little guy. Probably scared—he was 18 years old, he had an interesting life. He had his problems. Tommy and Robbie did *not* hit it off. Robbie always thought Tommy was arrogant, and Tommy always thought Robbie was stuck up and a stick in the mud. They were both right [laughs]! It was really hard to get Robbie to laugh—it was hard to get him to do anything.

Bobby Berge: I heard the first Zephyr album, and Tommy blew me away. That's when I really stood up and took notice—"God, I want to play with this guy." I loved what he did. Then he called me in May of '70, and invited me to come out to Colorado to play in Zephyr. I packed my stuff and went. Got in the van, and toured all over the U.S. all summer. Some of the local stuff was cool too—in Boulder, we used to do a lot of outdoor concerts. That was our home base, and we used to do a lot of mini-Woodstock type things. The 'hippie dippie thing' was full-blown. We used to open for some big concerts. In Cincinnati, Stevie Winwood was on the bill, the Bob Seger System, the Stooges—that was a big one. Grand Funk, somewhere in West Virginia. Fleetwood Mac at Central Park, New York City. Mountain. Then we did 'Going Back to Colorado' in New York, at Electric Lady Studios—living at the Chelsea Hotel for a couple of months, working with Eddie Kramer. The studio was beautiful. Used to go down to the Village all the time and hang out when we weren't recording. Tommy, John, and myself would go see Charlie Mingus, Mose Allison—it was great.

Eddie Kramer: I only knew [Tommy] for a very short period of time, which was the Zephyr album—one of the first albums he ever did. I remember they said, "You've got to hear our guitar player, he really loves Jimi," as a lot of guitar players do. I thought he was a really good guitar player. There was a bunch of stuff I was doing in '70 and '71—that album, Carly Simon, the Voices of East Harlem, Jobriath. The album went fairly well. I seem to remember that there was some difficulty with some of the songs, and not being as well formed as they could have been.

I do have another clear memory—I went to Colorado, and there was a concert. They opened for Jethro Tull. I actually got on stage with them—it was the first time in my life that I got on stage with a band. And I was terrified—I'm used to being on the other side of the glass, not up front, playing keyboard. Maybe it was because I'd done those keyboard parts on the record. But never again—it was just too scary for me. I remember being in Colorado and taking pictures of him and his girlfriend at the time. I have these very strange pictures I took at the top of a mountain someplace in Colorado, maybe Boulder.

David Givens: When Hendrix died [on September 18, 1970], Eddie Kramer called and said, "We won't be recording today—*Jimi's dead.*" Tommy's reaction to learning of Jimi's death was just a shocked look—I'm the one who told him. Eddie called me, and I went over to [Tommy's] room and told him what was up. He did a wide-eyed double take. We were all amazed. Eddie was going to introduce us—we were expecting to meet him, and then, suddenly, he was no more. We went down to the studio—pretty corny, but we wanted to play some of Hendrix's songs as sort of a tribute, because he was our hero. He and Miles Davis were our heroes. So we went in there, and Jimi's black Stratocaster was there. We all walked over and went, "Whoa!" Tommy put his hand on the guitar. Then we played "Hey Joe" and "Foxy Lady." Then the electronics guy—Shimon I think was his name, an Israeli guy—was super pissed that we were in there. He started yelling at us—and I understand, Jimi was his friend, and on top of that, his world had come to an end. He kicked us out of the studio.

Eddie Kramer: If you could imagine losing Jimi, and then having to work like a crazy fool—trying to keep the studio going. That's why I don't have much memory of it. It was horrendous. And then I did Carly's album, and that whole thing developed [Kramer and Simon had a relationship]. It was a very disturbing time, in fact. [Studio] A was finished, B was just about completed.

David Givens: That record was a mess because after Hendrix died, the fight went out of Eddie Kramer completely. He was totally preoccupied with trying to get 'Cry of Love' [an album of songs Jimi was working on at the time of his death, released in 1971] done—which I understand. The thing is, Jimi was deeply involved in the mixing and production. So for Mitch and Eddie to try and put that together without him . . . I mean, they were asking *us* for help! We picked a couple of songs that went on that album—me and Tommy—because they just didn't know what to do. One of them was "Belly Button Window," I can't remember what the other one might have been.

Johnnie Bolin: From 'Zephyr' to 'Going Back to Colorado,' you could tell it was a different studio/different producer, and Tommy's playing was getting far better every year. At 18, when he did the first Zephyr album, it was still early on for him. By the time he did the second Zephyr album, his playing was really something.

David Givens: Tommy wrote both "Showbizzy" and "See My People Come Together." "Showbizzy" we recorded in Studio B, with the guys from Lothar and the Hand People producing with us. Eddie Kramer wasn't really involved in that—it was sort of self-produced. Tommy played guitar through a Leslie on "Showbizzy." "See My People" I liked. That was one that we actually worked out and played live—one of the few—before we made that record. It was one that we learned at the Ford dealer's storefront rehearsal hall. That was a song that Tommy wrote the outline of, I filled in most of the blanks from an arrangement standpoint, and Candy reworked the words. Tommy played a phenomenal guitar solo on that—that was the first or second take. He blazed through that thing. I still like hearing that every now and then. It wasn't a real good time—I personally didn't like what Bobby Berge was doing. At that point, I wanted us to play more accessible music that had a better beat and better melodies. When Tommy first brought Bobby in, he'd been playing in top-40 dance bands, and he really knew how to play strong beats. But he became more abstract—that wasn't what I was interested in. Tommy liked it. Musically, during that record, is when we parted company.

Karen Ulibarri: They were different. I remember someone saying to me once—this is around the Zephyr time—"Tommy's music will mature when he matures." And I looked at him like, he was as mature as he was going to get at 18! But I realize later what they meant, because they were just bashing their heads. She was wailing, he was trying to get in as many licks as possible—for the sheer purpose of everyone hearing them, and thinking this was their last chance to be heard. But they realized—they let the second album show that they'd mellowed out a lot. They had to become sophisticated somewhat in their style, because they were very unsophisticated—as far as performing and as far as recording was.

Bobby Berge: After I was with them a year, we started to have differences. Candy and David wanted Robbie back for whatever reasons, and Tommy didn't want to play with Robbie.

David Givens: The record came out in early '71, and it seems to me that we broke up in the summertime of '71. We played some [shows in support of the album], but it started to be no fun—the fun was gone. The fact that the second album didn't turn out very well, we'd had high hopes that the new record was going to turn things around for us. The whole Hendrix death and the fact that it never got finished—the vocals and guitar parts—was a fiasco for us. It was half-assed from top to bottom. I mean, the photographs on the back of the album were taken by a friend, Wyndham Hannaway, because they realized when they were putting the album together that they didn't have any pictures! So they sent him down to the studio and he went snap, snap, snap—those are the pictures that are on the back of the album. The original album cover—the way they described it to us—was going to be these really beautiful, heavy-duty New York skyscrapers, with a puddle on the ground. And the reflection in the puddle was going to be the mountains of Colorado. And then this thing that they came up with—this smog-colored album with this little square in the middle—was like, "What?!" It was just a mess. We had developed no relationship with our record company, Warner Brothers, and we had no management. We made another record, 'Sunset Ride' [released in 1972], for Warner Brothers after Tommy left, and working with them afterwards was really pretty easy—they wanted to do the right thing. But Barry's management and the guy that we had for a business manager—it was just a steady stream of incompetence. They didn't do business. I'm a businessman now—I know how business works. And these guys were not businessmen. They were thoughtless and inconsiderate at best.

Barry Fey: Candy was good, Tommy was good—the whole band was good. The reason they didn't make it is because she sounded too much like Janis, and there was too much love for Janis.

David Givens: Barry is 'Mr. Personality.' One of the things that Tommy and I argued about—in fact, this is the thing that broke my relationship with Barry finally—Barry wanted to take out insurance policies on us. And Candy and I both were like, "*No fucking way* is somebody—besides a family member—going to be the beneficiary of an insurance policy on us. That's just not going to happen." And Tommy was like, "Barry would never do anything." I'm saying to him, "Geez Tommy, look at how he does business." There were several people he worked with. L.C. [Clayton] was a leg-breaker. Tough Tony—his job was 'muscle.' Barry used to have a guy named Shalom. Shalom was a Jewish biker—a great big guy with red hair, crazy. He, L.C., and Tony did security stuff for Feyline. But L.C. was like a human Doberman. Pretty formidable-looking person—not somebody you'd want to fight with. But he was an O.K. guy.

L.C. Clayton: I got to Denver in '70/'71, and that's about the time I met Barry. [L.C. played football for] the Kansas City Chiefs—I did the preseason, got into the season, and got hurt a week after the first game. It was their best year ever, and I didn't get no ring or nothing [the Chiefs would go on to win Super Bowl IV]. I remember getting hurt—other than that, it was all good. I'd just been in the South Seas—I got back from a little vacation called Viet Nam. I got my hip busted up, and they said, "I don't think you're going to be running anymore." Wide receiver—I tried running back later. But back in those days, rookies didn't play, unless you had special teams and shit like that.

I ran the security for Barry. I met Barry through a friend of mine named Tony Funches—he had been a bodyguard for the Stones and some other people. He used to come to a club that I was working here in Denver, and he said, "Why don't you come down?" Walked into [Barry's] office, and I met his secretary, Leslie Gorham. She was wild—she was in there yelling. I thought, "Oh . . . I don't know if I want to work here or not." When I went in to talk to Barry, he was sitting behind his desk—he was a little chubby thing back then . . . not a little chubby, *a whole lot chubby* [laughs]. He looked like he should have been sitting on a mushroom. We talked a bit, and then there was a big argument in the hallway, so I looked out there to see what was going on, and it was Barry's wife and Leslie—they were having a go at it. After that, I decided, "This is the kind of place I want to be at!" You could do what you wanted to do and say what you wanted to say—to whoever you wanted to. It was all good.

David Givens: We didn't like the insurance policy thing. And Tommy went to Barry. The next time I see Barry, Barry's says to me, "How was I going to do it, David?" I said, "Well Barry, I don't know. I don't like the theory, I don't like the concept." From that point on, Barry and I were never really too friendly.

Karen Ulibarri: It turned sour because of the disharmony in the group. And the need for Candy and David to control the whole situation. I think that's what was really difficult for him. And the fact that they really weren't going anywhere. They were 'the band' of Boulder at the time, but the two albums were the big breakthrough, and that was wonderful. It was great, but then eventually the disharmony . . . I think the dissention is what caused them to fall apart. But the struggles in Boulder at the time were the fact that there was a lack of money. I mean, you could play these clubs in a constant cycle—rotating them week after week. But at one point, you would be guaranteed that everyone had heard you. So I think they outgrew the sound, they outgrew each other, and they needed to go on.

Johnnie Bolin: Towards the end, I don't think it was too competitive . . . it was him and Candy, y'know? Because he was 'the Jimi Hendrix' of that era, and she was 'the Janis Joplin.' I don't think he was really trying to upstage her, but I think towards the end, she just kind of got in the way. He got tired of backing up a singer. He wasn't getting along with them towards the end.

David Givens: John, Candy, and I finally got tired of Tommy and Bobby going off on these excursions . . . Tommy was listening to John McLaughlin. Tommy was just fascinated by John McLaughlin—he sat up in his apartment practicing McLaughlin licks, listening to the records over and over. And the rest of us liked John McLaughlin—but *liked*, not loved. My idea of a really good drummer at that time was Tony Williams, who was playing with Miles. And Bobby was not that. I went and talked to Tommy, and said, "We want to get Robbie back." Well, what we didn't know was that when we fired Robbie and went to New York to play at the Fillmore East, Robbie and his girlfriend were hanging out with Karen a lot. Supposedly, they got into a strip poker game one night, and all ended up naked. I don't know what else happened, but Tommy was not happy about that. From that moment on, any potential for Robbie to get back into the band was over. We didn't know that at the time—I found that out a while later. The final discussion went as follows—Candy and I went up to Tommy and Karen's apartment, and told him we wanted to get Robbie back, and he said, "I don't want to do it." He understood about Bobby—he understood what we didn't like. But Robbie was not the answer. He said, "If you're going to do that, then I'm going to have to leave." We said, "We don't want you to leave, but we can't go on like this." He elected to leave.

Otis Taylor: It was all politics. Egos, politics—it breaks up every band. [Soon after, Tommy and Otis] had a band, it was called T&O Shortline. It was only for a month, because we were in-between things. We went and took some pictures. We'd just jam. It was, "Get the boys together and start jamming!"

We'd play songs for about 20 minutes—that was our signature thing [laughs]. And half of them wouldn't have chord changes—that was my style, because I was really into Howlin' Wolf. You just *played*.

David Givens: Barry brought in his friend, Steven Greenberg, who was a very wealthy stockbroker guy—he lived alone in a beautiful penthouse apartment on Park Avenue in New York. A real nice guy, but having a rock band for him was like guys owning racehorses—we were a toy. He knew nothing about the music business. 'Sunset Ride' got great reviews—people really liked the record, everybody was saying, "This is the best thing they've ever done." Radio stations were all excited about it. But, we didn't have a booking agent, and Steven couldn't seem to find one for us. Meanwhile, probably the best booking agent at William Morris was trying to contact us. We found that out after Candy and I finally quit—when he called us up at home. By that time, the band was dead. That was what our management was like.

Eddie Kramer: At the beginning, I thought he was much more into the Hendrix-y vibe. But obviously, there was a change that occurred the moment he left Zephyr and got more involved in the jazz world. But certainly in the beginning, I thought he had the potential to be a star. I guess he had different ideas.

Legendary 4-Nikators/Jeremy Steig

Harold Fielden: I was starting a band called Flash Cadillac and the Continental Kids, and needed a guitar player. I knew Tommy was around—this is 1969. I had everybody lined up, except for the guy to play 'Flash.' We were going to be greasy hair, '50s clothing, and dance steps. I don't know how I knew [Tommy], but I asked if he was interested, and he looked at me like I was on the moon. He had shoulder-length hair—this is when *everybody* had shoulder-length hair—and I'm like, "You have to cut your hair, you have to grease it back, you have to do this and this." And he has purple, green, and blue hair—just the whole concept of cutting your hair and greasing it back . . . it was not to be [laughs]. So that was the first thing with Tommy. But the way he got with the Legendary 4-Nikators was one time, we were at Tulagi's—we both happened to be there on a Friday—and said, "It would be cool to all play together." So I got Tommy, one of the guys from Flash, and David and Candy—there were going to be four of us, we were going to call it 'the Legendary Nikators,' and charge 25 cents to get in. With all the money we made, we would buy spaghetti dinner—this was probably 1970 or '71. With 25 cents, you could buy spaghetti for many, many people. And do it on very short notice. All these other musicians heard about it, and we ended up with eight, nine, or ten people on stage. So we called it the Legendary 4-Nikators. On one or two days notice, it got publicized—packed the place for a Friday afternoon, that was the only time that was available. That was it—we played oldies, because everybody knew it. Just had fun for one day.

David Givens: Dave Brown—Tommy's buddy—played guitar, he was in there too. Then Harold went to law school to become a lawyer [and the 4-Nikators went on hiatus].

Tommy Bolin: So I left the band and started getting very much into the jazz-rock fusion scene. Weather Report, Miles Davis, the Mahavishnu Orchestra—all that kind of stuff.

Bobby Berge: We got together at first and started jamming around with some local guys—Kenny Passarelli now and then. And then the next thing I know, Jeremy Steig comes out from New York. He's sleeping on Tommy's couch, we start rehearsing, and we do a few gigs—maybe a couple of places in Denver. It was great. But I guess Jeremy wasn't really into it, and he left right away.

Tommy Bolin: The way I got involved in jazz-rock was through a flute player named Jeremy Steig. He played on the second Zephyr album. He showed me various jazz relationships and put them into a rock perspective, and then through him, I met a lot of New York people, like Billy Cobham and Jan Hammer.

Johnnie Bolin: Jeremy went back to New York, and got Cobham, Eddie Gomez, and Jan Hammer. He said, "I've got this guitar player out in Colorado," and that's how Tommy met Billy. So Tommy went out to New York for a while. Played with Jeremy, had some dates out there—little improv jams—for about a month or something.

Kenny Passarelli: Let's say through 1969 to 1970, Tommy and I didn't have a lot of contact. I eventually went back to the University of Denver in 1970. I put my bass in the corner—didn't touch it. Tommy kept calling me to come up to Boulder to play, and I said, "I'm going to be a lawyer, like my dad wants me to be." Eventually, over spring break, I went up to play, because Tommy was bringing Jeremy Steig to Boulder, and he wanted me to play bass. So I did. I played with Tommy, Bobby Berge, myself on bass, and Jeremy. We played a few gigs at Tulagi's, and I went back to school. At that point, Tommy had told me, "You're crazy to be in school—*this* is what you need to be doing." He really made me see, "Am I fooling myself?" The Stephen Stills thing was a big letdown for me. I thought I was going to make it, and it didn't happen. Tommy convinced me to come to New York with him.

I took a break, and Tommy and I flew to New York—that's when the jazz thing started happening. We did at show at the Café A Go Go with Jan Hammer on keyboards, Alphonse Mouzon on drums, Jeremy Steig on flute, I played electric bass, and Eddie Gomez—who played with Bill Evans—played upright bass. And Tommy was playing like nobody's business. As a matter of fact, somebody sent me some copies of the recordings that were done there, that would blow your mind, man. We opened for Tony Williams Lifetime at the Café A Go Go. Billy [Cobham] came and sat in. I came in for a week, because I had to go back to school—Tommy stayed longer than I did. I think that's when he connected with Billy—afterwards. He had two different drummers when I played with Jeremy and Tommy—one was Bill Evans' drummer [Marty Morell], but he was a little bit too jazzy. He played a couple of dates, and then Alphonse came on and played. Then I left, and I think that's when Billy Cobham got involved.

We slept on Jeremy's floor in the Village. Tommy was a vegetarian, so all he would do is live off a slice of pizza. He was very particular—he would not eat meat, if it killed him. He would starve. We hardly had any money. It was like Tommy was a kid in the candy store—when we played, it was unbelievable. It was a magical experience. It was like I was his older brother. I was impressed by Tommy, but at the same time, we were really good friends. It wasn't like I was 'a Tommy Bolin groupie'—he liked my playing as much as I liked his. In fact, sometimes I'd say, "Tommy, slow down or turn down a little bit, man." We had a real camaraderie. We had a relationship where I wasn't kissing the floor that he was walking on—like a lot of people did later.

We were hanging out with Miroslav Vitouš from Weather Report—we were around the scene, man. There were free-fusion times in New York. I remember seeing Stanley Clarke playing upright bass—and he was a kid—like 17 or 18. The scene in New York was exciting, but also scary. A lot of the older players were on heroin, and it was spooky. Before I left, John Hammond Jr. came to one of our gigs, and hired me for the summer—to play with him. So I didn't return to Boulder to play with Tommy—I went off to do a tour with John Hammond. When I finished that tour, I didn't go back to Colorado. So if there was an opportunity for me and Tommy to play together, it never happened. After John Hammond, I went back to Vancouver, got in another band.

Gene Perla: There were a number of guys fucking around with smack [in New York City]. Mostly everybody I knew at least was smoking [pot], and if you could get any cocaine, that was fun. But I would certainly say the majority of us didn't fuck around with heroin. Maybe a lot of us would try it—I certainly tried it—but a lot of us did not get 'caught.' Other guys did. I don't remember having conversations with Tommy. I don't remember if he got high with us—I think he did, but I don't remember for sure if he took a smoke or some acid with us. Because Jeremy was a big acid freak—very often, if not always, we'd take acid before we'd play. Those days were involved in a lot of mind-altering substances.

Kenny Passarelli: There wasn't any heroin around us. Tommy wasn't around that scene at all. But we saw in 'the peripheral'—some of the Tony Williams guys, they seemed to be under the influence. Part of it was just that black New York scene, which was scary to us. I don't think it bothered Tommy, and I know he wasn't led down the trail then. I was told in the late '60s, he put a needle in his arm with speed. Denver around that time was called 'Crystal City.' But I never saw him put a needle in his arm. I was told at one point he might have early on—and never did it again. But once you've done it, there's a good chance that if you're around people who do it, you could be talked into it again.

Gene Perla: As far as the musical scene was concerned, the most exciting time for jazz was in the first half of the '60s. That's because there were three groups that blazed trails musically that had never been there before—Miles Davis' group with Herbie Hancock, Wayne Shorter, and Tony Williams, the John Coltrane Quartet with McCoy [Tyner], and Ornette Coleman's group with Billy Higgins, Charlie Haydn, and Don Cherry. They were three distinct types of music that these three groups created, and it was a fabulous time for us younger guys—the next generation—to hear this shit and try to incorporate it into what we were doing. Something I think that set our little circle apart was because of Don and my influence in Latin music, which those three groups that I mentioned weren't involved in at all. Then, when McLaughlin hit with this time signature stuff—it wasn't so much the time signatures, as it was the loud rock appearance of jazz. So we were doing that prior to that.

I don't know if you've ever heard Steig's record called 'Energy' [released in 1970], but that's one of the early records that started incorporating a rock feel into jazz. We went more towards a softer funk approach, as opposed to that screaming shit that McLaughlin did. So the drugs mixing with the tumultuous political times with Martin Luther and Malcolm X and all this other shit going on, and the war in Viet Nam and Kennedy's assassination—all this shit was swirling together in a big pot. It gave us the opportunity to explore all these new sounds and rhythms in song forms. And sometimes, no song forms! I had a loft at the time, so we could play there 24/7. I had a piano and a set of drums, so a million cats came by, and I've got tons of recordings of all this music. We made records that way. Very often, there'd just be a simple little riff, and we'd be creative beyond that. And other times, there'd be nothing—somebody would make something up, and away we'd go. So it was a tremendously exciting time for the development of music during that period.

Jan Hammer: The first time I met [Tommy] was through Jeremy Steig—I met him at Jeremy's house.

Gene Perla: Where I met [Tommy] and under what circumstances, I have no clue. What probably happened was I met him at somebody's apartment in New York—it could have been Jeremy's. I remember I took to the guy right from the giddy-up. We played a week at Slug's [Perla took Kenny Passarelli's spot on bass]—for the better part of a week. I remember that a couple of guys came in at the end, and I think they recorded us two nights in a row with a four-track machine. When they were doing the recording—it was a loud club—it was pretty tough to get separation. So they took a table that a patron would sit at, and put it on stage. They had Jeremy standing on the table, and they had a high microphone for him! The whole thing was dumb—the way they recorded it. But it was funny as shit.

I remember Don Elias was the drummer on some of that stuff. We fit like a hand in a glove—in our rhythmic feeling and understanding of different kinds of music, because of his knowledge of Latin, swing, and funk. And Tommy, you could say he got his cue from Hendrix—but I don't know what Jimi could do in terms of playing swing. Tommy could do that. Yet, the sounds he would come up with—with his foot pedals and his creative ideas—would lead us on great trips. We'd play these simple riffs, and he'd take us all kinds of places. We'd feed him and he'd feed us. We didn't play with him that much, but the few times that we did, it was just great.

Jeremy was the leader of the group—it was always 'The Jeremy Steig Group.' [Tommy] was hired by Jeremy, so I had nothing to do with that business. The thing is that Don Alias, myself, and Jan Hammer were living together in my loft in New York. One of the things we were doing as a trio was working with Jeremy. We worked a lot of gigs with Jeremy. Tommy shows up, and we did some things with the keyboard and guitar together, but then I remember we did this Slug's thing, and I don't think Jan was on that—I think it was just a quartet with Tommy. I don't know if there was any talk of [forming a permanent group with Tommy]. I mean, Jeremy would hire us, and if I was available, I'd make it. I was working *eight nights* a week—I was a very in-demand jazz bass player in New York at the time. I was busy as shit. But I would always try to play with Jeremy if Don and Jan were in the band, because it was always such an exciting experience to play with those guys—and Tommy as well.

Jan Hammer: We were going to record some demos of music—including my tune, that was later released with Mahavishnu Orchestra, "Sister Andrea" [on 1973's 'Between Nothingness and Eternity']. This demo was how Tommy met Billy Cobham—it was on this demo session that we did at Electric Lady, with Eddie Kramer. It's one of my favorite recordings of my music, *ever*. It's out on one of those compilations [the 1996 Tommy Bolin Archives release, 'From the Archives']. That was a demo we did of my tune. What Tommy did on that was just *mind-boggling*.

Eddie Kramer: That I think was an experimental thing—the fact that he was taking off on more of a blues/rock/jazz tangent. I think that opened him up to a lot of experimentation. I seem to remember that Jeremy was pretty enamored of his playing, and that there was a great jazz drummer, who had a terrific feel [Billy Cobham]. The problem that I always had with it was the flute sound versus the guitar sound—I'm not quite sure how that all went together. Jan Hammer was absolutely stupendous. So basically, Tommy was in a very good league, and couldn't help but be influenced by these guys.

Gene Perla: The story with the Electric Lady recordings was Jeremy hooked something up to go there. We were supposed to go with Don Alias, Jan Hammer, Tommy, Jeremy, and myself. We get ready to go to the studio, and Elias fucking got on a plane and split—to play a gig on the west coast! I later tracked him down, and I fucking read him the riot act. I said, "How could you do such a thing? Just walk out on us and not say anything to anybody?" But any case, here comes this session—rushing up on us. I call Billy Cobham, and that's why Cobham came and filled in.

Jan Hammer: You hear it immediately. [Tommy] wasn't really playing—he was just *allowing* the stuff to come out. He was channeling it—it was like no effort in what he was doing. It was wonderful, and I really learned a lot from it. It definitely influenced me a great deal. That's where I really heard him 'go to town'—especially the interplay with him and the repeats from the Echoplex. I'd never heard anybody do anything remotely like that. That totally blew my mind.

Eddie Kramer: I had very good feelings about him as a guitar player. I recorded Jeremy, [Tommy] came in, and everyone thought he was going to be the next Jeff Beck. He was an up-and-coming great guitar player. He had a great tone—I loved his feel, it was very bluesy. He could have been at least as good as Stevie Ray Vaughan. He was certainly in that league—he was potentially a great guitar player. He hadn't quite found his mark yet.

Gene Perla: The tunes that we were playing would give us an insight if you could listen to the 'Energy' album, because we played a lot of those tunes. You'll notice that there's one tune that always sticks in my mind—it goes [sings same riff repeatedly], and that's it! That's the tune! And then somebody would solo over that. The songs that we played with Jeremy were often little riffs that Jan and Jeremy would make up. If you look at the writer credits on that album, it's mostly tunes by Jeremy and Jan as writers. But they're just like little riffs. When Tommy walked in, we were already set doing this stuff. So he would listen, hear the riff, and then jump on with us. It was very seldom that Jeremy or anyone would say to anybody what to play. Somebody would say, "Hey, I've got this riff," they'd start playing, and then bang, an arrangement would come about.

Johnnie Bolin: Tommy never did any vinyl with Jeremy. After about a month in New York, Tommy came back to Colorado, and got Energy going. Jeremy has an album called 'Energy'—that's how Tommy came up with the name.

Energy

Bobby Berge: [Tommy] wanted to play with me, so we started our own thing—Energy. Then Stanley [Sheldon] came out to Boulder, and said, "My cousin really wants to play, Tom Stephenson." We were all set. Once we started jamming in '71-ish with Tom, Stanley, Tommy, and me, that was it. We were really happy with what were doing. We got Gary Wilson as a singer and Bobby LaKind [as percussionist, later of the Doobie Brothers]—we just jammed with a lot of local people. The fusion thing was happening at that time—Mahavishnu, Weather Report—we loved that stuff, we were into it. So we started doing that kind of thing—jamming. It was great.

Stanley Sheldon: I met [Tommy] over the phone. I was playing in a band when I first left Kansas and moved to Colorado—a band called Amadeus— with this guy Gerard McMahon, who went on to later write a lot of jingles for commercials. He's still in New York doing that, I think. So Gerard and I were playing together in this band, and he knew Tommy previously because they were both in Boulder together at the same time. Then, Tommy and I crossed paths a couple times—Amadeus moved out to California, we lived out there for six months. Tommy was playing there, and Tommy and I arranged to get together and do a jam for the first time. It was he and I, and Frosty from the Lee Michaels Band. Frosty came out and played drums with us, and we just had a kick ass jam. From that point on, we knew we were going to try and get this fusion thing together. We didn't know it was going to be called Energy at that point. Later on, my cousin, Tom Stephenson, met Tommy—just as he was leaving Zephyr. My cousin and I grew up in Ottawa, Kansas, playing in our first bands together, and here we are, playing together with Tommy—coming from completely different angles. And that's how Energy started. I'd never heard anything like it. I'd listened to [Miles Davis'] 'Bitches Brew' a little bit and a couple of those fusion things that were very early. But Tommy really was the one that turned us all on to this form of music, because he had been hanging out in New York. So Tommy brought this back to Colorado, and turned us on to his favorites—John McLaughlin and Mahavishnu. But Tommy was playing with Jan Hammer *before* Mahavishnu. There was no one more cutting edge than Tommy Bolin.

Tom Stephenson: Stan and I had a band together in high school, and then I went through all the bands in this area. I finally ended up with John Bartle—he grew up with Tommy and played guitar with Tommy a lot. He said, "Listen, you're too good to be playing in these crappy bands. I have this friend who just quit a group called Zephyr, and is putting a group together. You ought to call him." Literally, I called him that day—he was in Boulder—and he said, "Yeah, come on out." Within a week, I loaded up my equipment, went out in a U-Haul, unloaded the gear, had an audition that day, got the gig. Kenny Passarelli was playing with us at that time, Bobby Berge, Tommy, and I. Stanley soon joined the deal, and Kenny joined [Joe] Walsh. Stanley and I basically lived in Tommy's backyard—in a van.

John Tesar: And they were eating crab apples, because they didn't have any money. It got pretty grim there for a while.

Stanley Sheldon: [Tommy] was electric. He was *glowing*—the kid just had it. You knew it just by looking at him. He was so happy all the time—very much the comedian, and even in the early days, he loved to drink and get high. He loved life. *A little too much.*

Tom Stephenson: Barry Fey was our manager—which was a huge mistake. Barry tried several times to get some name [singers]—we almost had Paul Rodgers come over, and that fell through.

Gary Wilson: I was in Boulder—I was a student. I had gone to school in Kansas for one year, and then I transferred. I'm from Colorado originally. I had been in music since I was in junior high school—I had a band called the Citations. Then I started another group before I went to college, that was called Four Days. After that, I was at C.U., and was sitting in with different bands around Boulder. I got a pretty good reputation, and somehow, Tommy got my name. The first time I met Tommy was at a bar called the Skunk Creek Inn—owned by a guy named Alan Ross, who brought in a lot of national and local acts into this bar in Boulder. Somebody came in the bar and said, "Hey Gary, some guy's looking for you outside." And I see this guy with rainbow hair [laughs]. He said, "I'm Tommy Bolin, I'm a guitarist. I was with the group Zephyr, and I'm looking for a singer. I want you to meet me over my house." He was very aggressive [laughs]. It was almost like he was telling me, "Hey, *I chose you*. Meet me at my house on Pleasant Street," which was near the Hill. The Hill was a very popular, picture-esque, colorful area—where all the heads and all the students met up. There were different bars on the Hill—clothing stories and waterbed stores. I said, "O.K." So the next day, I went over to this house—he was living with Karen at the time—and he started playing all these different kinds of music. He was playing soul, Latin, flamenco—he was fluid in all these different styles. I was like, "Wow. This guy is something!" I didn't know much about him—I did like rock music a lot, because I was a big Jimi Hendrix fan—but I was blown away. I sat there and we sang and played music for two or three hours. He said, "Have you ever heard this?" And would play a little of this song and that, and I'd hum along. He said, "Look, I want you to be the singer of my band, Energy." I said, "Well, cool!"

Otis Taylor: Gary Wilson was more a soul singer, and Tommy was trying to get him more in a 'rock' mentality. So Tommy would have me come jam, so maybe Wilson would get the idea to be more 'rock n' roll.'

Gary Wilson: I remember going into Barry's office early on, and Barry was about 300 pounds at the time, and had a reputation as being one of those guys chewing the cigar, spitting it out, and hollering at everybody. Very coarse, Chicago, pushy person. I remember walking into his office with Tommy, and Tommy saying, "Hey Barry, we've got a new singer." I think the push was for Tommy to incorporate a singer with this band. Because I think Energy started out as a mostly instrumental group—the music was fusion-esque. It was very progressive.

Otis Taylor: Energy played Tulagi's a lot. One time, Tommy and I were at Tulagi's, watching a concert. I was not sitting with him—maybe the next table over. Tommy walks over to me, and goes, "Otis, this guy is really bugging me, can you go talk to him?" He thought Tommy was a girl [laughs]! Because he had long hair and kinda wide hips. I'll never forget that—I had to go talk to the guy. He didn't have a real androgynous look, but he *almost* did. But if someone was drunk and wasn't paying attention . . . back in those days, not everybody had long hair. A lot of stupid assholes got confused over that shit. Now it's not so common, but back then—if you've got long hair, you're a girl.

G. Brown: He was totally identifiable, because he was coloring his hair in red and green plumes way before anyone else.

Johnnie Bolin: I think Karen started making a living out of clothing—she was doing this and doing that for other people—and then she started doing 'rock n' roll clothes.' So he took advantage of that. And his hair, it was right around the time of the 'Todd' album, when Todd Rundgren had his hair colored like that. It seems like Tommy had that done right around the same time he did. Not that he was really into the glam thing, but that Bowie thing was happening at the time, and I guess he saw what Hendrix wore. I think it was time for him to change.

John Tesar: [Karen] was approaching color and coordination like an artist would with a canvas. And Tommy was her canvas. But Tommy would steer things. It seemed like he practically went without eating to save up enough money for a pair of snakeskin boots at one point. She had this cape/sash kind of thing. She had kind of a pirate look, and I always thought that had she been classically trained, she would have been a costume designer. Karen's color palette was strongly towards purple for him. Purple, grey, black, silver. Put him in silk and velvet. I'm sure that she was buying factory seconds at the sewing store, and putting them together out of old draperies or whatever. But Tommy absolutely loved what she did for him. That was really early on—she was decking him out, and a lot of the rest of us at Boulder at that time were in old Levi's, lumberjack shirts. In my mind, it was like total theater.

Mike Drumm: I was at a party—I think it was '71 in Denver, back in the brief period when Tumbleweed Records existed—when everyone moved to Colorado. That's when Joe Walsh was there—he started Barnstorm with Kenny Passarelli. Tumbleweed Records was Bill Szymczyk's label—who produced all the Eagles albums. Everybody wanted to move to Colorado. It was the high water mark of Colorado being, "Maybe this was going to become 'the new place'." Because everybody wanted to escape from what big cities represented. So there was this party at this old Victorian House—we were there, and in the basement, they had this intense ventilation fan that could suck all the air out really strong, in case the police showed up. So you'd go smoke pot downstairs, and at a moment's notice, try and get rid of all the smoke. I'm down there, and I witnessed Joe Walsh meeting Tommy for the first time—at that party.

Kenny Passarelli: Joe Walsh had quit the James Gang—this must have been '71. Tommy got my number, called me in Vancouver, and said, "Joe Walsh is looking for a bass player. I recommended you, he's going to call you." And that's what happened. Tommy Bolin made that happen for me.

Stanley Sheldon: I think it was an interesting time, because Boulder was a real musical mecca. Joe Walsh had moved to town, Stephen Stills was there. All these people were putting their bands together—Three Dog Night. And Jim Guercio had his studio up in the mountains, just fifteen minutes away, Caribou Ranch. A very famous studio. And Jim Guercio was Chicago's manager. So there were always musicians out there.

Gary Wilson: Our home base was Tulagi's—we did a lot of rehearsing at Tulagi's, which at the time, was the biggest spot in Boulder for music. We played there about a weekend or sometimes two weekends out of every month. Shortly after that, we started taking gigs.

Robert Ferbrache: [Ebbet's Field] was sort of a dingy, smelly club, that had the most superior sound system for a place of its size. It had Crown Amplifiers, clip speakers, nice microphones, and a nice P.A. It was a world-class place. You wouldn't believe the roster of people that played there—Steve Martin, Dolly Parton, John Prine, Steve Goodman. G. Brown is coordinating retrospective releases from Ebbet's Field from some of the recordings, and the personnel is unbelievable. [It held] 220.

Otis Taylor: It was a hip club. It was a Chuck Morris thing—the legendary promoter.

Robert Ferbrache: I met Tommy long before I worked at Ebbet's Field, because I went and saw him play numerous times. At times when I'd go see him, there'd be only five people seeing him play. I took a little notice. I'd be the only one there, and you get to know people that way a little bit. Energy was an amazing band at that time. I was pretty young then—19. I think the first time I saw them was at Tulagi's, and they did "Down Stretch"—that was going in a new direction. That was like hearing 'Sgt. Pepper' for the first time in '67. This would have been in late '71—I saw "Down Stretch," and I was just like, "*Whoa! That is the future of music!*" Just the first note of the song, when they started doing it, it ripped my spine in half. It was one of those things—the sonic quality just went right through your body. They didn't sound like anybody. I think the best they were was when they weren't trying to appease anybody. I mean, they tried a little bit to be a commercial band, but it was that time in the '70s where there was a lot of different stuff going around. They were pretty unique. To me, it felt like maybe heavy metal at the time, but obviously, if you listen to it, it's not at all. It's not fusion, either.

Stanley Sheldon: We were sort of . . . nobody really understood what we were doing [laughs]! We were playing in a lot of bars and playing this instrumental fusion music, which no one out there had heard before. So they liked it I think, but nobody knew quite what to make of what we were doing. They would just sit there flabbergasted, with their mouths open. *"What the fuck are these guys doing?"* Some people got it and some people didn't. Barry Fey took us under his wing, and his right hand man, Chuck Morris, ran a club in Boulder, [and] would hook us up with the blues guys that came to town. So we got to back up John Lee Hooker, Albert King, and Chuck Berry—all in the space of six months. That was fantastic. And we'd go and do little road gigs—we'd go down to Phoenix, for example. Wherever we could get a gig—Southern Colorado. But we never really got out of the bar circuit with that band.

Tom Stephenson: One thing that was fun, on my resume, you'll see there's Albert King, Albert Collins, B.B. King, Chuck Berry, John Lee Hooker, Bonnie Raitt, Big Mama Thornton—when those people came to town, the people they wanted as their band were Stanley, Tommy, Bobby, and I. Those gigs were just a great thrill, because sometimes, we got to open as Energy, and then we'd play as the back-up band for these great blues artists.

Gary Wilson: One of our first gigs was with Albert King. As we were performing, I remember seeing this Buick—an Electra 225. They used to call them 'a deuce and a quarter'—a big automobile. And I saw it from way in the distance—because the concert we played was outdoors on a big flatbed truck, with an electric generator. It would be just be a sea of hippies [laughs]. All types, all sizes, all colors were out there partying and having a great time. But I saw this car come through the back of the crowd, and it parted the sea of people as he drove closer to the stage, as we were performing. We were almost at the end of our last song, and I heard somebody from the side, "Albert King is here!" Everyone was excited. He parked his car—I guess he was slated to perform after us. He walks up to us as we leave the stage, and immediately approaches Tommy, and says something like, "You really blew me away, I really love your playing—I want you guys to back me up." Just like that. They immediately go in a huddle, and about a half hour later, they had put his set together. Albert proceeds to tell them what keys the songs were in, and I believe there was familiarity with his repertoire. They went on stage and blew everybody away. The set was fantastic—it was a number of songs they had thrown together quickly. Tommy was dueling with Albert King—playing the blues. Everybody just went nuts.

Mike Drumm: It was one of the most amazing guitar battles that anybody had ever seen. It was just incredible. Tommy was able to—from a blues idiom perspective—stand toe-to-toe with Albert. Song after song, just having the most blistering interaction. This showed that Tommy was able to play any genre—just step right in and blow everybody's mind. To be able to be so excellent in whatever genre you were playing in . . . what was so unusual about him—and what I appreciated about him—was he had a gift. Very few musicians in my experience come along where you think, "There's something special here that you just don't see." And this is what he had. A lot of people are very talented, but he had something *beyond* that.

Stanley Sheldon: Tommy and Albert King got on famously—they were grinning. Tommy had this Echoplex gadget—they'd be trading fours, and Tommy'd blast off this amazing thing with the electronic effect. Albert would just grin and say, "Boy, you got me that time, but you got that box!" Some of my favorite memories are those. My biggest disappointment is that no one ever taped it. We did a week with John Lee Hooker at Tulagi's. John Lee Hooker was a little more sedate—he was such a gentleman, too. To us kids, to play the blues like that and get that lesson from the masters was invaluable.

Tommy Bolin: I learned a lot about lead [from playing with Albert King]; learned that you don't have to blow your cookies in the first bar. At that time, I was playing everything I knew when I took a lead. And he said, "Man, just say it all with one note." He taught me that it was much harder to be simple than to be complicated during solos. If you blow your cookies in the first bar, you have nowhere to go. Blues is really good that way. It teaches you to develop coherent solos, because the form you're playing over is so basic. You have to develop leads that go someplace. The neatest compliment I ever got was when I was playing with Albert King at an indoor concert in Boulder, Colorado. He used to let me take solos, and I was very into playing that day. After the concert he came up to me and said, "You got me today, but I'll get you tomorrow!" I really respect him. He's a beautiful player.

Stanley Sheldon: [Chuck Berry] was kind of a jerk [laughs]. He showed up and played about 20 minutes, and he has to be paid in cash—the story's famous about him. He pulled up in his limo with a woman on his arm, got out, played the 20 minutes, barked a few orders at us right before we went on, and that was pretty much it for him. He wasn't so much fun to play with. We all knew the songs. I think he put a lot of people off, but we were glad to do it just to play with him.

Bobby Berge: We played Colorado Springs with Ten Years After—that was really cool. Met Alvin Lee. We used to back up Buddy Guy.

Gary Wilson: We did a number of those [outdoor shows]. In those days, there a lot of those 'baby Woodstock' type gigs. I would say during my time with the band—which was only seven or eight months—we did ten shows like that. We did shows with Leslie West/Mountain, Savoy Brown, Billy Preston, Little Feat—a number of groups. When we opened for Savoy Brown, they were from England and they were really wild, rowdy guys. But they seemed to know about Tommy. He always got his props from other musicians we performed with. It seemed like he was 'the young gun.' Whenever we played, either Leslie

West or the members knew of him—his reputation was growing as we spoke. He had a great aura, he was very charismatic. Tommy was a very soft-spoken person. At times, even effeminate. But at times, he had a very big aura about him—a big, friendly aura. He would change—by the time he hit the stage, he had this power, almost this 'strength.' On stage, he was so strong. Very fluid. And his personality when he was playing was so much different than his personality off stage. He was very quick—talked fast a lot. Tommy seemed to listen to what you were saying, but not *hear* what you were saying [laughs]. It seemed to me he always had his own agenda. He seemed to know where he was going, what he wanted. He had a power of controlling things. And people wanted to give him what he wanted a lot. We had a lot of groupies and people around that would always say, "What do you need? What can I do for you?" Him, being soft-spoken, might say, "I'd like a little Jack Daniels." "Here's your Jack Daniels!" "I need some strings." "Here's ten sets of strings!" Whatever Tommy wanted, he'd get it.

Stanley Sheldon: From the earliest days on, we were involved [with drugs]. Tommy and I were always the romanticists, thinking heroin would be fun. He and I were drawn to that one. I can remember one early point, when we were up in Cheyenne, Wyoming, he had shot up, and he almost died right then. I stood there and watched him almost die—he went into convulsions. At that point, I knew that Tommy's system was a little more susceptible to these things than mine. I was a little 'heartier.' He was only 20 years old at that point; this would have been late Energy. But from the earliest point on, Tommy and I were flirting with that stuff—big-time. The club owners back in Boulder used to pay us with coke. We'd do a gig for a week, and they'd give us like a quarter ounce or something. Or we'd do a couple of nights and they would just give us a big bag of coke. And then, Tommy and I would go to everybody's house and portion it out to the players. Of course, our portions were enormous and everybody else's were considerably smaller [laughs]! I remember Bobby and the other players grumbling about their portions.

Johnnie Bolin: We were in Denver—we were walking down the street and there was one of those pay phones. Tommy calls Barry, and we'd heard about the Stones coming with Stevie Wonder, and it's a Feyline Production. He says, "Barry, I just heard the ad. *You've got to make me a star.* I can't do this no more—playing locally." Barry could get you there—way faster than anybody else could. He had the vehicle to do it.

Gary Wilson: A couple of months after I was in the group, we went in and did this demo. ["Red Skies"] was my signature tune—my time to stand out. When I first met with Tommy, he briefed me on it, and it just fell into place. It was a basic blues, but with this prelude and this intro thing that was beautiful. The way he set it up was nice. We turned it around to something else—it was almost like a jazz tune. When we went to record that, man, we were just happy to be in the studio. I was hyped. We were very loose—what I mean is there was no tenseness in the studio. It was almost like a rehearsal—it went down so smoothly. Not a lot of overdubbing, just one take. I remember almost being in a trance doing it—we were locked into it. We were all energized and in a good space.

I remember a song called "Limits"—Tom Stephenson sang the lead. "Limits" was more of a pop-type song. It wasn't hard rocking, and it wasn't blues. We almost thought, "Does this fit?" But Tom did a real good job singing it. My part on that song was a lot of background vocals—we put a lot of real nice, pop-y type harmonies on it. It was almost like Jackson 5 background vocals. On the tail end of the song, I got this idea to hit this Marvin Gaye-ish, "What's Going On" thing, and I did some overdubs on the end of that. Tommy started doing these Wes Montgomery octaves. The beginning of the song was beautiful—it started off slow, kind of like "Red Skies." It had a beginning, an apex, and then it went into this ending that was like "What's Going On." But the music was rock and pop. The other tunes we did—we did a couple of instrumentals, we might have done Jackie Wilson's "(Your Love Keeps Lifting Me) Higher and Higher." I've never found a recording of that. I thought we did it that day in the studio, because that's a song that Tommy really liked to play. We were going to try and get a deal, and there were about five songs on total in there.

Bobby Berge: We were rockers—we could play anything. But Gary was more R n' B. And he's great—I love Gary—but it was more R n' B/funk, and we wanted a rock singer that fit in with us more.

Tom Stephenson: Gary was over the top—he's a great guy, great singer, but not the style we needed. What we needed was a Paul Rodgers. I don't know what Barry's deal was—he could get plenty of labels to come listen to us, and we tried obligatorily to write something like . . . "Rock-A-Bye," I wrote that song. It was a simple [song]—we tried to write some commercial stuff, but it wasn't what we were good at. What we were good at was fusion—"Hok-O-Hey" and "Homeward Strut" was the stuff we really shined on.

Gary Wilson: We did the recording, and I wanted to do my soul music thing. Being a black fella, I don't know if the market was ready for a black leader with a rock band—at the time. There was nothing like that happening. I mean, *maybe* Dobie Gray. The music was so powerful and really different—it couldn't really fit a niche at that time. I don't know if it could find its niche in the market. I don't know if Tommy was getting any pressures, but they were trying to break through. There was never a big disagreement where I said, "I quit the band," and nobody came to me and said, "You're fired." It was just kind of 'a drift apart.' Tommy and I talked a couple of times. At the time, you had Sly Stone and the Temptations. Being a brother, I wanted to get into that funk groove. I bowed out. Jeff Cook was actually a songwriter, and he was Tommy's friend before I was in the band. When I bowed out, he fit in right there. The Energy that a lot of people recognize was with Jeff Cook.

Jeff Cook: Actually, I lived in England [circa Tommy's Zephyr period], so I don't know anything about that. I came back, and the first Zephyr record was already out, and I didn't see him for maybe a year and a half. So I came up, auditioned, and they hired me to be the singer for Energy. That's when Tommy and I started doing our co-writing. Mainly, I would write lyrics and Tommy would write music. He also had another co-writer, John Tesar, so we would all submit stuff, and then he would pick the lyrics and write songs around them. But several times, we would collaborate on songs. It just seemed very natural. I was always critically analyzing my writing, but he never ever made a critical statement of what I wrote. He would always just dig it and then write a song around it. It was a very natural relationship.

Bobby Berge: Jeff fit the bill totally, as far as 'a rocker.'

Tom Stephenson: We had this incredible band—that was above everybody's head. We had a great following, but we could not find a singer. Jeff is a great guy, but was not the greatest vocalist—he had about a three-note range.

Jeff Cook: It was the very best combination of musical people that I've ever encountered. And I think each one of the members of Energy would say the same thing. There were times when the music would just take off and go places we never really intended it to . . . and we were anything but a commercial success. But Tommy constantly referred to the fact that this was his favorite band to play with, and it was because of the chemistry that we had with each other.

Max Carl: Tom Stephenson called and invited me to come see Tommy and Energy at a gig at an Omaha high school gym. I drove up from Lincoln on a dreary Nebraska afternoon, walking through a door into a space, which as a kid, was full of intense and sweet memories. A place where my two favorite things were played—basketball and music. Tommy and the band were soundchecking/rehearsing. It was the first time I had ever heard a Marshall amp, so you can imagine my astonishment. Tom Stephenson introduced me to Tommy and the band. Good vibes all around. Jeff Cook really impressed me. I recall him strolling off to a corner to run through the tunes, singing alone. Tommy and I sat at the edge of the stage and talked about mutual friends we shared, and how it was good to finally meet. Tommy and I hit it off instantly and began a connection that relied essentially on humor—I could make him laugh. It was a glue that stuck all the way to the end with us.

Jeff Cook: The tremendous level of musicianship—we played jazz-fusion, we played blues—there was a place for every kind of music there. We weren't really a pop band. We got fired from more gigs than we ever were successful at, because we weren't doing covers and stuff like that for club owners.

Johnnie Bolin: They were struggling. They didn't really get the breaks—they never got a record deal.

Bobby Berge: I'm not sure who, but a couple of record exec's came to a club called the Soundtrack in Denver.

Jeff Cook: That was a classic show business mistake. We knew that Barry Fey was going to be bringing an executive from Columbia Records to watch a show. So we came out, and the first set, we were *smoking*—really on top of our game, really nailed it. Barry came back with the record guy and they were very effervescent and very excited about the set, and said, "We love it—I think we can make a deal. We'll see you guys later." And of course, in the dressing room after hearing that, it looked like we were going to get a record deal. Between sets, we decided to celebrate a little bit—drinking shots. Well, we celebrated more than a little bit [laughs]! We were basically all shit-faced by the time we got to the stage for the second set. But what we didn't know was that the guy *stayed*. He saw the good, the bad, and the ugly.

Bobby Berge: That's one of the saddest things, that we didn't get signed, because that group was just fantastic. But back then, we were above a lot of people's heads musically. We weren't commercial enough.

Mike Drumm: The way artists are pursued now, [the labels] would have figured it out. But back then; they couldn't quite grasp that they should sign these guys. And part of it at that point was, "Was Jeff a good enough singer?" And Tommy was obviously loyal to Jeff—Jeff wrote a lot of the lyrics to some of Tommy's better-known songs. That might have been part of the reason—he just didn't have that great of a range as a singer. Whatever the reason, at that point, [Tommy] approached me, and said he wanted to buy a reel-to-reel deck so he could record demos, at this stereo store in Boulder, which is long gone. At that point, Barry had become his manager, and I'm thinking, "Why do you need my help?" It didn't quite make sense. I co-signed on a loan for him—I actually got the document back a number of years back, where we both signed. Karen made sure they paid that thing off. Here's this guy that's so amazing, has such a gift . . . yet he's broke.

Robert Ferbrache: Tommy had original tracks, obviously—all those [Energy] tracks ended up being James Gang songs. And all those songs turned into Deep Purple songs. He bailed both of those bands out, because they got him in the band, and they didn't have any material. There's a couple of them that Energy was doing, like "Lady Luck"—they were doing that in '72. Energy was doing most of those James Gang songs that were on that first album in particular. There's demos of Energy doing all those.

Stanley Sheldon: We were working on that song "Homeward Strut" for quite a while, but we never really played it in Energy. It was just a riff Tommy had. Some of the ones that I do remember he wrote with Jeff, like "Got No Time for Trouble." "Alexis"—we did record a version of that, early on in Boulder. And Joe Vitale played drums on it—Tommy, I, and Joe basically cut that track. It was a really good version, it never got to vinyl—he recorded it with the James Gang. But our version I liked a lot better. It could already be out—they've released so many of those tapes on Tommy's Archives label. That was the first time [Tommy] started singing, We recorded it, and we didn't know who was going to sing it, so he said, "I'll sing it." Joe Vitale really helped us out on that, because he's really good in the studio. He played with Joe Walsh and Stephen Stills—he was one of those guys in Boulder back in the day. "Summer Breezes"—I think we worked on that in Energy. "Standing in the Rain" we used to do. John [Tesar] and Tommy wrote a lot of those songs. Tommy and I wrote "The Grind" together.

Johnnie Bolin: I was at the studio when he first did "Alexis." It was during Energy—there were no drums on it at all. We just walked down there and he had it set up. Probably took an hour. It was right in downtown Boulder on the Hill. It was a 16-track, and he turned the lights off. He was unsure of himself as a singer. He sang all the time, but he didn't think he was a good enough singer to be a singer. But he had a unique voice—it's a loveable voice. He doesn't have to be Gino Vannelli or the guy from Queensrÿche [laughs]. He doesn't have 'a Glenn Hughes range,' but he's got a real loveable voice—and that's what I think really sold it. It catches you—you feel like you know the guy or something. I always felt that way 'cause I'm his brother, but there's a lot of people that feel like he's telling it from his heart—it's not just a song to him. It's like he's trying to tell you something. I don't know much about that song—Jeff Cook might know. Jeff was like a John Steinbeck—he could probably write a book as well as he could write a song. It made it sound like Tommy had been there—like the south of France, and Savannah. He'd never been to Savannah, but he'd written the song ["Savannah Woman"]. And he started writing like Jeff did—you don't have to go there to write about it. So I don't know if "Alexis" was really about an Alexis, or just something he'd made up. Tommy started to realize he didn't actually have to go to someplace to sing about it.

Jeff Cook: I think "Alexis" is one of the best songs he ever did. I wrote the lyrics to that. It had sensitivity, it had strong lyric imagery, and the music fit the mood of the song very well. I think "Savannah Woman" was that way, "Alexis" was that way, and on the rockers, "Teaser" was that way. The song was just a piece of fiction. When I wrote the song, I'd never been to Atlanta, I'd never been to New Orleans, and the lyrics were all just imagination. But what's very interesting is that whole song came true in my life. Ten years later, I ended up moving to Atlanta, meeting a woman younger than myself, marrying her, and having a daughter—so we named her Alexis. And her whole family was from New Orleans. So the song actually came true!

Max Carl: In late fall of '72, I was contacted by Tom Stephenson—Jeff Cook was leaving Energy and Tommy was looking for a new singer. I flew to Denver, then up to Boulder to see the band at Tulagi's. The band was solid with flashes of great technique, playing a strutting meld of electric blues and fusion. It was a great recipe as jazz is grounded in the blues and fusion borrowed from rock. Stanley Sheldon was playing a fretless bass—the first time I'd seen that. That was an amazing sound. Bobby Berge had a big rock kit with double kick drums—he had 'groove control.' Tom Stephenson was from the Winwood B3 school, with a big blonde Hammond C3 and matching blond 122 Leslie. Also, the Wurlitzer electric piano—as I recall, it was the 140 series. Tommy dominated the proceedings with his Marshall stack and Sunburst Stratocaster. He also did a great slide piece on a Gibson Cherry ES-335 12-string. Now *that* was a locomotive! Jeff Cook stood up there in the eye of the tempest singing like a New Orleans soul shouter. I grabbed him as he walked by me at the bar. We became lifelong friends on that night—I was best man at his wedding in 1991. I joined Energy in the end of '72. I recall going into Barry Fey's office in Denver, and Barry saying, "You guys are breaking records all over—everywhere you play, you get fired!" It was true; the band was a tough sell. We went into the studio that year, but the cuts weren't so inspired. We did "Standing in the Rain," "Dreamer," and a few others. Tom Stephenson's piano was simply great. Tommy's solo was my all time favorite—the Echoplex stuff is pure soul. Somehow, the greatness of that particular recording never saw the light, as is many times the case.

Johnnie Bolin: A little known fact is that Tommy did the music for a mountain climbing special on 'The Wide World of Sports.' It was '72 or something. It's called 'The Naked Edge'—Tommy watched the movie, and then played this space-y music. It's a 20-minute documentary. It's not really a song—like at one point, the guy is climbing the mountain and falls, and Tommy kicks in his Echoplex. It's 'space music.' It's a pretty good soundtrack.

Max Carl: For me, Tommy's creativity and playing was at its finest during his Boulder days. Energy was such a great four-piece. Wonderful players all around—in addition to the sum being greater than the whole. Tommy of course brought everyone's performance up to another level. Standing up in front of that band brought singing from me that I had never been capable of before.

Mike Drumm: Energy was really struggling. They couldn't catch on.

Tom Stephenson: I was the first to leave. Joe [Walsh] kept calling me about every six months, and it was a good starting thing—I ended up making $10,000.00 a week with Joe. We never saw $1,000.00 *a night* with Tommy. I just had to do it. From that point, it just went downhill, and Tommy decided, "Screw this, I've got to go out there and make some money." I know Karen was on his ass, because basically, she was supporting him. We weren't making enough money where he could have supported himself—she was paying for the apartment they were living in. Everybody just had to move on. Stan and I got great offers. I never had more fun than I had with Energy, but it just wasn't commercial enough.

Stanley Sheldon: We were just too bizarre. We were a little bit ahead of our time. That type of music was on the cusp, but it wasn't ready. And to tell you the truth, we really didn't have any arrangements that were tight enough that they would have made a fantastic record. We were a jam band. For that era, we were jamming very strange time signatures. There were some people doing it better than us probably—like McLaughlin, with more arranged stuff. The nature of that music is improvisation, so we had some wonderful 'skeleton structures' to play over. But it was really never tightly arranged enough for us to do it. And then we had some personnel problems—people dropping out, and always changing with what we were doing.

Bobby Berge: I ended up getting a day job, because I got tired of being broke. The next thing I know, Tommy gets invited to play on Cobham's album, and he's off to New York.

Billy Cobham/Legendary 4-Nikators

Johnnie Bolin: When Jeremy had Tommy come out to New York, that's when Billy heard him. They did four or five songs, and that's how the 'Spectrum' album came about—it was all through Jeremy.

Jan Hammer: The Jeremy Steig thing was very loose—we didn't know what we were after, just trying to lay some tunes down to see what they sounded like. It was really demos for a potential new Jeremy project—I don't even know if we got around to do it. It was something that didn't really lead to anything else after that. What did happen was the connection between Tommy, myself, and Billy. 'Spectrum' was a much more high energy and high profile project.

Stanley Sheldon: I was in his apartment the day Billy Cobham walked up his stairs, knocked on Tommy's door, and invited him to play on the 'Spectrum' album. Tommy had this little apartment in Boulder where he lived with Karen, on Euclid Avenue. Mahavishnu [who Billy was playing with at the time] was in town—they were playing at the university, and Tommy had obviously made some contact with him. He came up, knocked on the door, came in, and the next thing I knew, he was inviting Tommy to come play on his new solo record.

Tommy Bolin: It was really weird. I did sessions with Billy some time ago. They were like demos—this was before Mahavishnu. They were instrumentals, and he dug the way I played. Then he called me up out of the blue six months later. I was starving to death at the time. That album helped me a lot.

Barbara Bolin: Somebody like Billy Cobham would call, wanting him to be on his album. The first thing he'd do is call us up and tell us—we were as excited as he was.

Jeff Cook: That was something that happened very quickly. One day he got a phone call, the next day he was in New York, and in two days, they recorded the whole record. Tommy was the only person on the session that couldn't read music, but again, he was such a natural musician that they would just show him what parts to play and he had it in a second. He just smoked it. It was one of the biggest paydays that he'd ever seen—getting paid scale [for] a recording session in New York [laughs]. So that certainly was cause for celebration.

Karen Ulibarri: Quite honestly, it was really just a session. It was just going to do an album in New York at first—this is what we thought. He couldn't believe Billy Cobham was calling him up and wanting him to come play on an album. He just couldn't believe it—the chance to come to New York and play with jazz musicians of that caliber was just mind-boggling. The opportunity was just phenomenal, because the eventual outcome was just brilliant.

Jan Hammer: Tommy blew our minds when we first heard him on those demos. It was a great, lucky break to run into him at that time. And it was a big break for him, because he really got noticed out of that session. Everybody heard him and went, "What's going on here?" With 'Spectrum,' it was a real breakthrough, and everybody was sharp and on top of things. Everybody was focused. A lot of it was not ever written. So it wasn't any handicap for him— you hum whatever you have in mind, and it comes together in rehearsal. Even though Billy had written some things down, they were more for the other type of sessions, which Tommy wasn't on—the more jazzy things with the larger group. But as far as the things with Tommy and the four-piece band, there was a one-off riff, and just *go*.

Tommy Bolin: Cobham called me for the 'Spectrum' session, and I said, "I don't know how to read, man." He said it was O.K. So I went to the studio, and he handed me a chart. I told him again I didn't know how to read, so we had a day of rehearsal, then cut the album in two days. In rehearsal I'd just find out the changes—for example, Am to D9 to G6 to E13—and play around those chords and changes. I learned quite a bit through those people. You can't help but learn. All the different styles I've played have really helped me as a guitarist and helped me develop my own way of playing. I have my own style, but it's different for each kind of music. There are certain little characteristic things every player has.

Jan Hammer: Billy is sort of a reserved guy. It's funny, because you hear him, and he's this bombastic, great drummer. But personally, he's very much like a buttoned-down, straight, very square guy. He's not a very extroverted guy—total opposition to what he plays. He's not a demonstrative guy, so I couldn't tell you how friendly or close [Tommy and Billy] were—it was all business. But at the same time, it was *smoking* music.

Tommy Bolin: The sessions with Cobham were a gas. I'd be blasted out of my mind, and Cobham would down a couple of malts before each take.

Jan Hammer: It was just an amazing, lucky combination of the right people at the right time. We were able to do it. I remember it was very effortless. You rolled tape and it happened—I don't even think there were multiple takes. It was so inspired. On the tune "Quadrant 4," the opening solo, a lot of people thought that was Tommy. A lot of reviews kept mentioning that beginning, and it was *me*. Basically, that's why on my next solo album [1975's 'The First Seven Days'], I put a disclaimer—"For those concerned, there is no guitar on this album" [laughs]! It was sort of a jab at the reviewers who got it all wrong. ["Quadrant 4"] is all in the groove.

Johnnie Bolin: He went out there, and then he came back. I don't know if you've heard of Sugarcane Harris—he's a violin player, he played with John Mayall. He had some dates up in Vancouver—I guess I was 18. [Tommy] said, "Want to go with me and Stanley to back up Sugarcane Harris?" I said, "Of course!" So when I picked him up at the airport, he put the Cobham thing in there—in the cassette player. I knew who Cobham was from Mahavishnu. He started playing the beginning of "Quadrant 4," and we're like, "You sound really good there, Tommy." He's like, "That's not even me—*it's keyboards!*"

Mike Drumm: Back then, I lived six doors down from him, on the other side of the alley. I was really into the Mahavishnu Orchestra, and 'Spectrum' was Billy Cobham's take on what the Mahavishnu Orchestra had been doing. I was all excited and went down to his house after the recording was finished, and he gave me this white cassette—an advance copy of 'Spectrum.' When that album came out, it was so exciting. From where I had come from—seeing him in Zephyr and Energy—and the whole 'mind expansion' thing and being into jazz, that was clearly the high water mark for him. This was such a victory for him creatively. And then, the whole attitude in Boulder had to do with it was way hipper for you to be 'a creative star' than to be 'a pop star.' And here he was, doing his ultimate creative star thing, with these incredible world-class musicians that just embraced him.

Stanley Sheldon: When he came back, I was probably the first person— besides Billy's friends—to actually hear the acetate and hear what they had. When I heard it, I was just flabbergasted, I couldn't believe it. I said, "Oh shit Tommy, this is going to put you on the map!" Which it did of course—it's the greatest thing he ever recorded. As far as the world of fusion goes, you can't talk about fusion music without . . . that's in the canon. That's one of the major influences for all—you look at Marcus Miller today, the great fusion bassist, he produced Miles' last records. But on his most recent solo outing, he covered "Red Baron" from 'Spectrum,' that won a Grammy—it's called 'M Squared' [released in 2002]. That record is great, and they do a version of "Red Baron" that's just awesome. I guess what I'm speaking of is the influence it had on all musicians—that one record. It really did. When I tell a musician that Tommy was my friend, they'll quote the 'Spectrum' album. That touched everybody— every thinking musician, anyway.

Tom Stephenson: When he got back, the first thing he said was, "Stan, Tom, come in—listen!" Those were all first takes. He couldn't believe he was sitting there with Cobham. He was playing at his level. I don't think he was prouder of anything that he'd ever done than that. That was just phenomenal stuff. That was exactly what we wanted to do—that was what we were striving to do. He was used to being poor and not having any real feedback from his peers playing-wise—other than us. He was very gracious and had a lot of gratitude towards Billy and Jan for helping him out. It was a wonderful experience.

Martin Barre: I bought 'Spectrum,' and was amazed at the development of his playing.

Barry Fey: When he played on 'Spectrum,' my God, he was beautiful.

Robert Ferbrache: His most successful thing that artistically people really recognize Tommy for was the Cobham album.

Phillip Polimeni: That fucking blew everybody away. As a matter of fact, people were playing it and saying, "Listen to this guitar player, *Tommy Bolin*"— they wouldn't say, "Listen to this drummer, *Billy Cobham*." That is some of the hottest guitar playing.

Jeff Cook: That was the closest any recording ever came to showing his true brilliance as a musician. There were tapes of Energy that never got released, that had flashes of the brilliance and the depth of his playing ability. But as far as on record, clearly 'Spectrum' was the closest it ever came.

Karen Ulibarri: I cannot believe today how that album sounds, and what he did on that album—but it didn't surprise me, because this was a format, a chance for him to suddenly do what he loved. And to play on something like this . . . *did he shine.* Because he just thought to himself, "Maybe they just want me to lay back and play a few licks." He had no idea they were going to let him play as much as he did, with that many musicians. But he was the guitar player and he showed them—they were just blown away.

Jan Hammer: We always talk about influences—how Jeff [Beck] influenced me, and how I influenced him. But definitely, you can hear after he saw and heard Tommy that there was something that also added another ingredient to what Jeff was about. A definite influence happened.

Carmine Appice: That Cobham album is the thing that got Jeff Beck to move on to the 'Blow By Blow' [released in 1975] stuff. I was with Jeff with Beck Bogert & Appice, I had Billy's album and the Mahavishnu album, and we used to drive in the cars together. Pretty much, we would listen to Mahavishnu Orchestra and the Billy Cobham album with Tommy on it. The whole vibe of that jazz-rock mixture, Jeff really liked it. We did a song with B.B.A. called "Jizz Wizz," that came out on 'Beckology' [released in 1991], that was supposed to be on our second album—sort of the bridge between what Beck Bogert & Appice were doing over to what 'Blow By Blow' was. I ended up playing on

'Blow By Blow,' [but] ended not being on the finished product. I played on five songs—we just couldn't work a deal out with Jeff's manager, my manager, Epic, and all that stuff. So they ended up taking me off and putting some other guy—copying my licks and everything [laughs]. Which really sucked. And then the album went out and did really great. But 'Spectrum' was listened to quite a bit by me and Jeff on the road.

Tommy Bolin: 'Spectrum' to me was a kind of new music that could have had a wide appeal. It was not as complicated as the Mahavishnu Orchestra. But after that, [Billy] turned right about and went back to a jazz thing with horns.

Mike Drumm: Billy wanted him to go out on tour, but Billy was going to have horns in the band, and Tommy told me, "I'm not going out on tour with a band with horns. Forget it." He just wasn't interested.

Johnnie Bolin: Billy asked him to play on tour with him, and he said, "I can't go out"—because in Tommy's mind, he had the dream of having his own band.

Jan Hammer: I don't remember anything specific about [if there were plans for another Cobham/Bolin album]. I wasn't approached about it.

David Givens: After [Harold Fielden] graduated, he wanted to put the 4-Nikators back together—this is 1973. So we did.

Harold Fielden: Zephyr had quasi-broken up, I had left Flash, everybody was still in town, and said, "We ought to get the 4-Nikators back for one time and make some money," because we all had to pay rent. Got Candy, David, John Faris, Tommy, David Brown, and Otis Taylor. We had eight or nine people— we played at Art's Bar and Grill as the Legendary 4-Nikators, and it was every Monday for the summer of '73. It was $1.00 to get in, $1.00 drinks, and people would start lining up in late afternoon. It's now a strip place in Boulder, called the Bus Stop.

David Givens: This time, we brought in Mick Manressa, who was the lead singer—he was 'Flash' from Flash Cadillac. So we had Candy, Mick, Harold, me, Tommy, John, Otis Taylor, and a couple of piano players. We did all these big production numbers, like "Leader of the Pack"—we'd bring a motorcycle up on stage! It was just totally fun—it was a complete relief after all that bullshit that we went through in Zephyr. We had a Supremes medley—"Stop! In the Name of Love," "Back in my Arms Again," and "Baby Love." And we did "Fire" by Jimi Hendrix. We did a bunch of '50s stuff, like "Splish Splash," "The Stroll," "Rescue Me," "You Beat Me to the Punch." A bunch of Phil Spector stuff—"Be My Baby," "He's a Rebel." And Tommy would play guitar solos that sounded like sax solos. He could just cop that, "This song needs a sax solo," and he was able to somehow pull that out of his ass. We would do 'themes' for the night—Otis showed up in a kilt, like a black Scottish guy!

Otis Taylor: I was like, "Oh yeah, '50s music—*whatever*." Then all the chicks were coming, and I said, "Man, this is a mistake—I have to get on this" [laughs]! I used to ride my motorcycle on stage—just put exhaust all over the room. It was really stupid. We figured that out after the second time, we couldn't do that anymore—the club owner said, "You can't be doing this!" Because the whole room would fill up with motorcycle exhaust. I'd wear Hawaiian shirts on stage and shit like that. You name it, we played it—"Suspicious Minds" by Elvis. The only song I got to sing on was "Midnight Hour." Back in those days, either you did something interesting, or you had to go play the Holiday Inn circuit.

David Givens: We loved playing in the 4-Nikators. We made more money playing in the 4-Nikators, than we ever made in Zephyr. We were completely in control, there was no pressure, we got to play whatever we wanted to do. Harold the drummer was doing stand-up—it was a big laugh. We had naked dance contests—it was fun, it was an event. All that bad taste of bad records and bullshit was gone. We got to be friends again.

Harold Fielden: The great thing about this for Tommy is he didn't have to be 'a rock star,' because we were playing oldies—there wasn't the pressure on him that I had seen. He was just one of the group. Sometimes, he would come on stage wearing a baseball uniform, and he'd have his glove attached to his belt. He'd still have the Echoplex and do all this stuff, but it was really fun. We practiced a little, but with respect to Tommy, even if he wasn't familiar with the song, after two notes, he knew it. It was ridiculous how good he was.

G. Brown: You could see the joy on Tommy's face. He was being pulled in a lot of different directions by that time, and for him to have a good time playing oldies and making money was really fun for him. Some of my fondest memories.

Harold Fielden: Everything went so well that summer. That's when Zephyr got back together and did 'Live at Art's Bar and Grill,' because everybody had been getting along so well—because of the 4-Nikators. They did one or two nights at Art's.

Johnnie Bolin: I was 18, and Tommy said, "Do you want to come out and do a Zephyr reunion?" And I said, "Well, I'll do anything—I'm not going to say no!" We played Art's Bar and Grill, and Robbie—the guy Tommy doesn't like—walks in. I'm standing there, and Robbie goes, "What are you doing here? Where's your brother at?" I said, "He's right over there." He goes, "What's the deal? Who's playing drums tonight?" And Tommy goes, "My brother Johnnie is." He goes, "Well, *I'm* the original drummer!" He says, "O.K., you can play too!" So we both played—Robbie definitely knew the material better than I did. It was kind of an awkward situation.

Otis Taylor: The 4-Nikators still exist—they still play.

Harold Fielden: We were making the grand sum of $80.00 a night per person, which was awesome, because rent was probably $40.00 at that point. So not only do you pay rent, but there's food for the week. One Monday, we were playing, and Tommy came up to us just before the show, and said, "Well, this is the last time I'll be able to play with you guys." He had gotten contacted by the James Gang.

84

The James Gang

David Givens: We were playing together in the 4-Nikators at that time. I had gotten to the club, it was just the two of us there. He says to me, "Barry called up and he wants me to play with . . . now don't laugh, *the James Gang*." Back in our Zephyr days, when we were insulting other bands, especially Tommy [would say], "They're real commercial." That was the ultimate put-down. And the James Gang was one of those bands that was really commercial. The fact that he got the gig, he was pretty embarrassed. "But," he said, "Barry says I get to make my own record if I do this for a year." Couldn't argue. Things had been pretty tight for all of us after the band went under.

G. Brown: After the James Gang was getting famous, [Joe Walsh] was getting conflicted about that. So he dropped everything, moved out to the foothills of Colorado, woodshedded for a year, and formed Barnstorm. He was around town enough to see Tommy. I don't think it was an acrimonious leaving of the James Gang, he wanted to help them. He said, "Look, I've got a kid that's arguably better than I am. This is a good draft choice."

Johnnie Bolin: Joe and Tommy were really good buddies—Joe really respected him. Joe did an interview quite a while ago, and the radio guy asked what he thought of Tommy's playing, and he said, "Well, he plays circles around me—I can't play like that." He really loved Tommy.

Stanley Sheldon: Quite frankly, Tommy just did that one for the money. We were at a dead end with Energy. My cousin left to play with Joe Walsh, and we were in an interim period. Walsh gave him the opportunity, because Tommy had given Joe his bass player, Kenny.

John Bartle: When Joe started Barnstorm, he was looking for a guitar player, so Tommy recommended me. Kenny Passarelli called me—he was playing bass—and Joe flew me out to Nederland, and I was actually hired for Barnstorm. A long story . . . I ended up getting busted for draft evasion, so I couldn't go on the world tour. But Tommy got me the opportunity. They were almost finished with [recording 1972's 'Barnstorm'] when I got there.

Tom Stephenson: Tommy did his stint with the James Gang, which he hated. We talked several times—he just absolutely hated it. But it was money—it was the best money that he'd made for a long time.

Tommy Bolin: What the hell, I'll eat this month instead of starving.

Karen Ulibarri: To go from the extreme of Energy to the James Gang was just something no one expected. But he did it as stepping-stone. It was exciting to play with experienced musicians that had made it on a grand scale. It was exciting to work with new people and record with people like [producer] Tom Dowd, the opportunity to travel, to start making money. I think it was just another new stepping stone to eventually go on to what he really wanted to do. It wasn't the end, it wasn't his eventual happiness. It was just a progression, and for the time being, it was very good—he was able to get music heard that he had been writing, and put on these albums, that he couldn't have done with Energy or Zephyr. And it was at this time that he had collaborated with Jeff Cook and John Tesar, and they were writing some beautiful stuff—it worked well with the James Gang albums.

Mike Drumm: When they had Domenic Troiano [Walsh's initial replacement in the James Gang] and they did the 'Straight Shooter' album, sales dropped like a rock. Domenic just didn't have what Joe had. And Joe at that point, said, "Hey, you should get Tommy in there." Tommy was so broke that there was no way he could not take him up on it—because maybe he'd get a payday, make some money. And he had all these Energy songs built up—the James Gang's 'Bang' and 'Miami,' a number of those songs had been in the Energy repertoire. And they just re-did them with the James Gang. But he didn't want to be in the James Gang—he wanted to do his own thing.

Charlie Brusco: I actually went to college in Ohio and I used to go see the James Gang play a place called J.P.'s, in Kent, when they were playing bars—

when Walsh was in the band. When they got Domenic Troiano, I was kind of like, *"Eh."* Then, when they got Tommy, I was like, "Wow, this could keep this band going forever."

Jim Fox: We were finishing up a period of time when Donny Troiano was the guitarist. Donny was moving on and we were looking. I got a call from Walsh one day—out of the clear blue sky. "You've got a pencil? Write this number down—you'll like this guy, you've got to talk to him." So I called Tommy. He was pre-screened by Joe, but he seemed pretty interested. We arranged to fly him out to wherever the band was playing at the time. He came out, and we laughed awfully hard for a long time. It was a no-brainer—he was a brilliant guitar player. He had some songs that sounded real good, and we felt that he was a good fit.

Troiano never gets the credit he deserves—Troiano is a brilliant guitarist as well. He was sort of a buffer between [Joe and Tommy], because Donny went in a very different direction. Donny was very R n' B oriented—and Dale and I no doubt had a hot R n' B streak in us. We loved it; it was very different from Joe. Tommy was a step back closer to what Dale and I understood to be rock n' roll. And it was a very welcomed step back in that direction, because we felt it had been missing. Here comes Tommy, and he's 'balls out,' and we loved it. Compared to Joe skill-wise, they're two of the greatest ever. We feel really fortunate to have had the opportunity to play with guys like that. Joe had interests; Joe had a lot of things going on in his mind. Tommy was music and pretty much nothing else. You want to put a smile on Tommy's face? Just put him on a stage. Tommy was a guy that you could drive eleven hours, go up on a stage, play an overly long set, and Tommy couldn't wait to get to the local club afterwards. "Come on, let's play man!"

Dale Peters: Joe is a much more methodical, very deliberate kind of player. Absolutely phenomenal. But Tommy was just *wild*. Just this crazy, wild guitar player. Completely different. He seemed like the right guy, played the right way. He was a spectacular guitar player. He was incredible—he didn't sound like anybody else. He had this frantic, great style of playing rock guitar. He could play anything, he had a great sound.

Jim Fox: We had a road manager at the time, a Canadian fellow named Roland Paquin—an absolute lunatic. He was a ballbuster from way back. He went to the airport to pick Tommy up. From the airport to the hotel to meet us, he decides to set us up. He tells Tommy, "Listen, if you want this job with the band, let me give you some insight. These guys are *absolutely nuts* about Al Green. They think Al Green is the coolest guy that ever made a record. Everything he ever did, they think is the greatest." What Tommy doesn't know is although we certainly liked Al Green, he was the exact opposite of the music we were looking to play [laughs]. And Roland is telling Tommy, "You've got to tell these guys, 'That's all I want to do—play Al Green sort of stuff'." He brings Tommy in. "So Tommy, what kind of music are you into, man?" We sat there and he did five minutes on Al Green, and our faces fell. I guess it got so bad that Roland had to step in— *"It's a joke!"* Tommy was perfect man—he was perfect before we even met him.

Johnnie Bolin: He used [the Strat with a Tele neck] in the James Gang. He was going back and forth between the Les Paul and a Strat.

Jim Fox: We had signed with Atlantic Records, and they wanted a record. In order for Atlantic to wish to continue [working with the band], they wanted to know who the guitar player was we had in mind. When we told them it was Tommy, they were delighted, because they had a distant eye on Tommy. They thought, "That oughta work real good. How soon can you get a record to us?" Our attitude was, "Let's get together and play some." I don't believe we played any gigs in front of audiences before we recorded. We may have done some playing, and then a whole bunch of practicing, and prepared to work on the tunes that were available.

Johnnie Bolin: The James Gang 'Bang' album was pretty much already written with Energy. So when he got with the band, he'd already had the songs written—most of them.

John Tesar: The album with the James Gang, 'Bang,' he called me up in the middle of the night. I was in the Dakotas and they were just going into the studio, and he said, "I've got these nonsense lyrics, but I like the tune." So he told me over the telephone, and I rewrote them—from "Blah blah blah."

Jim Fox: I remember Tommy agonizing over singing [the song "Alexis"]. Tommy went through a whole lot of changes over, "How am I going to sing this?" I don't think that where he ended is very far from where he began. It was right in his head to begin with. I remember being very pleased with his vocal performance—"This is just what we need."

Phillip Polimeni: When Tommy joined the James Gang, he didn't have the confidence to sing—meanwhile, Tommy *could* sing. He just wasn't assertive enough and didn't have enough confidence in his own voice. He had a great voice.

Jeff Cook: I live in the constant hope that someday, somebody will cover ["Alexis"]. Because I still believe it could be a hit.

Jim Fox: As Dale and I not being major writers by any means, it's a little different situation. Here we have this band and we didn't really have writing capabilities—or at least not the kind that we felt we needed for success. So when we were looking for a guitar player, writing was important—or at least the ability to 'write with' was important. And here comes Tommy, and he has half an album's worth of tunes ready, and we liked most of them. So we took what we liked, and I think we maybe left a couple behind. The rest of them came together as we were getting ourselves together. The result is pretty much stuff that Tommy had written ready to go or came in time for the sessions.

Johnnie Bolin: They all lived in Ohio, and he still lived in Colorado. He didn't want to move to Ohio.

Dale Peters: When he joined, he came to Cleveland, and stayed with me at my house for a while. And that's when I realized he was seriously into drugs. He'd get up in the morning and take like a zillion aspirins. I mean, like 20, just to get going. Tommy was actually relatively quiet. Very nice guy, just the drug thing was hideous.

Jim Fox: I don't remember the aspirins. We were never 'a hard use drug band.' The culture around the Gang, certainly, all the drugs of the day were there. We weren't angels, everybody did their thing—we did our drinking, our drugging.

Heroin was not part of that culture. That was a surprise. Certainly Tommy—as far as we knew—was not involved in heroin at the time. In fact, he confirmed that to me later. I may have made a comment to him like, "Are you still getting high?" He made a comment back to me like, "I've found something *better*." That was a comment of concern at the time. I can't tell you when it got out of hand. I can only tell you that for the vast majority of the time, there were drugs and they were controllable. Dale remembers the morning, I remember the evenings—Tommy used to like to have a handful of joints before he went back to his room. Tommy could get pretty darned obsessive. But it didn't seem out of the ordinary. Within the community, [pot] certainly wasn't looked down upon. Whereas heroin might have been a different story. But Tommy, because he was such an adventure-seeking guy, was certainly an experimenter—Tommy would have tried anything. But we never missed a show—Tommy was never too sick or messed up to go on. Pretty much blew us away every night.

Mike Drumm: I think at the same time, the drugs started getting harder. His drug usage started evolving from the more innocent kind of stuff to more harder [drugs]. I think there was an arc each year where everything got crazier.

Dale Peters: Tommy was fun to be around. Oddly enough, when Tommy was high, he was fine. When he wasn't, he was miserable—very hard to be around. He was the opposite of everybody else. When he was 'flying,' his personality was great.

Jim Fox: [The 'Bang' recording sessions] went very easily. We recorded the basics here in Cleveland [at the Cleveland Recording Company]. So it was a very comfortable situation for Dale and myself—it was a studio we knew well. He just fit right in. I don't have that much in the way of specific recollections. It was really easy to work with Tommy. The stuff we set out to do, we seemed to be very much on the same page with. It was very easy to communicate ideas back and forth, to create arrangements, and to have the dialogue. It was a pleasure. Tommy was just a superior musician. Very flexible, very willing—not hung up about things. It was a great collaboration. He had a lot of stuff ready to go, and we were able to mold it very quickly and easily into stuff that we were all comfortable with.

Tom Dowd: Tommy was an extraordinary and sensitive human being, who sometimes sought help to face the world that we live in. But whether you heard him when he was on our planet or visiting another, he was an extremely sensitive communicant, master of his instrument.

Johnnie Bolin: Y'know the album cover? That's Tommy's head on Domenic's body! Domenic's hands were a lot bigger, plus he had rings on all his fingers. Tommy never wore rings, and his hands were fatter. So other than the hands, you can't tell it's Domenic's body—but it is. They didn't want to shoot the picture again, so they just took his head off and put Tommy's on there.

Jim Fox: I really did enjoy the time when Tommy was in the band. For the most part, they were great shows. Tommy was a pleasure to play with, because he was extremely high energy, and he was always inventive. For myself, what I liked about the format of the Gang, was we left room to play. When someone wanted to play, all they had to do was play. Tommy liked to play, and we liked to give him the room.

Jeff Cook: It was really his first taste of rock stardom—the groupies and all the hangers on were there. It was truly 'rock n' roll time.' I think that was really what he was drawn to, and was finally—for the first time—really experiencing that. Zephyr never really hit that level of success. But what came with each one of those gigs he took—he was filling some huge shoes. The constant critical attention and the comparisons with these giant guitar players, they took their effect.

Jim Fox: He couldn't see anything without his glasses. *Nothing.* He wouldn't wear them on the stage, and he wouldn't get contacts—I have no idea why. So he used to run at the audience, and run off the front of the stage [laughs]! The audience would push him back up on stage. After the second or third time, we got together with the road crew, and said, "What can we do?" We bought Christmas tree lights and strung them across the front of the stage, so he could stop in time to not run into the audience. You've got to love that kind of enthusiasm.

I remember playing Central Park once, a lot of fun. I remember a lot of the jams afterwards. I remember going to a local bar not far from where Tommy grew up in Iowa—we must have had a gig somewhere nearby. I remember walking into a club in St. Louis, someone told Tommy that Albert King was in town playing—St. Louis is his home. It was in his hood—this was his home joint. When we walked in, I have to admit that the thought occurred to me that maybe we weren't in the right place. Maybe this wasn't the smartest thing we could have done. But it would have never occurred to Tommy [laughs]! Tommy got in and had a ball. It was wonderful. I remember Tommy more for his enthusiasm—always ready to play.

I have very few board mixes of concerts—the record company has nothing. Quality-wise, there is nothing good. But there has been some stuff floating around online that I have either picked up or heard over the last number of years. Just tiny excerpts from what must have been board tapes of concerts. And boy, they're not the kind of thing you'd want to play for people. You almost have to be *us* to appreciate them—they're not high quality. But I do appreciate them, because it's the only stuff that I have from that period. It's fun, although on a one to ten scale, the quality is a one. It's terrible. It's not there—I wish it was.

Dale Peters: He was great live. Tommy was a real rock star—he was 'on' all the time. He used to dress like it. He'd get up in the morning and put on his silver lamé suit, his hair was all multi-colored and everything. So Tommy was like on stage 24 hours a day. He didn't really have a life outside of that—he had a girlfriend, but she probably hardly ever saw him. He was just into it, and it was fun to see him be so into it. It's a shame he had the drug thing, because he was a great guy under all that stuff. Very strange—usually anybody who's real into drugs, they're strange kind of people anyway. I mean, we grew up in the '60s, so believe me, I know a lot of strange people [laughs]! But Tommy wasn't, he was an absolutely regular guy—except he had this horrible, *unbelievable* drug problem. I have never seen anything like it—he didn't fit the mold at all.

Johnnie Bolin: He had a chance to play to a lot of people and see the United States. The James Gang didn't really limit his style; he still pulled off the solos with his Echoplex. They just said, "Go ahead and play." He liked the band and he liked all the guys.

Jim Fox: I think I remember we had most difficulties [with fan reaction to Walsh's replacements] when Domenic came into the band. The band was at a pretty strong creative peak at the time—we had records that had blasted up the charts, a lot of success, and Joe had moved on. And here's Donny standing there—and Roy Kenner [the James Gang's singer after Walsh] for that matter. I don't think that the record company did a very good job of preparing the world for the change. They kind of just let it happen, and didn't do much to let anyone know it was happening. And I think Donny's presence was a bit of a surprise to fans. We heard a lot of "Where's Joe?" in those days. When Tommy came into the band, some time had passed since Joe had gone. And I've got to be honest, I don't remember any "Where's Joe?" stuff to speak of with Tommy. Donny yes, Tommy no. The other thing—Tommy was formidable, man. If there was a "Where's Joe?", it was quieted within the first ten seconds of playing. Tommy's playing really stood up for itself.

Charlie Brusco: I thought that 'Bang' was the first good James Gang record that was made after Joe left the band. But it was still that situation that it was living behind what was the James Gang. It was tough for anybody coming in. I don't know what he could have done to make it work. I think he was behind the eight ball no matter what happened. They had to do James Gang songs that Walsh sang, so it was tough for anybody coming into that situation. But that was the biggest shot they had to bring it back, and that was a tough situation to try and bring it back. They were kind of in a no-win situation. That was the closest they came to recreating what they did with Walsh.

Jim Fox: I think we knew collectively that Roy was not the singer we wanted to end up with. In between the two albums we did with Tommy, we looked very hard and failed. Just couldn't find that 'Paul Rodgers type of guy' that we thought at the time was the thing we needed to convey these songs better. Personally, I think it was O.K., but there was an underlying disappointment, which could be said was the reason Tommy didn't stay with the band beyond two records. We weren't at 100%, and we knew it.

 Tommy wouldn't hear of [becoming the group's vocalist]. We had to beat him senseless to sing "Alexis." He didn't feel he had it. It's a common thing— we actually hired a singer once when Walsh was in the band. Walsh was like, "Man, I can't be a lead singer. I'm not good enough, I can't do it." So again,

Dale and I roll our eyes and hire a lead singer for a few weeks, until Joe came to his senses. Tommy had a certain voice that a lot of people found appealing. I don't think Tommy would ever allow himself to view himself as a singer. That's a shame. I think his confidence increased over the years.

I would have enjoyed more of Tommy singing. Again, being less than 100% behind what Roy was doing, it was great to have Tommy's voice in there. It's a shame, but I've seen it a lot. And you get into this whole 'personality thing,' where people who play an instrument are a certain lead singer, people who don't play the instrument are a different kind of lead singer. Tommy and Joe would have been the same in that category—neither one of them in those days had real confidence in their voices, because they had the instrument. Whereas you take a guy like Roy Kenner—he's out there naked. Like a Roger Daltrey type—there's nothing to hide behind. *You'd better sing.*

I think it was kept secret from Roy—to the extent that we could. I think our frustration must have shown. And also, Roy was having his own set of difficulties. Those were not difficulties that anyone in the band could do anything about—those were personal difficulties that he was going through in his life. He seemed apart from the rest of us. But Roy was not really able to overcome it and move on, and we were anxious to get through this, show improvement, and get to the next step. And it just didn't seem to be happening with the four of us. When we couldn't find a suitable guy, we went ahead with Roy, and I think the general feeling was, "We'll make the best of this." Not, "This is going to be the great thing."

Dale Peters: No, he didn't hang around with anybody. Tommy was always looking for drugs. He was either playing or looking for drugs. He was easy to get along with. Like I said, he was high all the time, so he was always in a great mood.

Jim Fox: I hadn't seen [the group's performance on Don Kirshner's Rock Concert] in years, when it finally turned up [on YouTube]. It was kind of interesting to me—it pointed out the strengths and the weaknesses of the band at the time. It wasn't the easiest thing to watch! The flaws are huge and the successes are huge. It's cool—I'm glad it's there. I wonder if that was the night we shared the show with Ricky Nelson? It might have been a half them/ half us kind of evening. T.V. wasn't our strongest suit—I don't know whether we got nervous about it. Don't know if Roy was ever captured well in those circumstances. Again, with Tommy, it seemed like all the negatives would melt away by the time it was time to get on stage.

John Tesar: He and I were almost never in the same city at that point—he was in Los Angeles and I was in Arizona, the Dakotas, or Chicago. All of the stuff on 'Miami' and 'Bang,' we did those long distance—by mail and by telephone. I did go to Denver at one time and watched him play around the James Gang time frame. There were too many drugs—I got spooked by that. I liked it too much, and he liked it too much. I couldn't afford to run with that crowd. I liked it and knew I had to stay away from it. It was mostly marijuana and cocaine. That was not the worst times for him—it got much worse later on. Those were sort of 'recreational times.' As I recall, during those times, he was pretty professional. It was later that it got the better of him. Around the middle of '74, it just got dingier and harder. I suspected there was smack and stuff like that.

Jeff Cook: He was elated at the beginning, because it represented financial freedom—which to him, represented freedom to express musically. I do believe that the James Gang thing became prohibitive to him on a musical level. There were the formula songs and the formula performances, and the rigidity of it probably bored him to tears. I think that's why he became discontented with it, even though it was providing a lot of money and a lot of notoriety. I think musically, he was very restless, and that the James Gang thing was pretty locked into being what it was. They weren't looking to experiment.

Tommy Bolin: They were tight among themselves, but it was like I was on one side of the river, and they were on the other. For instance, if I would be doing a guitar solo, be getting into it and all that, they would almost at points look . . . bored, y'know? They were straight-laced rock players, whereas I wanted to go out and explore other places.

Bobby Berge: In general, at first, it was very exciting, a big challenge, and he loved it. They did funk-flavored stuff, and it was his chance to break into the rock star mode. But then, I'm not sure what kind of differences went down. I think Tommy had his ideas musically, and they weren't happy with Tommy's ideas, and it kind of drifted apart there—because Tommy had so much going musically. In his mind, he wanted to play jazz from the get-go—back in Sioux City.

Jim Fox: By the time of 'Miami,' we were in conflict over direction. It wasn't an 'us against them' situation. Roy had his problems. And Roy was doing his best to overcome them, but they weren't getting overcome. We basically exhausted every vocalist that we knew between myself, Dale, and Tommy. And it was a revolving door for a while—trying people out and just being really disappointed that we couldn't find what we felt we wanted. So when it came time to make the record, there was a sense of, "Well, Roy is who we have, we're going to make the best record that we possibly can with Roy." I think that's probably what we did, but I don't recall it as being very satisfying. I remember working on "Red Skies." That was fun, because there were elements that touched me musically—jazz-wise. In fact, I think I got to play a little piano on it. It was just a fun thing. In general, the 'Bang' experience was a better experience for me than the 'Miami' experience.

And unfortunately, it wasn't our most successful record. But it isn't to say that some of it isn't good. There are a couple of songs—"Do It." Ray Charles came to visit during that session. He came to check out the new board in the studio. It remains a highlight in my life. I'm not sure if we were recording "Do It," but it was one of them where we had the instrumental down and Ray sat down at the board and played with the controls. But then the vocals got on it, and somehow, it was never the same [laughs]. Ray was basically in town, and he had been close with Tom Dowd forever—Tom had engineered records for Ray going way back. There was a new technology in use on this recording board—some things that hadn't been seen too widely in the industry. I remember Ray sitting down and going, "Man, the centers are *so close*." And I seem to remember Paul Anka stopping by one day, but that was less monumental [laughs]!

Dale Peters: It was great hearing what [Tommy] would do. You'd sit back and listen to him do an overdub or something, and you'd just go, "Wow, that's insane—listen to that!"

Johnnie Bolin: I was at his house in Boulder when 'Miami' had just come out, and Chuck Morris came over—he had something to do with managing

Tommy. He said, "'Miami' is out, and it's like #80 with a bullet." And Tommy said, "I don't care what it is. *I'm quitting.*" "You can't quit, you just did the album and wrote all the songs!" Plus he moved, he was starting to make some money, had a really nice house. No big huge mansion, but better than he had when he was in Energy. That's when he went back to trying Energy again and trying to get that record deal.

Tommy Bolin: I called my manager, Mike Belkin, in Cleveland, and told him I was quitting. And he told me that I was shortchanging myself because of the band's potential to make good money. I told him I wasn't happy anymore, and there wasn't much he could say about that.

Jim Fox: I'm not sure [if Tommy toured with the group in support of 'Miami']. If we did, it couldn't have been for a long time. There wasn't enough time in the chronology to have allowed for us to have toured for a long time.

Dale Peters: You know, I'm not sure why he left. When I think back, one day he was just *gone* [laughs]. I think the drug thing was getting even worse, and he was starting to hang around with a lot more drug people.

Jim Fox: I didn't talk to Tommy for the longest time—I was a little upset by that. I waited a month or two, and I called him. I said, "Hey man, you haven't been making rehearsals. Where the hell are you?" He laughed and I laughed, and everything was O.K. We weren't completely shocked, because it wasn't working exactly the way we wanted. But we were disappointed because I thought Tommy was a great player. We saw each other a few times after that.

Robert Ferbrache: Chuck [Morris] did a lot for him. Chuck bled for him—he tried all sorts of stuff. They were trying to put a band for Tommy together. At that time, they were going to have a band and Tommy wasn't going to sing—they were looking for a singer. They actually looked into having Terry Reid be the singer of Tommy's band. But they got a hold of Terry Reid, and when they tried to do something with him, he was all strung out on dope. I even saw one incarnation of the band that had Alphonse Mouzon on drums, Stanley on bass, this guy Ronnie Barron on keyboards—he was going to be the singer—and Tommy on guitar. They did a couple of shows. That's probably how Tommy got hooked up with Alphonse Mouzon. And they weren't doing fusion type stuff—they were doing 'Teaser' type stuff. I don't think there are any recordings around of that—but they were awesome. I became friends with him—I worked at Ebbet's Field and took a lot of pictures of him. It would probably be '74.

Johnnie Bolin: All the Ebbet's Fields [shows], he lived in Colorado. Ebbet's Fields was Chuck Morris, who is affiliated with Barry. So Tommy could play there—back up anybody or play any time he wanted.

Robert Ferbrache: My memory is clouded—even though I was in the front row, recorded that CD [released as 1996's 'Tommy Bolin and Friends: Live at Ebbet's Field 1974'], and took all the pictures of that. Obviously, time makes it seem different. I remember the electricity of it—those guys were really good, and they played with each other forever at that point. They could just step in. It was strictly fun for them. They were doing covers—all of those songs are blues covers, or even "San Francisco River," that's a cover, too [penned Flora Purim]. There wasn't one original track on that—it was just fun.

What happened was there was a radio broadcast from Ebbet's Field. I set my tape player with a timer, and recorded the show. I recorded everything—I had bunches of tapes. I always gave them to Tommy. Every time there was a radio broadcast, they were recorded on cassette. And cassettes weren't even made in the United States—I had gotten a cassette player from my brother-in-law, who was stationed in Japan, and he gave it to me as a Christmas present. I had to go to Buckley Air Force Base and buy cassettes—I couldn't even get them at Radio Shack at that time! Those tapes I recorded over the radio were the only existing copy of those performances that ever survived. And for the CD, I just de-noised it and remastered it—that's what I do, I'm an audio engineer. I have my own studio.

Stanley Sheldon: We were so high I can't remember a lot [laughs]. Back in the day, we were snorting so much blow that it's really hard to remember much. I do remember the audience was just enraptured. They were riveted, and it was a good performance—one of our better ones.

Carmine Appice: In like 1974, after I was done [playing] with Jeff Beck, I was on my way to California, and I had stopped in Colorado—Denver I believe. Tommy was playing at Ebbet's Field, along with a group called the Good Rats. The Good Rats had a drummer, Joe Franco, who was one of my students at the time. So I stopped in just to hang out with the Good Rats, say "Hi" to Tommy, and maybe think about doing something with Tommy in a project. When I got to the airport, Tommy picked me up. He had all these wild colors in his long hair. We hung out, his girlfriend at the time was Karen—we went to his house, she made some food, then we went later to the gig and had a jam. I got to L.A.—I ended up moving here. Never did get anything going with him.

Jeff Ocheltree: I was in a hotel in New York. He called my room and said, "I'm Tommy Bolin, I got your number from somebody"—I was with Billy Cobham—"I know you guys are playing tonight at Carnegie Hall. I want to come see the show." I said, "No problem." We started talking, and he said, "You're from Iowa originally, aren't you? That's where I'm from, too. Iowa guys have got to stick together—nobody understands how much talent comes from that state." I started telling him about musicians—famous jazz musicians— that even he didn't know about. He started telling me about other musicians that I didn't know about. It was a really nice conversation—it was like 10:00 in the morning. That night, he came to Carnegie Hall, saw the show, and afterwards, we had a really good time chatting. That's how I got to know him. I liked him. He was flamboyant and he was very interesting to talk to about music. He wasn't 'the rock n' roll kind of guy' that most people thought he was. He was more well-rounded and knowledgeable about music.

Robert Ferbrache: He was being managed by Chuck Morris. Then I worked for Barry Fey, and there was a whole thing where Barry sort of stole Tommy away from Chuck. I went into [Barry's] office, and Tommy was there one day. We hung out, and I took him up to Boulder, and he was telling me that Barry approached him about doing management. And of course, nobody said "No" to Barry Fey—*ever*. I know he was pretty conflicted about it, because Chuck put his heart into it. Then, Tommy basically jumped ship to Barry.

Barry Fey: When he left [the James Gang], he called me up when he was home. He said, "I want you to manage me, *please.*" I said, "Tommy, come on—we've been through that. I don't know how to manage." He said, "All I know is you're the only one who won't rip me off." I know what he was talking about, but I don't know what the basis was. He said that everybody who he had been with—starting with the first manager—had ripped him off. He said, "I want to form my own band," and I said, "I'll help you as much as I can."

Alphonse Mouzon/Los Angeles

Alphonse Mouzon: I heard Tommy on 'Spectrum' and loved the way he played the guitar—and his use of the Echoplex. I called him up and asked him to play on my 'Mind Transplant' album. I flew him in from Colorado, and put him up at the Hyatt Hotel in Hollywood for a week.

Tommy Bolin: I also did the 'Mind Transplant' album with Alphonse Mouzon. I really like the L.P., but every tune is about a minute too long.

Alphonse Mouzon: Tommy was a pure genius at what he did. No one played guitar like Tommy. Tommy was always funny and making jokes. He was really happy and sincere—it all showed in his guitar playing. He didn't read music but it didn't matter, because he had a special gift that allowed him to memorize melodies and chord changes immediately. He would add harmonies to the melodies because Tommy had great ears.

Jeff Cook: Alphonse was a very respected musician, and he had his own set of issues—just like all of the rest of them. I think [Tommy] really enjoyed playing with Alphonse, but I think it was also a little bit overwhelming in terms of all that went with having him in a band. I don't feel comfortable talking about that. The guy had some 'issues,' you know what I mean? But I will say that when they played live, it was extraordinarily energetic, because Alphonse was like an express train on drums. I mean, he was non-stop. And powerful—a very strong drummer.

Alphonse Mouzon: Tommy was a very caring, sincere, and funny guy. Tommy used to call me 'Fonzie' instead of Alphonse. We never did go on the road as far as I can remember. But we did jam a lot after the recording sessions. There's a bootleg [released via the Tommy Bolin Archives as 1999's 'Fusion Jam'] that has some great playing on it.

Tommy Bolin: I think the rivalry between Cobham and Mouzon is really funny, but personally, I like Billy's drumming more. They play very similarly. But Alphonse has an amazing ego in the first place, and Billy plays with more sensitivity. He'd play a country and western tune if you asked him, but Alphonse is more a lead player.

Johnnie Bolin: I think he knew that moving out to California was the next step to take. He'd worn out Colorado, and it was time to go to an actual 'music city.' To do it right, you have to go out there. There's definitely a nightlife out there, it's quite a bit different than Boulder. I think he kind of changed when he got out there, too. It just does it to you—staying out all night, doing this, doing that.

David Givens: Tommy—when he became 'TOMMY' with capital letters— went to L.A., and he changed a lot. As anybody would.

Stanley Sheldon: Tommy and I decided we were going to move to L.A.— [with] our girlfriends. That was about '74. We moved out there, struggled for a while looking for singers, did a little thing with Mike Finnigan.

Mike Finnigan: I think he heard me when I played with Jerry Hahn—he's a guitar player. And I think he knew about me from playing with Jimi Hendrix [Finnigan played on 1968's 'Electric Ladyland']. Stanley Sheldon was playing with him, who was from Kansas, and I used to live there, too. He was aware of me, and I think that's how we got together. I think the first time I met him face-to-face was when Barry Fey approached me about getting in the band with him. I played with Tommy and the guys for a couple of days. Ultimately, I decided not to do it—not because I didn't think he was a great musician. It just wasn't a good idea for me at that time. It *probably* would have been a good idea, but I wasn't thinking that clear, either. I can't remember what my thinking was. I had no musical objections. He was pretty much on a fast track to hell. But I was too—I was just on a little slower track [laughs]. One thing I remember was I thought, "Man, *this guy is really fucked up.*" And that is very much the pot calling the kettle black, because I drank too much and used drugs—I had to stop drinking entirely 22 years ago. It wasn't too long after that that I found myself in a fucking hospital! But there was a lot of people doing that in those days—you could have a meeting with a record label, and the guy behind the desk would be high.

It was really fun [playing with Tommy]—I enjoyed it a lot. I remember somebody sent me something not too long ago that said the reason it didn't work out was because I tried to run the show. And I went, "What the fuck? What is this bullshit?" We had nothing but a good time. I really don't have a memory of why I decided not to do it other than I think I thought he was really fucked up. Barry Fey came to my house when I said "No." He appeared at my door—it blew my mind. He said, "Nobody says 'No' to me!" As it turns out, it wasn't too long after that I made a solo record deal. Me and him together would have been a bad deal. Musically it probably would have been great. There was wild inconsistencies in his performance. He was not somebody that could get loaded and still be good. If he had a little 'glow' going, he was fine. But if he was really fucked up, he couldn't play very well.

He came like three hours early [to a barbeque Finnigan had at his house], and he was already ripped to the tits [laughs]! Of course, I was always ripped to the tits myself in those days, so for me to think that about somebody meant that they were *major fucking league.* He was gaked out by like 1:00 in the afternoon, when everyone else started arriving. He was really out of it and passed out. I remember that was the 4th of July. He wasn't like one of these guys that got tore up and turned into a mean guy. He was always a sweet guy. He showed up, and obviously had a nice glow going already. I had some beer, booze, and probably some blow—he probably brought some of his own, too, and whatever else he might have taken. So they're cooking ribs, I look over, and he's sitting in a chair, and he went from Chatty Cathy to passed out. I didn't think too much about it. My wife was in the kitchen, and she said, "What the hell? You can't let him sit [outside]—he's going to get sun burned to shit!" So me and some other guys tried to rouse him and we couldn't, so we just carried him inside—because he was pretty fair complected [laughs]!

Tommy Bolin: I'd like to call the band 'Energy,' because that was the name of the best band I've ever been involved with. Right now, I feel so inspired; it's hard to believe. I've written about 20 songs in the last two days. I'd gone about four months without writing a thing.

Stanley Sheldon: Played with a few other singers—Ronnie Barron, a few of these blues guys. And we could never really nail down a singer.

Bobby Berge: January 1, 1975, of all days, I get a call from Tommy. I'm pretty much doing nothing, and he says, "Hey, come out to L.A. and play in my band." I packed up the '64 Rambler, and hauled ass out there. When I got there, I think he had already been doing the thing with Alphonse. See, there's so much going on at once here that to separate it . . . but I went out there, to start the first Tommy Bolin Band. It was Tommy, Stan Sheldon, Ronnie Barron, and myself. We rehearsed a few times, and we got an audition with a record company. It went pretty good, but it didn't fly. And then that fell apart.

Johnnie Bolin: Tommy did play sessions, but he wasn't out trying to find session work. I think with Alphonse, he grabbed him because of Cobham. And then Dr. John played with Tommy during stints in Colorado. Actually, maybe that's how he met Dr. John, was through Barron—he was from New Orleans. Dr. John thought the world of Tommy. He thought he was really a great guitar player. They had some good experiences playing together. He wasn't in his touring band, but he did play with him—there's a lot of pictures floating around, kind of like what he did with Albert King. He was just really big into Dr. John.
    Tommy had done some rhythm tracks [for the Dr. John album, 1975's 'Hollywood Be Thy Name'], done some lead. But then through the record companies or something, it wasn't going to work out where they could put his name on there. They took Tommy off it—they scratched him and probably re-recorded it. Tommy was affiliated with somebody—where they couldn't put his credit on there. Dr. John wanted credited people, and I don't think they could swing it. It's like three songs he was on originally. He did a lot of slide on [the song] "Hollywood Be Thy Name," and the other two, one is kind of a ballad, and the other one is real funky—he does a solo, but it's more of a rhythm thing he's doing, whereas the other two he solos a little bit more.

Tommy Bolin: I don't know why. I heard he went back and recorded it again— but it was a beautiful L.P., away from all that New Orleans stuff.

Johnnie Bolin: Tommy began working on demos at Brothers Studio—which was run by the Beach Boys. I don't know if he hung out with the Beach Boys, I think Dennis Wilson was running it—he was the one that was around mostly. Tommy played with Ricky Fataar—Ricky used to play with the Beach Boys. Actually, Tommy had him in his band for a while in California—doing some recording. He's on some of the tapes that we've got from the Archives.

Bobby Berge: [Bobby, Stan, and Tommy jammed on] a lot of the 'Teaser' stuff, but we did some blues too. Dr. John—a few covers. Tommy was always into blues, so we did some blues shuffles. But we had gotten into some of the 'Teaser' stuff, which we had already done in Energy. It just carried over.

Tommy Bolin: I want the new band to work together for a while, and when we're ready we'll probably play a week at Ebbet's, and invite every major record company to see us.

Phillip Polimeni: I moved in '72 [to Los Angeles] with a band, and I created a studio underneath a house—it was an actual garage carport. It was called Glen Holly studios—it was on a street called Glen Holly, right off Beachwood Canyon. It was up near the Hollywood sign. There would be deer on the lawn—it was that far up in the mountains. Imagine driving up in the hills, there's deer, and you're going to go in a studio and play rock n' roll! It was an unbelievable sound for a homemade studio. It was an accident, and it turned out to be the most incredible place—everybody wanted to use it. The guy that did Stevie Wonder's A Studio helped me set up the room. He showed me how to build a room *inside* of a room. Tommy came to California with the James Gang, and he started coming back in forth. [When] he moved there, he started using [the studio] regularly. That's when he was there every night—he would sometimes fall asleep with a girl, sometimes two girls, on the floor. I'd go downstairs, and there would be a bottle of Bombay gin and Tuinals spread around the floor. The reels would still be going around, and he would be sleeping with his guitar and amps on. I would play what he had done, and it was just amazing.

What he used to do is go party at the Rainbow, and whatever musicians were in town would end up back at my house—playing all night. It was soundproofed [and] on a dead end street—Diana Ross' keyboard player lived on the same block. Everyone was using it at the time—everyone from the Motown crew, all of Diana Ross' backing band. And the guys from New York—Earl Slick, Richie Zito. It was a room that was so comfortable—you literally just had to walk in with your guitar. There was every kind of amp you could think of there. Tommy had his equipment there. He used to invite musicians back, and I would tape it—whether they wanted it or not! Because through the floor, I drilled a hole, and I had a Beyer microphone, and a four-track upstairs in the house. Some of the guys would say, "Listen—don't record me," and I'd say, *"O.K."* Tommy would give me 'the wink,' and I'd go upstairs and hit the machine. There was a microphone that dropped through the floor—it was an overhead—and it would catch everything. There's hours and hours of tapes.

I remember Jeff Beck came up, and Tommy pulled out a vial of coke. He took a hit of it, and he said, "Want some?" And Jeff said, "No, I don't touch it." Tommy put it away and didn't pull it out again. We had a couple of drinks, they jammed, and then Jeff played bass for a while, and then played guitar for a while. But the real hot jam was when Tommy moved out to Malibu. My friend [who was a realtor] had one house that had a panoramic view of the water, and Tommy said, "I've got to come out here and write." And he said, "You're welcomed to—take one of the rooms back there and bring your stuff." So Tommy had Jeff Beck out there and he called me up, and said, "Get a machine over here, he's got some kind of fucking box. I want you to record this!" I've got three songs—nobody's got a tape of this. These [songs] were things that happened all of a sudden—when Jeff had the guitar on, Tommy would pick up the bass. And there was a kid out there—J.P. his name was. He was a bartender in one of the local bars, and he idolized Tommy. The kid died later—his mom told me he went over a hill drunk and died. He was about 20 years old, and he had his whole drum-set set up at one of the houses Tommy was staying [at]. So when Tommy would have a jam, Tommy would call this kid and have him come over, or he would have a drummer sit right down, and there would be a drum set there. It was a multi-purpose thing.

When Todd [Rundgren] played with Tommy, it was real short. It was a thing where he kept insisting, "I don't want to be recorded." It was more about he wanted to listen to Tommy—he wanted to hear Tommy play. Tommy loved him from Nazz—he loved "Hello, It's Me." He kept asking him about that. And [Todd] said, "That's been many years ago Tommy, I've been through too many things since then." Tommy was stuck on that—"Play that one for me!"

It got a little sticky. But they did just a little guitar playing—both of them. It wasn't really a jam set-up, so I don't have anything spectacular, where there was a drummer and a full thing. Just about a half hour cut on that. Now when [the Wailers] came up, that was really fun. Bob Marley wouldn't let them do any drugs, so they were freaked out. They said, "Please—don't tell anybody about the coke!" They were snorting it, but they were saying, "Please don't say anything, or Bob will kill us! We can't do any chemicals—chemicals aren't our thing." They were rolling these fucking . . . I can't tell how big these *cones* they were rolling! I was telling them, "Hey man, that is Thai stick, what are you doing? We don't roll them like that!" And they were rolling joints that were literally like ice cream cones. I couldn't get over it. They were smokin' and smokin'. The keyboard player and the bass player were up there, and I've got some really great jams with Tommy, and Stanley Sheldon sat in on a couple of them. I've got a real good jam of that—Tommy and the Wailers.

Rick Grech came up, and we had to ask him to leave! He was tripping—he was on D.M.T. or something. He started off playing great, and then he started screaming into the microphone. It was so irritating. Tommy turned his guitar up and tried to drown him out, and finally, Tommy said, "You know what? *Shut the fuck up!*" He turned to the roadies, and said, "Get him out of here." That's one of the [few] times I'd seen Tommy pissed off. Rick went out, and about in a half hour, he came back and apologized. He acted like he was O.K., but then he got the guitar on—he laid down on the ground and started strumming it. Tommy said, "That's it, that's it!" He goes over and unplugs it, and goes, "Get him the fuck out of here—and don't let him back!" That was the end of that. But I've got a couple of songs with him playing good, and then all of a sudden, whatever he took came on and he really went off.

Bobby Berge: Out in L.A., coke and booze was more into the picture. I got into it. Out there, it just kind of grew, escalated. '75 seemed like no problem, everybody was doing it—I was trying to keep up with everybody. The main reason why I can share all this is because I'm clean and sober now. I made some real doozy mistakes because of what I was doing—partying. But now, I can look at it and learn from it, 'the dark past.' So '75 was pretty much high old times, and everything was on the up and up.

Stanley Sheldon: In a word—*volatile* [on describing Tommy and Karen's relationship at this time]. I could elaborate on that, but volatile would suffice. It was volatile because of the nature of the business. They were apart a lot, and there was some infidelity involved. When they were together, they loved each other hard, and they fought each other hard [laughs]. I can remember my future wife, Judy, had a Volkswagen, and we were driving around in L.A.— they were sitting in the back. And Karen was kicking the shit out of Tommy in the backseat, with her high heels! And her feet were coming up and hitting *us*. So I slam on the brakes, and Judy kicked Tommy out of the car. He had to walk. Then we left and drove home. Is that volatile enough for you?

Johnnie Bolin: And then they had Guille Garcia, who was in Captain Beyond, playing drums. They had two drummers—Guille and Marty Rodriguez. The only real 'Energy guy' was Stanley.

Stanley Sheldon: Before we ever got anything together, we were still trying out singers, when the Peter Frampton audition came along, and Tommy said, "Yeah, go for it Stanley." And then about two weeks after that, he got a chance to play with Deep Purple.

Moxy/'Teaser'/Deep Purple

Johnnie Bolin: The thing with Moxy, I think Tom Stephenson played on that record. They asked Stephenson how to get a hold of Tommy, and he said, "He lives out here." He was getting those calls. At that point, he was kind of in limbo.

Earl Johnson: Regarding Tommy—I loved his playing, but never met him personally, and wish I had. I wrote about 95% of Moxy's first album [1975's self-titled release] as the guitar player. I got into a fight with the producer about the guitar solos I was playing at the time—more like Page and Beck—and Tommy was brought in one night when I was thrown out of the studio by the producer. It actually made me a better player, as I felt challenged, and knew I had to improve my playing. Tommy had a great feel and style, and I admired him for that. Moxy went on to record two more albums, and by the third album, I was ripping and completely confident—much of that was derivative from the first album. I was lucky in that our two biggest songs from the first album were songs that I played all the guitar tracks on—"Sail On Sail Away" and "Can't You See I'm A Star."

Johnnie Bolin: He did that because they paid him in coke. That's all he remembered about it. He played good on that though. That song "Train," that's not even Tommy playing that guitar solo. *Really listen to it*—put on any track before that or any track of Tommy's. He does the first part of the solo, but the actual solo itself is not him—it's the other guy.

Earl Johnson: I deeply resented the producer as he took the feel to a different area—but it did work, and the hype on Tommy helped the band.

Phillip Polimeni: There was a time when Tommy was up—believe it or not—for the Stones, before Ronnie Wood took over. He was supposed to be going over for the part of the other guitar, and they decided they wanted an

Englishmen. But he was being considered for the Stones. He never got to rehearse with them, but they'd heard about him, and he was on 'the list to be considered.'

Johnnie Bolin: As far as having a band, he was figuring out who he was going to have. It wasn't a slow period, it's just I think he was unsure of what he was doing as far as a band. That was the era of Peter Frampton, Steve Miller, and Gary Wright—the solo male singers. So Tommy got his solo deal with Nemperor Records by saying, "Would you like some stuff with Energy?" The record company said, "Why don't *you* be the singer?" And he's like, "I don't really want to sing." But they said, "If you do, then you've got yourself a record deal. If you don't, you probably won't have one." He wanted Stevie Winwood and Terry Reid to sing. They knew he could sing, but it was hard for him, because he was so used to just playing and singing in the studio—now he has to sing the whole night and play. He didn't start really singing until he was 22.

Barry Fey: When I started managing him, he put a group together, and I got him a record deal with Nat Weiss—Nemperor Records. When we were getting the deal together, he gets a call from Deep Purple.

David Coverdale: When Ritchie Blackmore decided to go [from Deep Purple], Ritchie had invited me to go with him to do the Rainbow project. But I felt uncomfortable about it—I didn't think it was appropriate. And that's what led to some abrasive aspects of Ritchie's and my relationship for a while, unfortunately. When we had a meeting without Ritchie, my recommendations were number one, Jeff Beck, number two, Rory Gallagher, and number three, this guy called Tommy Bolin, which no one had really heard about. I'd heard Tommy Bolin on the 'Spectrum' album by Billy Cobham, and I'd heard him on Alphonse Mouzon's album, 'Mind Transplant.' I was really impressed with this work, and I had no idea if he was a 70-year-old African American—I had no idea. So everyone went, "Oh wow, he's pretty good!" So we sent the word out. Now at that time, Purple was this huge global entity—one of 'the rock n' roll aristocratic bands,' before the market was so oversaturated, as it is now. Even *we* couldn't find out where he was. And we found him a few miles down the road from where I used to live in Malibu—he was living there. We arranged for him to come down and jam with us. This guy walks in with multi-colored hair, lime-green Arabian knight . . . they weren't trousers, they were like pre-Steven Tyler *floating pants*. And on four or five inch sole platform . . . they weren't platform shoes, they were kind of platform *sandals!*

Glenn Hughes: He wasn't nimble with his feet; he was falling over a lot.

David Coverdale: He was a sight to behold—this exotic creature. He walked up to this line of amps—which had been pretty intimidating to whoever else had been there—and turned them all to eleven. Hit a chord, and the chord got everyone off their smug ass and started jamming—immediately. All his guitars were in hock—for whichever reason—so he had borrowed a guitar for the audition. It was quite an extraordinary, explosive audition.

Glenn Hughes: We were rehearsing at Pirate Sound—that's where we were 'auditioning,' if you will. We only auditioned two people—Clem Clempson, and then Tommy. Clem didn't get the gig, not because of his ability as a guitar player—I think it was because to fill Ritchie Blackmore's boots, you have to be a character. Tommy on the other hand . . . when I walked in and saw him, I shouted across the room, "Whatever happens, you're coming home with me!" We were just peas in the pod together. Tommy's a Leo; he's a sensitive, funny, and very sweet man. *An artist*, y'know? I saw he had the Echoplex set up on a stand, his Hiwatt's, and just the way he picked up the guitar—he was going to get the job. I particularly wasn't looking for a Ritchie Blackmore clone. Let's just say that if Yngwie Malmsteen would have been present at that time in the '70s, I probably wouldn't have wanted to go for a clone of Blackmore. As we didn't clone [Ian] Gillan and [Roger] Glover with Coverdale and Hughes. So I think getting him in, we weren't interested in jamming old Purple songs that day. We wanted to just forge ahead. And lo and behold, I think we started coming up with stuff immediately—that first day. For me, Paicey, and Lordy, that's what we liked to do anyway—jam a lot. We probably shouted out some chords and drifted off into some jazz stuff. And then we probably picked up the tempo and played some really intense rock stuff. It was a very brief audition, because we knew he'd probably got the gig.

Tommy Bolin: When Purple first called me for an audition, I hadn't slept in a couple days—not a wink—because I'd been up writing stuff. The rehearsal was for 4:00, and I was lying there thinking, "I gotta figure a way to tell them, y'know, tomorrow or something." And I thought, "Well, fuck it, I'll just go down." So I walked in and I was like a zombie. But in the first tune, right away, it was smiles all around. You know, I was shocked to see how good they were, because I had never heard that much Deep Purple.

Glenn Hughes: It probably was [the best Purple's 'Mach IV' line-up ever sounded]. Because as the annals of history know, there was some other stuff going on with substances that we didn't really know too much about. The 'darker' substances were being probably used or dabbled in—opiates. Even I, who was participating in some of the things with Tommy. But yes, he did sound good at the Pirate Sound rehearsals. He got the gig, and he moved straight into my house until we found him a home. Tommy stayed at my house for about a week. We had impromptu sessions, where I'd tape stuff on my TEAC. I've got a bunch of those tapes—it's just me and Tommy jamming. I would play Fender Rhodes and he would play my Les Paul—just him and I going off. I'd been going to Herbie Hancock's quite a bit—learning how to play Fender Rhodes through Herbie, and hanging out with the Weather Report guys. And having Tommy come into my life, I was learning how to play triads on the keys and guitar—a very new way. I was learning to branch out in that world, and that's what you heard on my solo record, [1977's] 'Play Me Out.' We ate from the same plate, went out a lot together, got a little high together—this was back in the years when it was kind of cool. But nobody realized he was ill with a horrible addiction.

Carmine Appice: I got a call from the guys in Deep Purple, asking me about Tommy—what I thought of him, was he a cool guy, and this and that. I remember telling them I thought he was a real cool guy and a great guitarist. The next thing I know, he was in Deep Purple.

Barry Fey: I said, "Why don't you try to have a dual career—a solo career and a career with Deep Purple?" I talked to Bruce Payne—who was the manager of Purple—and they went along with it. So Tommy was going to be their lead guitar player, and also have his own band. I was his manager. They got none of his earnings from his solo career. They were never his manager. They had him sign a contract.

Bobby Berge: The first thing I really remember was going down to Beachwood Sound Studios, and watching them rehearse. It just blew me away. The place was huge—had a big stage set up. It was just like a huge wall of sound. When I think of Deep Purple and Tommy, I think of Glenn Hughes—because those two were really tight, and I love Glenn's playing and singing. I think I was with Stanley Sheldon, watching their rehearsal. Frampton popped in there. What was real exciting for me at that same time was when Ritchie left Deep Purple and started Rainbow, I got a chance to audition with [Rainbow]. I didn't get the gig, but hell, it was a real treat getting a shot at it.

Tommy Bolin: I was very depressed at the time, and when I went along to play with Purple, it was like a tonic. I didn't know what to expect, but it was great. Purple are so tight, they're a great outfit. I don't think my playing has ever been better.

Robert Ferbrache: Let it be known that Tommy Bolin never listened to Deep Purple, and he used to *loathe* that kind of music before he was in the band. The only thing he liked about Deep Purple was he realized—when he started playing with them—that Ian Paice and Jon Lord were incredible musicians. He only did that band because of money and Barry Fey—he didn't do it because he loved the music at all. It gave him 'the rock star attitude.'

Mike Drumm: For us who had 'the Boulder attitude' back then, him being in Deep Purple was not cool, because Deep Purple was felt as commercial. They were mining a certain base music to be successful. In retrospect, they're better than what we all thought back then—it wasn't quite such a terrible thing to be in Deep Purple. One of the things it meant to him was he had access to a lot more drugs and alcohol.

Karen Ulibarri: I think it was more business than anything—he wasn't a fan of theirs. You may say they weren't good musicians, but he was surprised to find that they were all really incredible musicians. They just hit on a good formula, and took the money and ran.

G. Brown: He said he'd never heard any of Deep Purple except "Smoke on the Water." But then he went in and I think co-wrote over half the tunes on 'Come Taste the Band.'

Tommy Bolin: It's an ideal situation for me, because I can get my cookies off playing rock while taking them in a new direction. I'm not replacing anyone. I'm joining a new band.

Ritchie Blackmore: Tommy Bolin is very good. He's one of the best. I think Purple will probably be quite happy with him. He can handle a lot of stuff, including funk and jazz. Maybe they'll turn into a rather different band, but I really don't think so. I think they know that if they did they'd be just another funk band. They'll still keep to the rock side of things, I'm sure of it. In fact, the next album will probably be a lot rockier than my last record with them, 'Stormbringer.'

Johnnie Bolin: Tommy ran into Ritchie when they both lived in Malibu—he invited Ritchie over. Ritchie went over to Tommy's house, and there's no furniture at all—there was a bed and a couch. He lived in L.A. at the time, so he had two different places. He showed Ritchie his Strat, Ritchie went to play it, and he must have had the strings on there for months. I think I remember him saying in an article, "He was a really nice guy, and he's a really great guitar player. He kind of reminded me of Elvis!" I think they got along O.K. He appreciated his playing.

Glenn Hughes: Look—Ritchie was a genius. In the early '70s, him and Page stood alone in the rock era. When 'Burn' was completed, we started to make 'Stormbringer'—Ritchie sort of lost the plot in a way, because my [funk] influence was very strong, and I don't think he liked it. He sort of dropped the ball and disappeared.

Ritchie Blackmore: I just didn't like the way things were going with Purple. In the studio we'd be five egotistical maniacs, pushing up the faders so each of us would be progressively louder than any of the others. It wasn't a team effort any more, and the songs seemed to have been forgotten. But at the same time, it was all becoming too classy, too laid back and . . . cool. That's not Deep Purple, Deep Purple are a brash, demanding band.

Glenn Hughes: Well he was he different, wasn't he? I mean, at the point, I'd only played with two [guitarists]—Mel Galley and Blackmore. Ritchie came from a very melodic, European, classical way of playing guitar. And Tommy came from a very South American-flavored, Brazilian, reggae-ish twisted, Americana way of playing guitar. It wasn't European. It was very be-boppy, it was jazz—it was everything Deep Purple weren't. Which I liked—and having another guy in the band that wasn't frightened to do that, or play on instinct. So I'd bring in the soul and the funk, and Tommy would bring in that Brazilian, be-boppy, jazzy flavor. Which was a very interesting aspect.

David Coverdale: Weeks later, we were at a party, and somebody put 'Spectrum' on. Tommy and I were standing over by the record player, and I said, "Oh, I love that!" And he goes, *"That's Jan."* And I go, "Oh . . . what about this? I love that!" he goes, *"That's Jan."* But still, there were enough licks there to keep me more than happy.

Tommy Bolin: I consider myself a full member of the group. But Deep Purple isn't gonna take up that much of my time each year. The other months, I'll probably go out with my own band, which will probably include different players each time.

Johnnie Bolin: 'Teaser' and 'Come Taste the Band' was about the same time. I think he was going back and forth with recording each album. In the music stores, they hit about the same time—that was kind of confusing to people.

Bobby Berge: It was really great, because so much was happening at that time. I ran into my old friend, Buddy Miles—we went to school together in Sioux Falls. We started rehearsing, and he said, "Hey, do you want to play on my album?" So I'm starting to play with Buddy, Tommy is doing his own thing and he's hooking up with Purple. In the meantime, we're rehearsing 'Teaser' demo stuff at Phillip Polimeni's little studio. At the Record Plant—the spring going into the summer—Buddy's doing his first solo album there, [1975's] 'More Miles Per Gallon,' Tommy's doing 'Teaser,' so I'm hanging out there a lot, which is a beautiful studio. Really big studio, and there's all kinds of rock stars—George Harrison, Bad Company, Stevie Wonder. *I* did "The Grind" [Jeff Porcaro is listed as the drummer on the 'Teaser' album credits]—I don't know how the record company got the wrong idea—and "Lotus." It was great, fantastic. I'd be doing "The Grind" in Studio A, and then I'd run down and do a cut with Buddy down in Studio C. Back and forth.

Jeff Cook: By the time they were in the studio, I wasn't a part of it. We collaborated in the oddest ways. We wrote some of the songs for 'Teaser' over the phone, with me in Denver, and him in California. We'd get on the phone, knock ideas around, and talk about things. I'm pretty sure "The Grind" was written over the phone. I do remember him playing me the lick to "Teaser" and saying, "Do you think this will work?" So we were on the phone discussing how that song was coming together. I know we wrote "Spanish Lover," "Gypsy Soul," and one other song on the phone. Most of the songs had been written well in advance. I just remember that the 'Teaser' album was recorded at a time when everybody was partying their brains out. It's funny, because I got a call not long ago from somebody that was remixing the 'Teaser' record, and his first question was, "I want to ask you guys one thing—how high were you when you were making 'Teaser?' Because I'm finding tracks that were never even listed on the track sheet [laughs]!" So the fact was that it was a huge party. He had some of the greatest musicians in the industry coming together to play on that thing. While it wasn't a huge sales success, I think it was a pretty good critical success. Tommy didn't seem to be intimidated by anybody or anybody's musical credentials, and was completely at home playing with a jazz player, a rock player, a country player—whatever kind of genre of music. He was chameleon-like in that way—he could just fall into it and play with the best of any genre of music.

Stanley Sheldon: Tommy had come to New York, while we were mixing 'Frampton Comes Alive.' We had come back from San Francisco in the winter of '75—with our tape of 'Frampton Comes Alive' from our Winterland show. We were at Electric Lady Studios, mixing it down, and going to release it in January or February [of 1976]. So we had a couple of weeks at Electric Lady to do that. Well, Tommy comes to town, and books Electric Lady Studios, and that's where we recorded 'Teaser.' Half of it—we did the other half in L.A. But for the New York stint, I was there doing both those projects at the same time. So it was a wild time—I would be going from studio A to studio B. I had no idea that these records were going to as enormously successful as they were . . . well actually, the 'Teaser' album was not enormously successful, but it's a great record. But 'Frampton Comes Alive' was certainly an enormous success. I knew it was good, don't get me wrong—I knew I had the world by the balls right then—but I didn't really realize the deep impact of all that stuff. I was just there having some fun, making some music.

Prairie Prince: Lee Kiefer engineered the first Tubes album [1975's 'The Tubes']—it was shortly after that record, I got the call from Lee saying that he and Tommy were doing a record. He had mentioned my name, and Tommy remembered me from playing out in the desert. I was working in San Francisco and flew down to L.A. I went in there, and Paul Stallworth was on bass— from the Attitudes—and I saw Tommy. It's like we'd been old friends—he was just so sweet and warm. We immediately set up the equipment and started jamming—I didn't hear any songs previously. I think he started playing "Savannah Woman"—it was kind of a bossa nova groove, pretty easy to fall into.

We just jammed around for a while, and then he broke out "Wild Dogs." We jammed on that for a long time—several takes of that, that went on and on, which you can now hear on the 'Whips and Roses' record [released in 2006]. I'm so glad they found that stuff—I have to commend Greg Hampton for digging all that up and re-engineering it. I thought they had pumped up the sound quality—the drums especially. I always loved those two songs, but I was disappointed in the drum sound that they ended up with in the [original album's] mix.

So that was just like a marathon session—we got in there at 1:00 in the afternoon, and we didn't get out until 1:00 the next day. I remember after I had done a lot of playing that night, we took a little break, and everyone turned the lights down in the studio, and Tommy started overdubbing on the two tracks. Everybody was lying on the floor, just completely lost in the genius that was coming forth. We were all astounded. It had *a little* something to do with the drugs—'cause I knew there was a little of that going around—but other than that, it was all music and very innovative for the time. I don't want to condemn myself, but there was definitely a fair share of 'marching powder,' let's put it that way [laughs]. But he seemed to handle it pretty well at the time. We were all younger then—it was easier to do more and enjoy it more.

John Tesar: Although ["Savannah Woman"] was always credited to Jeff Cook, if you asked Jeff, he'll say I wrote the lyrics. That was a song about women who are leaving their boyfriends for other women. So then I started to think about what those storylines would be like. Somehow, it got into a wealthy woman who was keeping young women in Brazil. Tommy liked bossa nova and Brazilian stuff very much, so I put it in Brazil, which is why it's "Savannah Woman" and not "Boulder County Woman."

Narada Michael Walden: I think we were upstairs at Nat Weiss' office in New York—[Tommy] was signed to Nat's label. I was working with Mahavishnu Orchestra, and Nat was manager of the Mahavishnu Orchestra. And then we didn't really meet again until . . . I remember being down at Electric Lady, and I was doing something there—I'm not quite sure what it was. He was there, and was very excited about working with me. I just chimed in and said, "Sure—let's do something." And we did—fast. We recorded a piece called "Marching Powder" not long after that. That session was quite something—a live session at Electric Lady, in the same configuration when I'd done the album with Mahavishnu Orchestra, [1975's] 'Visions of the Emerald Beyond.' My drum set was in that same corner, and I loved that sound that comes out of there. They brought in Jan Hammer, David Sanborn, Stanley on bass, Sammy Figueroa on percussion, myself on drums, and Tommy. Tommy taught us the song, and I think we cut it once or twice. That was it. Pretty blazing. It was fun to play like that—live, with everybody in the same room.

Jan Hammer: Narada was scheduled on the ["People, People"] session to play drums. We were in Electric Lady, sitting there hour after hour, waiting. [Narada] was stuck in traffic somewhere in New Jersey—but his drums were all set up and mic'd. So we just said, "Let's have a run through," and I played drums—I can always overdub the organ later. So we did it, and it ended up being on the record. I played drums all along—I played drums on many records. For instance, the famous record with Carlos Santana and John McLaughlin [1972's 'Love Devotion Surrender'], I played drums on that. That was around the same time. That was just a wonderful thing, but the atmosphere was very 'stoner-like'—everybody was chilling. Again, nothing wrong with that—lots of fun. It's just eventually, Tommy took a wrong turn, and it became less 'chill' and more frightening.

Prairie Prince: I was really taken by his voice—I thought he had a really beautiful voice. Maybe even more than his guitar playing—I thought his voice really stood out.

Johnnie Bolin: People go, "I fell in love with his voice." That's cool, because he didn't even want to sing! I mean, he did want to sing—but he didn't think he was going to be good enough to carry a whole song. Tommy sang from the heart. He was a real a romantic—he had it in him. He liked guys like Terry Reid and Marc Bolan—he liked that little 'lightness,' and saved the heaviness for his guitar playing. He wrote everything acoustically, and then when he plugged in his guitar, he decided if it was going to be a rock n' roll song or not. If you listen to Tommy's acoustic demo of "Teaser," that could have been the way the song could have went. He plugged in his guitar, and went that way. Maybe because of the neighbors downstairs—he never really had his guitar plugged in. He always had his acoustic laying on the bed—I don't think he played his electric much at the apartment.

Jeff Cook: "Teaser" [the song] to me, the music and the lyrics are a really great fit. I remember every night when we played as Energy, the band maybe looked better than they played—even though they played pretty well! There were always a bevy of beautiful women around the band, and all of us had women. There was one woman that I wrote the song about, that was just 'unavailable.' And to me, she became the biggest challenge of all time. And that's what that song was about—the one woman that wasn't making herself available. I really wrote that hoping that Energy would record it, and then Tommy decided to record it on his solo record.

Glenn Hughes: Tommy asked me if I would sing on 'Teaser'—not all of it, but three or four cuts. But I convinced him I didn't want to do that. Like Hendrix had his own great style of singing, you have your own style of singing these particular songs. I mean, I can't imagine myself singing some of those songs. He really loved what I did vocally, so he was always pushing for that. I went to London to record it, but I couldn't use my name because it was a tax thing. You won't see my name actually on the record, but I sang on "Dreamer." I probably would have sang more, but I convinced Tommy that he needed to sing this record.

Tommy Bolin: I really love the whole album. I'm very proud of the whole album. It's doing tremendously in the States. You know, far beyond which I thought it would do. I love "Lotus," "Homeward Strut," "Marching Powder," "Dreamer." Those four I think are probably my favorites, and "Wild Dogs."

Jan Hammer: If I were to contrast [the 'Spectrum' sessions] to the sessions for 'Teaser,' there was much more of a drug fog descending. ['Spectrum'] was very laid back.

Johnnie Bolin: I remember he was really happy—he was proud of the 'Teaser' album. He finally did something that he really wanted to do. All those breaks that he had were all for the better. I don't know how to explain it, because I didn't know how badly he wanted it. That's why he did what he did, because it was very puzzling to me and a lot of people—like when he said, "I can't go out with James Gang." He had to do the Purple thing . . . he didn't *have to* do anything. I mean, Mick Taylor quit the Rolling Stones because he wanted to do his own thing. But Tommy, if you think about it, that's why he did what he did. He just had this drive. It wasn't real noticeable in the things he would say—in his actions of quitting or leaving.

Tommy Bolin: I think I will be bringing out my own individuality with [Deep Purple], and bring some things out in them. The L.P. we're making will surprise a lot of people. We start recording on August 3rd in Munich.

Glenn Hughes: Tommy coming in was a breath of fresh air. I've always evolved in my music, I don't stand still. I won't mention names, but certain bands stand still. And we were always evolving. 'Come Taste the Band,' look at that—it's 'an evolving record.' Tommy came over to my home, and he'd already gotten a barebones structure of "Gettin' Tighter." I helped with some of the music on that.

Tommy Bolin: I love that song. I wrote that at one of the rehearsals. I just thought, "Oh man, you know they would probably enjoy" . . . y'know, because I was starting to feel them out, and they were starting to feel me out, and it was like a give-and-take situation—even musically. I just kind of presented, with all the tunes, mostly the music—a riff, or whatever. I would construct the tune around it and David would take it from there, and do the lyrics, or Glenn would do the lyrics.

Glenn Hughes: He had come in with "Lady Luck"—wrote the lyrics with Jeff Cook.

Jeff Cook: Well unfortunately, my memories of that are not happy ones, because David Coverdale basically changed they lyrics to the song. The song was originally a sort of Steinbeck type, 'Cannery Row' song about living in a certain part of town and wanting to break free of the poverty and so on and so forth. But a lot of that was lost when Coverdale started making up lyrics [laughs].

Glenn Hughes: Came in with some riffs maybe on one or two other songs. Pretty much wrote the rest of the record together as a unit. In Musicland in Germany, we were still sort of writing the record when we got there. "This Time Around" was written in the studio in Munich. "Owed to 'G'" was Tommy's instrumental that we added on to "This Time Around"—it was written separately, but we forged it together.

Tommy Bolin: Jon and Glenn were going to call their half 'Gersh,' and I was going to call my half 'Win.'

Greg Hampton: Some of the songs and riffs that ended up on 'Come Taste the Band' are from parts of sessions from early '74 to '75. I've heard a lot of those riffs in these multi-tracks that I've been listening to, that inevitably became Deep Purple songs.

David Coverdale: Those were interesting times. Not having the strong presence of Ritchie Blackmore was very noticeable. It was a lot more casual. Ritchie was much more work-focused and oriented—I favor that, personally. The 'hanging around' is interminable for me. And it was a couple of 'social aspects'—not necessarily with Tommy, but within the band—that could have been extremely damaging. I'm very happy that we actually came out with a worthwhile project.

Glenn Hughes: I guess if Tommy and I had our own druthers, we would have drifted off into our own camp—we were definitely a 'Hughes-Bolin camp' going on. But remember, you've got the lead frontman, Coverdale—that's the way it is and that's the way it was. But Tommy and I began to feel really comfortable playing together 'after hours' and hanging out.

David Coverdale: It's one of my favorite projects that I've been involved with. It actually works very well with my Coverdale/Page project—I put a lot of my stuff in an iPod shuffle, that magically spins around like some kind of crazy digital jukebox—and whenever either 'Come Taste the Band' follows a Coverdale/Page track or vice versa, it stands up very well. To be honest, I have no relationship with the management company of Deep Purple, who consistently scrape the barrel with Deep Purple compilation stuff. Unfortunately, for such a powerful band, we have no say in the matter. I would love to present the albums to modern rock engineers to remix, with that perspective. Y'know, like your Brendan O'Brien's or your Kevin Shirley's—I'd love to hear them brought up to date in a sonic way. Because I think they'd stand up very well.

Glenn Hughes: When you listen to 'Come Taste the Band,' it's a great album. It didn't sell as much as 'Burn' or 'Stormbringer,' but from most people I ask from any age group; 'Come Taste the Band' is their favorite.

Tommy Bolin: I think they're going to love it. The new album is more sophisticated than the old Purple stuff, but I don't think that'll matter. The kids are more clued in than they were a year ago, so I think it'll be accepted. Highly. Very highly.

Bobby Berge: When 'Come Taste the Band' came out . . . shit, here we go again—it just blew me away.

Otis Taylor: We were so proud of him. It was like, "Now he's a star." Everybody was happy for him—"Deep Purple, that's so fucking cool!" In those days, when people made a record it was a big deal, when people got elevated it was a big deal. If they were your friends, you were happy for them, because if they were a star, you knew a star. For me, there was no jealousy. I was really happy for him.

G. Brown: When he left, that was kind of 'it'—everyone thought that he's only 24 and he was in the ranks of the masters, and everyone believed in him. But that was probably a bad thing, because in retrospect, he was always able to get what he wanted from people.

Tommy Bolin: Nothing's going to stop me now.

Deep Purple II

Glenn Hughes: I met Karen three or four months into Tommy's arrival into Purple. They had been boyfriend/girlfriend on-and-off for years. When Tommy joined Purple, he had another girlfriend—a sort of South American looking gal in L.A. I think she was Asian actually, I can't remember her name. But Karen wasn't his girlfriend at the time. I met Karen at one of our rehearsals with Tommy, and we hung out a little bit—nothing was going on. They got back together again around the time of our world tour. Karen came on the road with us in America, maybe for three or four weeks, and she came to Hawaii in November of '75. She also came to the U.K. leg—at this time Karen and I were becoming really good friends. I was dating Vicky, who became Vicky Lord—now Jon Lord's wife. We were all friends.

Karen Ulibarri: He always had these stars in his eyes—"Wow, if I could be like so-and-so and travel like that." When he did it with Purple, it was like he was now one of these people—he was now on the superstar status. And some people handle it well, and some people don't. He didn't handle it well. He was a cocky little guy that could outsmart most people, but he still had that little Midwestern quality about him, that didn't know how to deal with the big boys. He didn't know how to handle himself on a superstar status, surrounded by people who were very used to it. That is very damaging when everyone around you wants to give you things—thinks it's an honor to give you drugs and get you high. And he was surrounded by this whirlwind of money and drugs and attention. It just engulfed him.

Johnnie Bolin: I think he could handle the James Gang fame, but when he was in Deep Purple, that was a totally different ballpark. He was traveling *all the time,* and these guys had done it forever. Touring with the James Gang was a little bit hard on you, but these guys, you're out for 60 days, and 50 of them you're playing. I know that Deep Purple's United States tour went really well—he was playing just fine. But when he went overseas . . . he couldn't hide it in his playing. He was doing some serious stuff there, it wasn't just like coke—which is bad enough—but when you start getting into heroin, then it's uncontrollable.

Tommy Bolin: It's about junk [the Deep Purple song "Dealer"]. It's the best thing in the world when you have it, and the worst thing in the world when you don't.

Jan Hammer: It was a gradual change. Things were sort of slipping. For the longest time, it didn't really involve his playing—he was able to play right through it. But I'm sure it eventually influenced that too.

David Givens: After Zephyr had broken up, Candy, Tommy, and I would bump into each other when he'd come to Boulder and hang out. There were nights when we did mountains of coke, and drank huge glasses of 151 proof rum. Tommy was doing heroin and drinking heavily. Coke, morphine— whatever he could get. And it was so out of character for him, because he was 'the clean liver' out of [Zephyr]—he was always looking for health food stores, always giving us shit for smoking cigarettes.

Candy and I were hanging out at the Good Earth club in Boulder, and Tommy came up to us. He said, "I owe you guys an apology. I used to think you guys were fucked up, but after what I've seen, I think all you really wanted to do was do the right thing. What I do now, everything I do, I do so I can have my way." Which was really weird—we never talked in depth about stuff. So for him to have that conversation with us was remarkable. But he was *so* fucked up. And Candy—of all people—said to me when we were on our way home, "Man, he's not going to last much longer. *He's going to be dead in a year.*"

Jeff Cook: I think [drugs] really became a problem in Purple, because there was so much access and so much money. That's when I think it really started getting out of hand.

Barry Fey: Glenn Hughes—you had to keep those two apart. They were so friendly, but so bad for each other.

Glenn Hughes: Here's the deal. In the early '70s, I started to use cocaine with another member of Deep Purple, which will remain nameless. It was social. Back in the day, you could actually do a little bit of blow with an executive at Warner Brothers if you'd like. It was kind of 'hip' to do that. Back in the early '70s, we didn't know about cocaine—we didn't know it was an addictive drug, we just thought it was a thing to do if you're in the industry. Tommy came in the band, and we did some lines together. But we did not know that Tommy had opiate problems—'opiate' meaning downers, or as we later found out . . . I found out from Karen that Tommy had a slight heroin problem in the James Gang. Or maybe even before the James Gang. And throughout his time with Purple, there were times on the Starship—our private plane—where I would look across at Tommy, we'd sit across from each other, and he would nod out. His face would become ridden with scratch marks. And we always thought it was cute—because we didn't know about the effects of heroin or opiates. None of us did. We didn't enable it, because we didn't know he was doing it. Tommy would do blow with us or drink Vodka and grapefruit—that was his drink. But when he did any opiates, he wouldn't discuss it with us or share it—we wouldn't know it. And we were very naïve and vulnerable to the fact that we didn't know that Tommy was on opiates or heroin. He wasn't on them all the time, but I can tell you that if he had the chance to get a sleeping pill, he would take it. I remember back in the day, all of Deep Purple would have our sleeping pills from the Harley Street doctors. And I think I gave Tommy most of mine, because I was never really 'a pill guy.' But we did not know the extent of Tommy's addiction—or let's call it 'the flirtation'—with opiate drugs at that time.

David Coverdale: I have fabulous memories of getting stoned with Bob Marley and the Wailers and Tommy—at the Sunset Marquis. And Bob Marley being really impressed that we could deal with this *unbelievable* amount of grass that they were smoking. My God, I'm surprised I don't have dreadlocks! It was a profound life experience.

Tommy Bolin: That was the first Purple concert [in Hawaii, on November 8, 1975]. I got my small pox shot. It was like, the small pox shot and the T.D.T. also. My week in Hawaii was watching everybody swim.

Glenn Hughes: By now, the Hughes-Bolin camp was definitely set up. Tommy and I were traveling together, we were hanging out together. We were 'doing our thing.' It was definitely split into two camps.

Tommy Bolin: For a first gig, I think it went great. I was very loose, but by the time we head for the States, I'm sure everything will be very together. We're playing dates in the Far East just to feel each other out.

Johnnie Bolin: They ran into some weird gigs, like the Indonesia thing, where the roadie [Patsy Collins] was pushed down an elevator shaft, and then the riots. It's just a different world when you get over there and play with that big of a band.

Tommy Bolin: He fell down a locked elevator shaft in the hotel after being hit on the head. That's accidental? But Indonesia was weird anyway. There were voodoo tents set up in the crowd against the band. I pinched a nerve in my arm and could hardly play.

G. Brown: Word came back of what had happened over in Indonesia, when his roadie was killed. I remember those little signs from the hinterlands . . . wasn't he named a co-respondent in Blackmore's divorce, with a dozen others or something? I just remember thinking, "Gosh, he's really having to deal with this stuff now"—being this sweet kid we all knew.

Johnnie Bolin: Yeah, Blackmore's divorce papers said that Tommy was messing with Blackmore's wife or something. I think everybody was, but I don't know for sure. It also said in Rolling Stone Magazine that Tommy was supposedly dating Olivia Newton-John. Tommy said, "I don't even know who she is!"

Glenn Hughes: Well, Japan was a miss because of the Indonesia accident, where he was given some morphine, and he fell asleep on his hand, twisted. He kind of passed out, feel asleep, and ruptured some tendons or whatever—he put them to sleep. So when he woke up, we had to get him into therapy with his hands in Japan. The 'Last Concert in Japan' record [released in 1977]—his right hand was dead, so he couldn't play.

David Coverdale: It's unfair for me, to be honest [to compare Tommy to Ritchie Blackmore]. Tommy, as it's pretty well documented now, embraced the peripheral aspects of the music business—to a debilitating degree at times. My disagreements at times with Ritchie Blackmore were more personality-based, and not alcohol or drug-based. That was an uncomfortable spiral downwards, I felt. I think one of the things that was really difficult for Tommy is that he was looked upon as 'a replacement guitarist.' Y'know, he replaced Joe Walsh in the James Gang. He told me people would shout out, "Joe!" The more insensitive members of the audience.

Tommy Bolin: If someone yells "Where's Blackmore?" at one of our concerts, I'll just do what I did when people yelled "Where's Joe Walsh?" at me while I was with the James Gang. I'll have cards printed up with his address and throw them out to the audience.

Jeff Cook: Again, it was one of those things where he was stepping in to replace somebody that was really considered 'a guitar God.' I think the same set of issues came up—immediately. The press was saying, "Is this guy as good as Ritchie Blackmore?" And the audiences were going, "Well, is he a Blackmore or is he not?" I think Tommy felt a certain pressure there, and was also upset that he wasn't accepted on his own terms. If Tommy was anything, he was definitely an individualist, and really cared about trying to put his personal mark on anything he did. To just play note-for-note what other players had played was not what Tommy was there for. So again, it was a step up, but it also had its downside.

Johnnie Bolin: [An odd-shaped guitar shown in pictures of Tommy touring Japan with Deep Purple] was given to him. I thought it was a Yamaha, but they don't ever show the headstock very well in pictures. That was real heavy too—he didn't like all that weight. You can tell by looking at it, it's really hard wood.

Jon Levicke: I never heard of him until he joined Deep Purple. I was a big Blackmore fan. I said, "Who the hell is Tommy Bolin?" And somebody told me that he replaced Joe Walsh in the James Gang. I said, "An American guitarist stepping in to replace Ritchie Blackmore?" The first song I saw him do [at the Swing Auditorium in San Bernardino, California], it just floored me—he was one of the best guitar players I've ever seen. And I've seen them *all*. I used to shoot [pictures] for about ten years—in the '60s and '70s—so I saw all the good ones. And he was by far one of the best I ever saw. He blew me away. I can still remember it like it was yesterday. It was a small place—held about 3,500. Probably like the Hollywood Palladium. It was festival-style, meaning first come/first serve—we camped out overnight, because I wanted to get right up front to the stage. I got up right in front of Tommy Bolin. It was about 200 degrees, hotter than hell. The opening song was "Burn." I turned to my friend, and said, *"Ritchie fucking who?"* I was just totally blown away—he completely did the whole solo backwards. It was unbelievable. He was one of the cleanest guitarists I've ever seen. I flew to one of the Tommy Bolin fests in Sioux City—I flew there with Glenn Hughes, and talked to Glenn a lot about Tommy. He insists that Tommy never took the stage unless he was really fucked up. But he never missed a note—he was just so clean it was unbelievable. He would come out on stage in a full coat, velvet pants, and a hat. He played an old, beat-up Stratocaster. It was just amazing. There is no way to describe how good he was.

Greg Hampton: I saw him with Deep Purple in Houston—it was definitely a life-changing experience for me. He came out, and it was really loud, but he was really 'on' that night. He had on this little brown cabbie hat. He played an amazing Echoplex solo—he played all the stuff from 'Come Taste the Band' pretty much spot on, *but about five times better*. It was really a great gig. I've read reviews and I've heard bootlegs of different shows from that tour, where it wasn't nearly as good. The interplay between he and Glenn was one thing that was very impressionable to me. Before Glenn joined Deep Purple, he had Trapeze, and it was a funky band—it seemed that they were already on the same musical wavelength, so you could see the interplay . . . they were just great. I do remember David Coverdale not coming out front a lot—I could definitely tell there were some negative vibes in the atmosphere. The 'Come Taste the Band' record was just amazing—it was brilliant.

Johnnie Bolin: In Chicago, me, my mom, my dad, and my brother came out. Tommy was happy—in good spirits, good shape. Now he was playing in the big league. I'm not saying the James Gang was the minors, but there's nothing like Purple. And once again, he got the chance to play the way he wanted to—they didn't hold him back any.

Mark Stein: I first met Tommy when he was playing with Deep Purple at the Long Beach Arena. The first time I actually saw him was on stage—it blew me away. He had an amazing vibe, and he looked incredible. I remember him dancing around the stage with that long scarf he used to wear, that fell towards his back. Kind of looked like some great 'spirit' up there, and he had an amazing sound. I met him backstage, when I went to say "Hi" to Jon Lord.

Jan Hammer: There was one time—I was playing somewhere in Philadelphia, and Tommy was playing with Deep Purple. He came to see us play. I was standing there backstage, and he walked right by me! He kept saying, *"I have to see Jan, I have to see Jan,"* and he just walked by me. A classic case of 'too much of a good thing.' He eventually found me.

Jeff Ocheltree: I think because of being in Deep Purple, he got to know Zeppelin. Did Johnnie tell you about the time that [John] Bonham went up onstage during a Deep Purple concert, and yelled, "We've got a new album out, these guys suck!" He almost got into a big fight—Tommy was going to club him in the head with his guitar. He just jumped up on stage and started yelling—drunk out of his mind. I talked to Ian Paice about that a few years ago, and I think he remembered seeing Bonham come up there, but he wasn't up there very long, and he did see Tommy almost get into a fight with him. I don't think Bonham liked Tommy. I think he just didn't dig the idea of having this American guy playing guitar with them.

Bonham was a very wise person about music—he had an incredible knowledge of lots of different kinds of music, and listened to different types of music. His thing was 'big band.' Until this last article came out in Traps Magazine, they finally got Bonham's sister to contribute, and she said the same things I've been saying—he listened to swing and big band. That's why he had the big drums. I thought that was really interesting—that most of the great rock drummers were jazz drummers. Bonham could have played jazz with anybody. I don't know why anybody says the shit they say about him unless they're going to talk about the musicality. He was just a great musician—he had great ears and he listened. Played great anytime, all the time. He was never screwed up before he went on stage. And yeah, he didn't like people who didn't talk intelligently about music, so he reacted. He didn't like being away from home. He covered up his fears of being away from home by being drunk. And if you got him pissed off, *look out.* It's too bad, because he was a very generous, loving person. But you're never going to know that about somebody, if you keep talking shit to him. So most of the people that have negative things to say about Bonham usually are the ones that talked shit to him.

Tom Stephenson: [Robert Plant and Tommy] were friends. Robert admired Tommy and Tommy admired Robert. But Robert had an agenda—to get at Karen.

Jon Levicke: It was different [than the previous version of Purple]. He had a completely different style than Ritchie Blackmore. I was a diehard Deep Purple fan—I liked Ian Gillan a lot, but I liked Coverdale just as well. They were harder, they were a lot louder, and they were more raw—that's the best way I can explain it from the previous Deep Purples. Blackmore was real flamboyant in his early days. He was all over the stage. They used to end with a song called "Mandrake Root" off their first album [1968's 'Shades of Deep Purple']—they'd go into a big instrumental at the end, strobe lights flashing, and Blackmore would be twirling his guitar and rubbing it up and down the stage. That stopped after they did the Cal Jam concert [in 1974]. Then he just kinda stood there.

Tommy was all over the place. Personally, I think Tommy was a better showman than Blackmore. He changed a lot of the songs—that's probably a big difference. In the solos, he put his own spin on it, so he didn't play the solos exactly like Ritchie used to. Especially "Burn"—he completely changed the solo. He tended to put his own spin on everything, which was really cool. He was hated in the beginning. Deep Purple were around so long, the real diehard Blackmore fans had a hard time accepting Tommy. I did too when I first heard the album. I thought, "*Eh,* it's O.K." But after seeing them live, it was a whole different thing. Even a lot of people after they heard Tommy, they never accepted him. Why, I still don't know—I don't get it. The only thing that I can figure out is Deep Purple were different—they had the nucleus members, but they weren't the same band. Especially with Coverdale and Hughes in there. Personally, I thought the line-up was a much better line-up. Glenn was a much more superior bass player to Roger Glover. Coverdale was much more of a raw singer—it was before Whitesnake—they were more gritty. As far as doing the old standards, I didn't see a problem. And as I said, I was probably one of the most diehard Deep Purple fans you'll ever meet—I saw them every time they came to L.A. I *never* missed a Deep Purple show.

G. Brown: He felt like he'd met that challenge. He told me he did it mostly for the money—the fact that he was able to pull that off, it really validated him.

David Coverdale: Ritchie Blackmore was such an icon—it was difficult. I think American audiences embraced Tommy much easier than U.K. audiences. When we got to the U.K., I actually wanted to cancel that tour, because I felt that the band was in such a debilitated state—it would reflect very badly on the image of Deep Purple. But the acting manager at the time, I had a very good friendship with. He asked me—and I'm deadly serious—to "Please, do me a favor and do this tour. Otherwise, my reputation . . . " y'know. And that was the last time I did anybody that kind of favor, because it was this huge source of regret for me.

Glenn Hughes: In the U.K. tour, I think the shouts for Blackmore were overwhelming. "Blackmore, Blackmore, Blackmore!" And Tommy just could not deal with that. A young man growing musically, mentally, or spiritually couldn't deal with that aspect. He basically gave everybody the finger, and he played below par.

Tom Stephenson: People were booing because Ritchie wasn't there. And it started effecting Tommy really badly.

David Coverdale: I left the stage at the end of the Liverpool show [at the Empire Theatre, on March 15, 1976], and that's when I left the band. They asked me to keep it quiet, until they decided what to do. But somebody had to make the decision. I was looking from the stage to the audience, and I could see this bemusement, like, *"What the hell is going on?"* It was not the band that I had actually joined.

Karen Ulibarri: Again, it was another situation where he wasn't happy. A very sad stigma that followed Tommy joining these groups was the fact that he was always a replacement for Joe Walsh or Ritchie Blackmore in the eyes of a lot of fans, and this is what they wanted to hear. It was very hard for him to be on stage and hear somebody yell, "Joe Walsh!" Y'know, "Where's Ritchie?!" This is what haunted him during the English tour—was "Where's Ritchie?!" Booed him off the stage—he played terribly. He was just so unhappy to be responded to like this—the reception was miserable, so his attitude was miserable. And that was just the end of it after that.

Glenn Hughes: And lo and behold, when the band broke up, that's when he really got into [drugs].

Solo Tour/'Private Eyes'

Phillip Polimeni: I would say in early '76, he started doing more and more coke because he was doing so much alcohol. We had Tuinals back then—barbiturates—and he was doing those to counteract the amount of coke he was doing. Rather than someone saying, "Why don't you just stop doing the coke?", they would tell him, "Why don't you do Tuinals, to slow down from the speed of coke?" It was a vicious cycle. Tommy would come over the house and the first thing he would say was, "What have you got to drink?" *Right away.* Even in Iowa—Tommy was always with a drink in his hand. Tommy was always a drinker. And he could handle it—he didn't get mean, sloppy, or rude. He would be 'right' after three straight martinis—he would be calm, perfect, and ready to get down. Play his ass off. When most people would start getting stupid, he would just be becoming right. This didn't happen overnight—this went on from Iowa, to Colorado, to Beverly Hills, and then the Hollywood Hills.

Barry Fey: He was living like a superstar in L.A. Tommy was dotted on by the superstars and he lived like a superstar. He just didn't have the money. And it was costing at least $3,000.00 a month for the house, and I was paying for everything. I didn't care—I loved Tommy.

Johnnie Bolin: He couldn't tour in support of 'Teaser,' because he had to go out with Deep Purple. He postponed his solo tour until '76. Even though 'Teaser' was several months old, he hadn't toured with it.

Karen Ulibarri: Well that was it—that was what it was all about. All these bands, all the things that he had done, had finally come to fruition. He had the band he wanted—he hand-picked all the musicians, he was going to play his music, and no one was going to tell him to play "Smoke on the Water" or "Funk #49." He was going to do Tommy's music, and he was elated. He had the support of the record company, the management, and everyone around him wanted to be a part of it. It was exciting for him because he finally had some control—he didn't have anyone telling him what to do, and he was able to be as creative as he possibly wanted. But what being in all these other bands taught him was that you still have to be commercial. You still have to do something that sells, you still have to play what people want to hear. And I think he tried to stay along those lines, and be somewhat sell-able to people. So he learned from those experiences, and I think he tried to do that in the Tommy Bolin Band. And be creative, talented, and also free—but there were the restrictions from record companies, the fans, and he knew he had to stay within those guidelines. But it was a happy time at first, and also with having your own band came the responsibilities. And that was hard on him. Fronting your own band was suddenly very hard. Also singing, that was hard on him— to suddenly have to carry the whole show doing all the vocals as well as the guitar work. He was terrified. The pressures started setting in, and I think that was the beginning of the downfall, because the pressures were phenomenal.

John Tesar: I asked him one time—this is when he had left Deep Purple, and he was headed back out on his own—"Would you ever join anybody else's band?" And he said, "Absolutely not." Then he thought for a while, and he said, "Oh, of course I would play for James Brown if he asked me" [laughs]!

Narada Michael Walden: Tommy asked me if I'd go on the road with him. I said, "O.K.," and we put a band together—with Reggie McBride [on bass], I brought Norma Jean Bell from Detroit on sax to sing, Mark Stein from Vanilla Fudge on organ, myself, and Tommy. We had a fantastic band. It took about a week and a half to rehearse to get it really super tight. I felt every day it getting stronger and stronger.

Mark Stein: At the time, I was doing a lot of songwriting—I wasn't on the road for a couple of years. About three years, since 1971. I had moved out to California from New York, because that was where everything was happening in the music business at that time. I was putting together a band with some friends of mine, and I remember making a few calls. Wanted to go down and play with Tommy—that would be a great way for me to get back on the road, playing with Tommy's band. I remember it was an exciting vibe, going down to S.I.R. on Santa Monica. We played about three times, before he said, "O.K., you've got the gig." I think he was busting my chops, because he knew I really wanted to be in the band, but he didn't tell me until the last minute, so I didn't know for sure if he wanted me to be playing with him. I think all the time he did, because he was a Vanilla Fudge fan, but just didn't want to let on at the time. So that was it—we started rocking.

Reggie McBride: I had left Rare Earth, and during that time, I met Mark Stein. He and I started getting together at my house to write and jam. Soon, Bruce Gary [drums] joined us, along with Bobby Cochran on guitar, and we had started a band. While we were rehearsing, Mark got a call from Tommy's manager. They needed a bass player and a keyboard player, so Mark recommended me for the gig.

Mark Stein: Between rehearsals, we used to hang out with [Tommy] and Karen. Karen and my wife Patty were good friends. We used to sit and talk about his upcoming recordings that he was doing at the time, which eventually became 'Private Eyes.' [We'd] talk about just general things in life, not everything was 'rock stardom'—he was a kid underneath it all.

Jeff Ocheltree: Because of talking to him those couple of times after shows, he called me up and said, "I want you to come work with me." I happened to be in L.A. at the time, and I went down to where they were rehearsing. I'll never forget that rehearsal—it was at S.I.R. down on Santa Monica Boulevard or the Sunset Strip, I can't remember. They're rehearsing, I go in there, and he wanted to talk to me about a tour he wanted to do. He starts a tune, stops it, and then says to Narada, "Hey man, this isn't how I want this played." Narada stands up on his bass drum, says something to him, and Tommy says, "Get off your bass drum—this is *my* gig. I don't need your feedback on how to do this." Then he says, "We're going to run rehearsals a little different tonight. When I stop to do something, *listen* to why I'm stopping you." He was capable of being a really good bandleader—with any musician that came on that stage with him.

Narada Michael Walden: I remember even the rehearsals in L.A. were buzzin'. Everybody wanted to come in just to hear the rehearsals. There was a lot of love and high musicianship. And then we went on the road—*we killed.* I remember being at the Roxy on Sunset, and George Duke and Billy Cobham were up in that kind of pier that looks down on you. I remember looking up and seeing those guys and being a little intimidated, because those are heavyweights. But we played so hard, it didn't really matter anymore. Billy Cobham said, "You played so hard, you knocked the paint off those drums!" And Tommy had a good time at that time. He was really enjoying playing and being a little bit loose—which was always his thing. His typical thing was, "Fuck 'em if they can't take a joke." He was a spiritual guy, but really wanted to have fun—didn't want to take things too overly serious. We toured quite a bit—went down to Denver. But I remember the intensity. And I always liked playing really intense, anyway—hitting hard and playing fast and furious. Just pushing Tommy. And he would really react, man—he would just catch a fire.

Johnnie Bolin: When I first went out and saw his band on that tour, that was the first time I ever heard Tommy sing live. It was really cool, because they all sang. They were all good singers. Five-part harmony—it's like, *wow!* That was an incredible band.

Reggie McBride: I thought Tommy was one of the nicest people I ever met. He had a very strong persona that brought you into his world musically. His guitar playing was phenomenal. He was a very strong and soulful rhythm player, and his leads were way different than I had ever seen or experienced in a band. Of course, his writing was classic.

Narada Michael Walden: I turned down a gig to join Weather Report to join Tommy Bolin. The reason was . . . I wanted to experience what it was like to have girls' panties on the stage in a rock n' roll band! As opposed to all the jazz-rock-fusion stuff, where it was so heady, *but no panties.* So I went through a phase in my life where I wanted to be around that side of it. Well, I didn't really get those many panties on the stage, but it sure was fun though. The pandemonium that makes that kind of wild, screeching sound—it just makes you want to go crazy.

Bill Graham: [From a Western Union Cable] Dear Tommy: Sorry I couldn't be with you for your San Francisco gig. Best of luck tonight, and all the rest of the nights on your tour. You're a winner.

Prairie Prince: I went and saw him play at Winterland. I recall him being really animated and extremely excited. It was an awesome performance. We went back to the Miyako Hotel and partied with him a bunch. We had a meal—that's when I passed off some t-shirts to him. I remember him lying on the bed, and me and my girlfriend were sitting on chairs. We were laughing and joking, smoking cigarettes, doing a little bit of marching powder, and drinking some champagne. He had a couple of girlfriends around . . . and he was lounging around in a kimono [laughs]. And a hat—he had a big velvet hat. I remember him being real mellow. We talked about if we could ever go back to the desert and jam again—I kept bringing that up, because it was one of my great memories of my teenaged years, jamming with Tommy out in the desert.

Mike Drumm: When he came back in May of '76, everybody had heard rumors of his lifestyle becoming much crazier. He did this meet-and-greet party at this long-defunct club which I went to, because I was still running record stores back then. And I'm like, "Geez, is he going to remember me?" As soon as he saw me, it was like no time had passed. He gave me this huge bear hug. He was genuine and so 'there.' And, I couldn't help but notice that in this party that was being held in his honor, he and two other people were spending a bunch of time out in the lobby by the pay phone—trying to score drugs. That had obviously become supremely important in his life. And then there were all the rumors about the management friction—whether his manager wasn't also caught up in a bad addiction of gambling, and that a lot of money was disappearing. There's a number of people who have stories about all the fights between Tommy and Barry Fey during that period. There's a perspective that the ultimate demise of their relationship was about to happen.

G. Brown: '76, that spring, he came back to Denver and played Ebbet's Field. Just a phenomenal set. He played two nights—it was a triumphant return. He was doing it on his terms.

Reggie McBride: The tour was long. I remember finally getting to New York, and getting a second wind.

Narada Michael Walden: I could tell whatever he was taking or doing was getting a little out of control, so I talked to him about it privately. He was always very kind—he understood that I was concerned for him. He would listen to me, and say it was hard for him—whatever it was, he'd do better. The last concert I remember being in New York at the Bottom Line. That place was always very important to me, because I had lived in New York, and I always wanted to do well in New York. Tommy—for some reason—couldn't even stand up at one point without leaning up against the pole on the stage. And I didn't like that—I wanted him to be at his best in New York. I just realized that I should quit the band. And I did. I think that was a sad time for all of us—I did love him and I really cared about him. If you're going to get it together, then fine. But if you're not going to get it together, what am I going to do? But our friendship and love for each other was always divine, always special. I had this song I was writing, called "Delightful," and he wanted to record it on his album. And I said, "No—I'm probably going to use it for my own album." As it worked out, I did use it for my own album [1976's 'Garden of Love Light'], and I had Raymond Gomez play with me. But Tommy always loved "Delightful."

Barry Fey: I—believe it or not—never did drugs. I don't know how in this business, but I never did drugs. I knew he had a terrible problem when he fell off the stage at the Bottom Line. When Tommy fell off the stage at the Bottom Line, he was still on Nemperor Records. And Nat Weiss called me into his office, and said, "Barry, I love Tommy, I love you. I have a small label, but I only want people on it that I want, and I no longer want Tommy. I'm not going to make any announcements, I'm not going to make it any harder on you—but go find another label." And I think 48 hours later; he was signed to Columbia Records.

Narada Michael Walden: It was a sadness. But he was still kind of 'druggy-druggy.' I don't know what he was going through that was making him so sad. I couldn't get to the bottom of it. We had a powerful band and a powerful sound, and we were ready to just *explode*. I don't quite know what it was—I wasn't able to get that deep. Musically, we could get deep. But not when it came to just sitting there and Tommy [saying], "This is what's really bothering me—if I fix this thing, I will be alright," I couldn't get that out of him. So I just said, "Listen, I'm going to have to move on—this is going in a direction that I'm not comfortable." You must also know, I was a disciple of guru Sri Chinmoy—there was no smoking, no drinking, no nothing going on. So it was really ailing to me at that time to be around too much of that 'out of control-ness.' It's one thing to play rock n' roll, be hard, and be strong. But it's another thing to be like you're embarrassed because you can't stand up on the stage. So he understood man, but it was sad, because we loved each other. And I—to this day—love Tommy.

Bobby Berge: It just seems like in general—and I saw it happen to other people too, including myself—I heard talk of heroin use. I was drinking way too much, I wasn't eating good, and I didn't have a whole lot of money, so I couldn't afford much. But '76, that first part, I was still working with Buddy, and Tommy was gone a lot. Then the next thing I know, going into May/June, I'm invited to do the 'Private Eyes' sessions. Well, it still hadn't hit Tommy yet, but it had hit me in the spring of '76—*big time.* I was struggling, but the 'Private Eyes' sessions, [there were] some really great/fantastic moments. But I pulled some boners there myself. I was the first one there kind of falling on my face. I would say the summer of '76, I knew what was going on—the heroin—you hear stories and everything. One of the saddest things in my life is I almost died from alcohol poisoning during the 'Private Eyes' sessions. I recovered, actually finished the last few cuts totally straight, and we finished up the album.

Jeff Cook: I remember that about the time of 'Private Eyes,' I got a call from management to try and go see Tommy, and maybe talk to him about the drug thing getting out of hand. The fact that they sent me was like sending a fox to the henhouse, because I had as big a drug problem as he did—if not worse. So all we ended up doing was partying the whole time I was there. As I recall, I did say to him, "This is too much, we're doing too much." But I think it fell on deaf ears, because I think it was already too late.

Barry Fey: I don't know where Tommy passed the point of no return—because there was one. I just don't know when it was.

Phillip Polimeni: ['Private Eyes' producer] Dennis MacKay was such a beautiful soul, and he loved Tommy. He came up to Tommy's house, and they were sitting across from each other—they were having martinis. At this time, Tommy was on to vodka, and they were drinking vodka and talking. Tommy had a stack of stuff, and an acoustic guitar in this big living room. Tommy was like a king out there. He's playing him this stuff, and they're great songs. As he's downing these drinks, Dennis notices that he hasn't eaten. *This is his breakfast*—having drinks. Dennis is going, "Why don't we get something to eat?" And Tommy's like, "Well, I'm not really that hungry." He was little on eating and big on drinking.

Mike Drumm: Dennis MacKay told me about how Tommy was so drunk all the time that he had open sores on his chest. All that he would do is drink—he wouldn't eat.

Phillip Polimeni: Dennis worked with him and they picked out tunes. We'd go into the studio—Cherokee or the Record Plant—and Tommy would tell him, "Let's run through it." They'd go through it once or twice, and he'd go, "That's good. I'm leaving—I'm going to party. You take care of it—you know what to do." And he'd leave! Dennis and I used to eat lunch together, because Dennis was a health freak and I was a vegetarian. I remember avocado and cheese sandwiches with sprouts. We'd sit at this table—he'd write a list and say, "I need you to get him to do this and do that. You're his best friend, and I need him at the studio at this time and that time." Tommy called me his 'P.A.'—his personal advisor.

Mark Stein: I remember rehearsing the material for the album—again, we used to rehearse a lot at S.I.R. I had a good time helping arrange some of the vocals on "Bustin' out for Rosey" and "Shake the Devil." I remember having fun with Norma and Tommy—it was almost like gospel rock backing vocals to some of those arrangements. I think they went to try out some of the studios in London after we were done with the backing tracks. The backing tracks were done in California, but they mixed it at Trident in London. I remember we had a little listening party back at S.I.R., and Tommy came in with Dennis. They put the final product over a big system, and blasted it. Everybody was pleased with it.

Reggie McBride: I remember recording at Cherokee, which was one of my favorite rooms—Studio B. I had recorded there before doing R n' B and jazz. However, recording there with Tommy was very different for me. Dennis MacKay really dialed us in as band, and I was impressed at the playback when we came in to have a listen.

Carmine Appice: After Deep Purple, he moved to L.A.—we started seeing each other around. We used to see each other a lot at the Rainbow Bar and Grill. So we were hanging a lot. Then when he did 'Private Eyes,' he asked if I wanted to play on it. So I said, "Yeah, definitely." I don't remember much about the recording to tell you the truth [Carmine played on the track "Someday Will Bring Our Love Home"]—I don't know why. I think we did it at the Record Plant or one of those big studios in L.A. Y'know; Tommy had a problem with the drugs obviously. I don't remember a lot of him being sober very often—he was always pretty out of it. And that was really a drag. So the sessions were taken over by the producer. Just did the tracks—they went down easy and they were fast—I do remember that. On my part, anyway.

Jeff Cook: 'Private Eyes' was another expression—very different record. If you listen to both 'Teaser' and 'Private Eyes' side-by-side, you see that he was continuing to experiment and grow. There's a softer side more prevalent there than on the first record. And there's a much more commitment to the imagery of the lyric. I think he was becoming more respectful of the song structure. He'd certainly proven that he could play, but it seemed that the songs were more 'song-like.'

Mike Drumm: Once he got to 'Private Eyes,' he started writing his own lyrics. Because up until then, it was always John and Jeff writing all the lyrics. That was the whole thing—it was all coming together. His voice had really developed, he was writing his own lyrics, he was doing the kind of music that would have guaranteed massive airplay. And it would all come together in the second half of 1976.

Jeff Cook: When I heard the 'Teaser' record, and heard "The Grind" and "Teaser"—those giant guitar licks—I thought about "Shake the Devil." I thought we should try and write a song that addresses 'the dark side,' and also the kind of women we should all be fearful of [laughs]. So that's when I wrote the lyrics to "Shake the Devil." My memory was, "This is going to be a huge, loud rock song." And it sure turned out to be that. I think it's been released two or three different times since the original recording on different compilations that Columbia has done. I'm very proud of that song—I think that song's a survivor. Then "Sweet Burgundy," I was listening to a lot of Van Morrison, and I was trying to capture that kind of feel and imagery that Van Morrison did in the 'Moondance' period. Plus, I was in the middle of taking a tour of France with wine—I was drinking a lot of French wine [laughs].

Tommy Bolin: Well, I went in the studio and got this basic idea that's playing now [the song's opening riff of "Post Toastee"], and just thoughts started coming to me, things I thought would add to the thing. It goes into a reggae thing, to like a ballad thing, and then back to the theme at the end. It was originally like fourteen minutes, and I had to splice it all up.

Johnnie Bolin: 'Private Eyes' was all brand new stuff. Once again, 'Teaser' had a lot of stuff that Energy had done—he had that album written before he had a record deal. But 'Private Eyes' was totally different. A lot of it was written in the studio. So when I heard it first, I was like, "That's kind of different." It was kind of a different mix, too. And Rolling Stone got down on him about the reverb—which later, people praised. I don't know if it was ahead of its time. I thought it was kind of recorded weird, too. It's way different than 'Teaser.'

Tommy Bolin: Well, it gets to a point where you have to release yourself without playing 120 decibels all the time. So, "Gypsy Soul" I think kind of speaks for itself.

Mike Drumm: At that point, he was obviously focusing on a much more commercial direction with his music. He was going to become a star—it was time to head that way. The first solo album wound up being thought of as 'too eclectic and too creative.' So 'Private Eyes' was really drawing in the reins, and coming up with just a commercial oriented rock record. And in retrospect, they did a great job—even though he was really blasted a lot of the time. They were still able to create this really commercial record. That's when 'album oriented rock' and all those radio stations were blowing up all over the country. This is how you became a star. You look at the bands that made it all through the '70s, and then as we got to the later '70s—when the Kansases and the R.E.O. Speedwagons became big—he was positioned to be the next big thing.

Phillip Polimeni: I felt they rushed out 'Private Eyes' a little too fast. But Dennis was happy with it.

Greg Hampton: The playing on 'Private Eyes' was good—it wasn't great. I think when he was playing and surrounding himself with some of the best players in the industry, it would keep him on his toes—to push himself past the boundaries. And that's why I think some of those great things would come out of him. I think the musicians on 'Private Eyes' were more of 'a band unit,' to facilitate the songs getting documented. So that was the reason why I think 'Private Eyes' was a good body of songs, but he could have had a lot better record. I think that record could have been way better if he had more time, because he really didn't have the songs finished. He would write them in the studio, and literally cut them—they would cut up and edit them. He would write them in the studio on one day—on a Wednesday—and then record them on Thursday or Friday. He only spent a few weeks doing that record, as opposed to the 'Teaser' record—those songs had many demo versions. He had some of those songs that he and Jeff Cook had written since '72 or '73. Some of those songs could have potentially been on James Gang records. And he subsequently moved to L.A. and had a lot of those songs in tow—where he did demos of in various locations.

Prairie Prince: He called me. He said, "Can you paint a t-shirt for me?" 'Cause he'd seen all the airbrushed t-shirts that I had been painting for the Tubes—Michael Cotton and myself did all the costumes and set designs. He had seen the face t-shirts we had done—we did portraits of everybody in the band, kind of caricatures, and we wore them on our second album's back cover photograph [1976's 'Young and Rich']. I said, "Sure. I really like that photograph of you from 'Teaser'." And he said, "Yeah, that would be a great one." So I copied that picture from 'Teaser' onto a t-shirt for him, and he used it in a photo session—they used it as the sleeve of 'Private Eyes.' So in doing so, we struck up a rapport in my artistic career. He was always saying, "I would love it if you could paint me some more costumes to wear on stage." That's the way I painted him a shirt that was a Tubes shirt—we had done some of them for the Tubes, and he said, "I really like that intertwining tubes design." So I painted him one of those, and he had someone design him a red velvet jacket—with feather epilates on his shoulders. I painted eyes on the sleeves for him. And I think I did something else, but I can't recall right now. Johnnie told me that they're framed now in his mother's house. I was proud to hear that.

Mark Stein: I know during the recording of 'Private Eyes,' he was really happy and positive about it. He was excited when it was being played on the radio.

Bobby Berge: I was in bad shape. By some miraculous thing, Tommy must have loved my playing, because I got to do a short tour with him after 'Private Eyes.' And as far as I know, he was holding it together there—June/July. I still have my itinerary. Albuquerque with Santana—Tommy and I got up and jammed with Santana. The next gig in Dallas at the Electric Ballroom, then Kansas City with Fleetwood Mac. Austin, Texas, and Jan Hammer came to that gig. Then we ended up in Houston, and I was pretty much a mess. I came back to Colorado after that tour, and then Johnnie Bolin took over on drums. It was kind of later in the summer, going into the fall—I knew what was going on [with drugs], but he was still holding his own. I was real happy for him; I was trying to just survive myself back in Colorado.

Greg Hampton: I saw him solo also, in New Mexico. He cancelled in El Paso—he said he was sick, he was opening for Santana—and Freddie King played. Two nights later I believe, he did the show in Albuquerque, and we went to that. He played great. I think the Deep Purple performance overall was better—he was just opening [for Santana]. He was able to really stretch out, and I think the prestige inspired his playing with the big stage with Purple. I wouldn't say he felt it was beneath him . . . *he kind of did*. It was kind of two steps back, opening [for others]. Any opening act has to take 'the humility aspect' and be humble, because there's some things they're just not allowed to do. Unfortunately, it's something I think he never got accustomed to. Once the Purple thing was over, he still had it set in his mind that he should be treated like that, and he lived like that. He always carried on like that. And from what I understand, that's why he was so broke.

'Private Eyes' Tour

Reggie McBride: I used to hang out at Tommy's house sometimes. I would see Linda Blair hanging out—she was good friends with Tommy and Karen. He used to call her 'the blugly blugly girl.' I got a kick out of that!

Johnnie Bolin: Tommy and Linda were just friends. She was a Black Oak Arkansas fan, and then she hung around Lynyrd Skynyrd and Rick James. Tommy had just moved out of his place in Hollywood, was kind of in limbo, and she was off doing 'The Exorcist II,' so she said we could stay at her house. Real nice house—it was Robert Shaw's old house, from 'Jaws' [Shaw played 'Quint']. He had 'R.S.' on the stove, and in the attic, there was a hidden bedroom. It was a beautiful house—it was in Beverly Hills, on Roxbury Drive. She said, "I'm going to be gone anyway, I want somebody to watch the house." We would go out to parties. One night, the three of us—me, Rick, and Tommy—went up to Jon Lord's house. He and Paice had a place up on Mulholland Drive. Took a cab up there, and they'd never heard 'Private Eyes' before, so Tommy played it for them. Jon and Ian really liked it—they all remained friends. Now *that* was a party—went there about 7:00 at night, and didn't get home until 8:00 in the morning!

Glenn Hughes: I started my Trapeze tour in St. Louis—mid-August '76. I got into St. Louis, called Tommy's house—as I always do when I get to the States—and Linda was over there. Linda was a good friend of Tommy's. She got on the phone; she was on her way to New York. I said, "If you'd like to pop in and see my show at Kiel Auditorium, I'm playing there Friday night." She came in on Thursday, and we started an immediate relationship that lasted about two months.

Johnnie Bolin: Tommy and Karen were separated. A month before that, we were at Linda's house, and they were together there, but not really 'together.'

You could tell there was a problem. We all lived together at Linda's until August. It just got sour—I don't think it was what you would consider a break-up . . . they just kinda weren't together. After we went on the road, he got out of Linda's house—I don't know where he was staying. He was on the road most of the time, so he'd come back and get a room. I don't think they had an actual breaking up, but they weren't happy together at that point. The thing is, he didn't really talk about Karen at all. I don't know if he was trying to get over it—but he wasn't happy about it . . . yet he wasn't happy with her. I think the time away was supposed to be a time where they got it together to try it again. I could have brought it up, but he didn't want to talk about it. Valeria [Tommy's subsequent girlfriend] was around some of the time, and of course, he didn't want to talk about it *then* [laughs]. Valeria came over to this country to Hollywood [she was Swiss]—that's where Tommy met her. She didn't speak good English at all—she was very quiet. She didn't know the language good enough to talk. But yeah, she hung around—we'd go to rehearsals and she'd be there, we'd go to the Rainbow and she'd go with us.

Jeff Ocheltree: Dating Valeria was actually more of a friendship. It was a nice friendship, but it wasn't like Karen.

Otis Taylor: I have a theory, that it really broke him up. After they broke up, I saw him, and he seemed different to me. It was hard, because they were childhood sweethearts. He met Karen when he was 15 or 16. So I think that's hard on people.

Mike Drumm: They were always a team. Karen's really beautiful, and she was from the Denver area—they were this 'Boulder couple.' It was always Tommy and Karen. Then they moved to L.A., and I just think as the drug and alcohol consumption increased—and as the craziness increased—Tommy was tempted. Any guy who's 23/24 years old still has a high testosterone level, and all of a sudden, all these women will have sex with you. I'm under the impression that's what started happening. He started fucking around, and it put a lot of strain on them. And ultimately, she hooked up with Glenn, who'd been Tommy's best friend in Deep Purple. So they had this really sordid kind of situation. But they were still all friends—it's kind of like 'the George Harrison and Eric Clapton thing,' with Pattie Boyd. They had a bond as musicians, and the women were below that. So some woman went from this person to that person—you still maintained your relationship as a musician. That's the impression I have—things got crazier and crazier, he was philandering, and it got to a point where she was uncomfortable. So I don't know if ultimately she got back at him by getting with Glenn.

Glenn Hughes: I actually had an argument with him. It was about 6:00 in the morning, he was asleep—I went down to his room [at the Beverly Hilton, after a release party for Led Zeppelin's 'The Song Remains the Same' movie]. I'd been up at Bonzo's room. Knocked on the door, we rolled around on the floor. It was all about his breaking up with Karen and I may have already started a relationship with her, prior to me going to my home in the U.K. I was angry that he dumped her because of the drugs. There was a rumor going around that he was on the needle. And she didn't party, she was a normal gal. I didn't think Tommy wanted to be around Karen when he was getting high, and I think as most couples do, when one is using heavily, they break up. Karen wasn't enabling Tommy, she couldn't stand him getting high. What does she do? She jumps ship to a guy who was a cocaine addict, which is me! See, here's the deal with Tommy and I—we weren't nasty volatile/drunk volatile. We were sort of always 'hands on,' always like touching each other, loving each other, and fighting—laughing a lot. For us to be seen fighting on a Hilton floor was not a sight that was uncommon. But I was angry at him. I may have spoken to him a day later and apologized to him, but we loved each other, regardless. I mean, I don't feel to this day, that I left him on terms that were wrong. I loved him dearly, and he loved me dearly, to the very end. There's no doubt in my mind. And although I was with his girlfriend, he was the one that gave me 'the thumbs up' to start a relationship with her—because he was I think too sick at that time.

Carmine Appice: Glenn was on his way to killing himself, too. But he straightened his act out, thank God—he is an amazing talent. He used to live in Mark Stein's house. This is all like, co-mingled stuff. It's amazing how everybody hung out together.

Reggie McBride: I became more aware of Tommy's drug problem, and it was cause for concern for me. I never sat down and talked to him about it, but as a band and management, we all had an open discussion about what to do about it. I wanted to explore my options as a L.A. session player, and do some writing and producing [McBride exited Tommy's band in the summer of '76].

Kenny Passarelli: I finished with Elton John in August of '76—and I got a call from Barry, asking if I'd be interested [playing] with Tommy. I think I ran into [Tommy] at the Sunset Marquis, and he was a different guy. He was really out of it and really arrogant—not the person I used to know. He didn't say anything bad to me, he just wasn't the kid that I knew—he was kind of numb, and very high. I mean, we'd gotten high, taken acid, and done all kinds of shit together—but he was a different person at this point. He and Karen had broken up—he was alone. I think he'd gone through the Linda Blair thing—he'd been through all kinds of different incarnations. He was mostly into drugs at this point. So when I got the call from Barry, after seeing Tommy the way he was . . . and I was busy, I'd signed a deal with the Robert Stigwood organization. I probably could have taken the gig, but I didn't, because Tommy was just a different person. The kid I remember was a smiling, happy guy. Maybe when he strapped on that guitar he turned into a monster, but the demeanor that Tommy had was always super kind, super friendly. And the guy that I saw wasn't somebody that didn't talk to me—he was somebody that wasn't 'available.' Stood right in front of me, I looked at him, he looked great, but he wasn't friendly—he was cold. And that wasn't the person that I knew all those years. I knew he used to like to take soapers and barbiturates. I thought, "Well, he's really fucked up." He just wasn't the person that I knew.

Jimmy Haslip: I met Tommy through Mark Stein. He was playing with Tommy; they had recorded 'Private Eyes' and just finished a first leg of a tour. I had done a few recordings with Mark and Carmine Appice—I was hanging out with those guys at the time. It was time for Tommy to go out on the road and promote 'Private Eyes'—they had been out on the road for a while. They came home on a break. Reggie and Narada decided to leave the band. So when they split, Mark got me an audition in Los Angeles at S.I.R. I went down there and played with Johnnie Bolin on drums. We both got the gig at that time. I had already been out on the road with Harvey Mandel's band, and I'd been playing with a bunch of cats locally—I had a band for a while with drummer Vinny Appice and guitarist Phil Brown. I'd been out in L.A. for a year or so before I got the call for Tommy's band. I was psyched! [The tryout] was pretty straight ahead. I got there, and Mark, Tommy, and Johnnie were there. There was some crew. There were a few tunes I was asked to review prior to the audition, so I practiced a bunch of the tunes and went in there prepared. We played a bunch of tunes, like "Post Toastee" and maybe "Marching Powder." It all went well, and Tommy liked it. We were just about the same age at that point, and we hit it off. I was happy and excited to join the band. I believe there were some rehearsals scheduled after that, because the next leg of the tour was getting ready to start. The first date was an opening spot for a rock festival at Mile High Stadium. It was with five bands, and we were one of the opening acts—we came on first or second, I can't remember. Then there were performances by Gary Wright, Steve Miller, and Peter Frampton.

Carmine Appice: [Tommy] was rehearsing at S.I.R., in Los Angeles. I went down there—I knew everybody in the band. In those days, everybody used to rehearse in S.I.R. At any given day, you'd walk in there, and you'd see Zeppelin in one room, and Tommy Bolin in another. *He was out of his tree.* I know he was taking Quaaludes, cocaine, drinking—anything they gave him, he'd take it. So I remember going up to him, and saying, "Hey Tommy, what's up man? You've got to stop doing this stuff, you're going to kill yourself. You're never straight anymore." [Mimics Tommy's voice] "Ah Carmine, I'm fine. I'm alright, I'll be good." I said, "Yeah, well you better watch it, bro." And then I think it was Jimmy Haslip or one of the band members, I said, "You guys got to keep an eye on him, because he's not looking good." They said, "Yeah, we know."

Johnnie Bolin: Off and on, we played quite a bit together. And then he asked me to join the Tommy Bolin Band. Our first gig was at Mile High Stadium. I remember we were staying at a Holiday Inn, and we were right next to Mile High. We got there, and it was kind of neat, because Stanley Sheldon was with Frampton, and Tom Stephenson was with Gary Wright. So we went and had cocktails. I woke up in the morning, opened up the shade—it was 10:30, and there was already about 30,000 people. I had just come from playing this truck stop in Sioux City—Thursday through Sunday, wearing a cowboy hat and cowboy boots. By the time we started, there was about 50,000 people! We played 40 minutes—that was *the fastest* 40 minutes. It was really weird to think I'd hit my snare, and a mile away, someone could hear it. But it was a great experience. Definitely the highlight of my life.

Jimmy Haslip: It was awesome. I'd been playing locally around in L.A., and I had gone out with Harvey Mandel's group—playing in clubs mostly. But we also did a tour up in Canada opening for Jeff Beck and the Jan Hammer Group, which were larger venues—everywhere from 5-10,000 seat venues. But it was nothing like playing at Mile High Stadium for 50,000 people! That was surreal. That was my first experience with that size of a crowd. And Tommy's music was great—it was fun to play, the band was great. It was quite an incredible experience. I was blown away by the scope of being in front of an audience that was that large, and it was all about having fun—and rockin' out, too. I was also really enjoying playing Tommy's music. Mark was my close buddy on the tour, and I was just getting to know Tommy, Johnnie, and Norma Jean. The whole crew was very cool too, so the vibes were good all around. I also had friends in Colorado out in the audience, and they were completely blown away. Tommy was very well known in Denver—he had hung there quite a bit. It was like playing in front of a hometown crowd in that respect.

Tom Stephenson: Everybody and their mother was there that knew us from Energy. So everybody expected it to be a great reunion. Stanley and I were really looking forward to seeing him after so many changes. And it was just not what we expected—it was really sad.

Stanley Sheldon: I was with Tommy getting high before he went on. Then after his show, we were getting high again before our show, while Gary Wright was playing. And Tommy was crying. I remember he was just so upset that he wasn't the headliner—I think it was really getting to him at that point. I mean, he was happy for me of course, but he was a little frustrated at that point. And definitely way too high.

Tom Stephenson: He was really down about it, really depressed, strung out on heroin at that point. Tommy, being what I consider much more of a guitarist than Peter [Frampton]—nothing against Peter, but Tommy was just a prodigy at what he did—that type of stuff really ate away at Tommy. *A lot.* So Stan and I went over to visit him at [the hotel]—he was strung out and almost in tears. He talked about this thing going on with Karen, and he actually said to Stan and I, "*I* was supposed to be the star, and look at you guys? You're out doing all this stuff—why can't I get something going?" And was doing heroin right in front of us.

Stanley Sheldon: Well, I wasn't the right person to talk, because I was probably as involved—if not more so—than he was at that time. I had my own 'increasing tolerance,' y'know? And when I hooked up with Frampton, then I just felt God had given me license to abuse myself ad infinitum. Like I'd earned it somehow. So I never did give Tommy a lecture, no.

Johnnie Bolin: He would tell me, "I know I'm getting kind of fucked up—I've got to straighten it up a little bit." But as a younger brother, I couldn't . . . we had a couple of really good talks on the road. Because he was gone all the time, I talked to him on the phone, and when we got together to play, we really didn't have a lot of time. I could have said something, but who am I to say? Look at what the guy has already done, and maybe it's something he's going through. A passing phase. And as long as we continue to play and he's playing well—he has his nights, he has his moments. I guess I didn't really say much—he knew it was time to slow down a bit.

Tom Stephenson: Stanley and I begged him that day in Denver at that concert, "Please man, *slow down*. You're going to kill yourself." And [Tommy said], "I don't care. I don't even want to live." He was fucked up 24 hours/seven days a week. And a big factor was that it was heroin and downers. When he got with the Deep Purple thing, God, he'd have doctor's prescriptions for *thousands* of pills. Valium, Quaaludes, speed, I can't even remember all the stuff he had.

Jimmy Haslip: On a personal basis, I really liked him. He was a very personable guy, and had a great sense of humor. That really was a big plus for me—when your boss has a sense of humor and likes to have fun. It was just an ideal situation. I was involved in this established group of musicians—with a recording contract and touring dates. I mean, what else could you ask for as a young musician? I just felt blessed and that Tommy was a good guy to work for. Personally, I think we had a nice connection.

Johnnie Bolin: We did some dates with Earl Slick, we played with Blue Öyster Cult. The Blue Öyster Cult thing was kind of weird. We played two nights, and on the first night, we were doing the King Biscuit Flower Hour. We're playing "Post Toastee," our last song, and all of a sudden, the house lights come on. It looks like the concert's ended—why are the white lights on in the auditorium? So Tommy threw his guitar down and flipped out—we played too long, so they turned the lights on. We were recording, so we felt like idiots up there—a Spinal Tap deal. He went back, trying to beat up Buck Dharma or somebody. He got really mad, because when those guys used to open for the James Gang, they didn't care how long they played. But tables turn, and it was hard for Tommy to go from Purple to putting up with bullshit. It's like riding around in a limo, and then all of a sudden getting it taken away, and you're going back to your Corvair. You're starting back over again. We had to cancel a couple of gigs because his voice was wearing. The headlining ones were more like large clubs—we weren't really doing auditoriums, unless we backed up somebody. No real big venues after the Frampton thing.

Charlie Brusco: I've been a manager since '73—I got the Outlaws signed to Arista with Clive [Davis]. The business at that time was completely different. It was business of a lot of relationships—you had relationships with radio people that meant a lot. You could use the leverage that you had. The Outlaws in '76 were headlining 3-5,000 seaters, and we were on our way to being a headliner in most arenas. And that gave me a certain amount of power with being able to get acts on different shows—and power with agencies, radio stations. It all ran together. A lot of times, suggestions came from the record companies, like, "You need somebody stronger management-wise." Record companies would call and go, "Listen, these guys are going to be leaving this guy. He can't get some of the things done that need to get done."

I was managing the Outlaws, and I was very close with all the guys in Skynyrd. Barry Fey and Chuck Morris were involved with Tommy, and they wanted the band to go out and play. I put him on a bunch of dates with the Outlaws. We started hanging out together, and [Tommy] and I struck up a friendship. I would be in L.A., and Tommy would call and go, "Hey, I'm going to be in L.A., why don't we get together?" We would go to the Rainbow Bar and Grill and hang out—chasing chicks together and all that stuff. We became really close. If you walked into that place with Tommy, you were going to leave with a number of girls—because wherever Tommy went, they all followed right behind him. He was like 'a woman magnet.'

Henry Paul: He was a special guest on the Outlaws' tour. We would hang out, maybe do a little cocaine. We'd see him if we'd be down there recording. Tommy seemed like a really sensitive and smart guy. His style of play was a little far to the left for me. I wasn't so much of a rock n' roller as I was a country rocker—melody, lyrics, and acoustic instruments. He was a Strat player, and played 'out there'—more mainstream rock n' roll approach to his music. He seemed like a really soft, sensitive character. He wasn't an asshole-big-mouth-rock-star. He was quiet and he had a quiet confidence about him. He didn't seem too caught up in who he was or what he was doing at all. He was a little odd for us, because we were these country fucks, and he was more of an urban rock n' roll star. I thought the Outlaws and Tommy Bolin were an odd combination, but not a bad one. The Outlaws were doing pretty good at the time, and Tommy was up and coming. He put it together thinking it would be a good bill, and it was.

Charlie Brusco: They used to have these big CBS record company extravaganzas—whoever was president of the company at that time would have all of the record company come to town. At the time, Barry Fey was one of the biggest promoters in Colorado. We go to this convention [in the ballroom of the Century Plaza Hotel], and there is a promoter who's a really good friend of mine from Atlanta, Alex Cooley. Somehow, the four of us were seated at this table. At the time, I would guess Barry weighed 300 pounds, and Alex probably weighed 400 pounds. They were gigantic guys. We're at the table, and Tommy and I were doing a little cocaine here and there. We get up during dinner, and they're bringing out these prime ribs. So Tommy and I go into the men's room. In those days, if you went into the men's room, you went into one of the stalls—usually, there were two guys in the stall together, and they were doing coke. We go in there, and we hear people coming in, and one of us is standing on the toilet so it doesn't look like there's two guys in there. Everybody knew what was going on—drugs back then were rampant. We started talking and laughing—we're not paying any attention to anything that's going on. We're probably in there for half an hour. So we come walking out of the bathroom and go to sit down, and Alex and Barry had both eaten our dinners while we were in the bathroom! They introduced Tommy at that thing, because ['Private Eyes'] was getting ready to come out. I remember him standing up, and the place going crazy.

Johnnie Bolin: Norma had been playing with Zappa and Narada a bit—these unbelievable drummers. She liked the way I played, but she wanted someone like Narada again. Someone who was *astronomically* good. I was developing my style, but I was playing just fine. So that was kind of the reason why I left Tommy's band. The way Tommy presented it to me was like, "I've got to keep her happy." He wasn't for getting rid of me, but that's the way it was going down. I played with them for three months. Then he got the drummer who had been playing with Jean-Luc Ponty—Mark Craney—who once again, is a jazz-fusion drummer. Everything was alright though.

Jimmy Haslip: As time wore on, I started to notice that Tommy had some problems with substance abuse. That was a bummer to me—I was concerned and wanted to help him chill that out.

Dale Peters: He came and played Cleveland. Jim and I went and saw him, and boy, he was in a nasty mood. I mean, it was just not a good situation. And we looked at each other and said, "This guy's done for, he's gone way too far." It was amazing, I'd never seen anybody do that many drugs. *It was staggering.* I grew up in the '60s, but Tommy was hundreds of times more into drugs then anybody I'd ever met in my life. He literally could not function without them.

Jim Fox: I think that may have been that earlier conversation, about "I might have found something better." He was playing solo—it was in a club. And Tommy didn't look good.

Dale Peters: We tried to talk to him, and he was just nasty. Like he hardly even knew who we were. Very, very messed up.

Charlie Brusco: He was very introverted, until he started drinking or doing drugs. He was really a sweet guy until he started drinking or doing drugs. For as cocky as he seemed, I really don't think that he realized how good he was. And some people may say I'm nuts for saying that, but that's how I viewed him from what I saw. In a lot ways, he was like a little kid. He was 'the guitar player's guitar player'—there's no doubt about that.

Mark Stein: Well, it wasn't any secret. Everybody knew it. He was very open about it; it wasn't like he did it in a closet. It was just a fact—it was a known thing. It got worse and worse. It's hard for me to talk about it, because I can see him in that kind of state right now. I used to talk to him all the time about it. Again, it got to the point where he just couldn't overcome that. A lot of people tried to talk to him, but to no avail. It was a real shame. I told him I would help him up the ladder, but not help him down. I left the band because I was having a little bit of a hard time with Tommy. Trying to get him to be more 'normal minded,' for lack of a better word. I felt he was going down a negative path, and I didn't feel like there was anything that I could do to get him out of it at the time. I thought it would be best for me to bow out. It was after a tour was over, and was just getting ready to start rehearsing for a new tour. Also, I was at odds with some of the management and some of the other things that were surrounding him at the time, as well. I just made a decision that it was time for me to leave.

Stanley Sheldon: I saw [Tommy] on the Sunset Strip in Hollywood, we hung out and talked at a nightclub there. I remember vividly standing in front of the Roxy; I think we'd just seen Bill Evans play, the famous jazz pianist—one of his last shows. So we were standing out front, getting ready to say goodnight, we hugged each other. I was getting ready to go on the road, and he was getting ready to tour. We just hugged each other and said, "Hey, as soon as we finish this, we're going to get right back into it and do what we were going to do." So that's kind of a nice bittersweet memory I have.

Johnnie and Tommy Bolin—two and five years old
[Photo provided by Tommy Bolin's family]

Johnnie, Rick (aka 'Pudge'), and Tommy—1963
[Photo provided by Tommy Bolin's family]

Rockin' teens! Johnnie and Tommy—1968
[Photo provided by Tommy Bolin's family]

Tommy at 17, shortly after joining Zephyr
[Photo by Wyndham Hannaway]

Candy Givens—1970
[Photo by David Givens]

Zephyr live in Houston—1971. L-R: John Faris, Candy Givens, David Givens, and Tommy
[Photo by Wyndham Hannaway]

Tommy backstage with the James Gang at the Auditorium Theatre in Chicago—February 1974
[Photo by Jim Summaria - www.jimsummariaphoto.com]

Tommy in concert with the James Gang at the Auditorium Theatre in Chicago—February 1974
[Photos by Jim Summaria - www.jimsummariaphoto.com]

One of Tommy's favorite guitarists, the Mahavishnu Orchestra's John McLaughlin
[Photo by Jim Summaria - www.jimsummariaphoto.com]

The great Joe Walsh
[Photo by Jim Summaria - www.jimsummariaphoto.com]

Jeff Beck—one of Tommy's greatest admirers
[Photo by Jim Summaria - www.jimsummariaphoto.com]

Keyboard wiz Jan Hammer
[Photo by Jim Summaria - www.jimsummariaphoto.com]

Tommy with Deep Purple bassist Glenn Hughes
at the Oklahoma City Fairgrounds Arena—February 17, 1976
[Photo by Richard Galbraith - www.myspace.com/richardgalbraith]

Tommy with Deep Purple singer David Coverdale
at the Oklahoma City Fairgrounds Arena—February 17, 1976
[Photo by Richard Galbraith - www.myspace.com/richardgalbraith]

Tommy (in all his suspendered/snakeskin booted glory) with Deep Purple
at the Long Beach Arena, California—February 27, 1976
[Photo by Marvin Rinnig - www.musikfoto.com]

Tommy live at My Father's Place in Roslyn, New York—1976
[Photo by Ken Bowe]

Tommy live at My Father's Place—1976.
Note 'Tubes shirt' Prairie Prince made for Tommy, and Tommy's trusty Echoplex on a stand
[Photo by Jamie Bateman]

Another town, another gig—1976. L-R: Tommy, Jimmy Haslip, Johnnie Bolin, and Mark Stein
[Photo by Ken Bowe]

Max Carl and Tommy on their way to the stage,
opening for Foghat at the Oklahoma City Fairgrounds Arena—November 10, 1976
[Photo by Richard Galbraith - www.myspace.com/richardgalbraith]

Tommy live—November 1976
[Photo by Robert Ferbrache]

Tommy on Fender Strat and Ibanez Destroyer, respectively—November 1976
[Photos by Robert Ferbrache]

Jimmy Haslip—November 1976
[Photo by Robert Ferbrache]

Max Carl—November 1976
[Photo by Robert Ferbrache]

Norma Jean Bell and Tommy—November 1976
[Photo by Robert Ferbrache]

Tommy and his long-time guitar tech, Dave Brown—November 1976
[Photo by Robert Ferbrache]

Tommy's last Thanksgiving at home in Sioux City, Iowa— November 1976.
L-R: Tommy, Pudge (standing), Johnnie, Barbara Bolin, and Richard Bolin (standing)
[Photo provided by Tommy Bolin's family]

Carmine Appice and Johnnie Bolin at the NAMM convention—2006
[Photo provided by Tommy Bolin's family]

Tommy's gravesite in Sioux City, Iowa—2008
[Photo by Tamy Thomas Morgan]

The Tommy Bolin 'Teaser' Tribute Guitar by Dean—2008
[Photo by Sean Vennett - www.musicalpeace.com]

'Private Eyes' Tour II

Jimmy Haslip: Mark Stein left the band, and was replaced by keyboardist/ vocalist Max Gronenthal [a.k.a. Max Carl]. Max and Mark [Craney] were really interesting and smokin' additions to the band. They were seriously talented musicians. Mark had just left Jean-Luc Ponty's band, and Max had been playing around Los Angeles. He was—and is—a very talented singer/ songwriter and keyboardist. I think Max and Mark had played together before in another band or some other situation, so they knew each other well. It made the band more cohesive in a way. I'd been playing with Tommy and Norma Jean at that point for about three to four months. When the personnel change came about, an interesting connection also came about for me. Hanging with Mark Craney was a total groove—we were both vegetarians and really into eating lots of ginseng and bee pollen. Healthy foods—that was our daily regimen. I was into yoga, too. So we were trying to get Tommy into that kind of a regimen, or we at least wanted to introduce him to health foods and stuff, and see if we could curb his appetite for all the other bad things that were going on in his life. And on some levels, we were successful. He was certainly curious about what we were doing, because we focused on being healthy guys out there on the road. And it was helping us with this intense, grueling schedule.

Max Carl: From '73 to '76 I bounced around the Midwest and Southwest, working in clubs, practicing and keeping in touch with Tommy. In late summer of '76, I drove to L.A. from Denver. In an encounter that still seems mystical, I was walking through an alley in Hollywood on my first night in town, and as I rounded a corner, I literally bumped into Tommy. We hugged and he instantly said, "I need a keyboard player—*now!*" I stepped in—that night. That was that.

Jeff Ocheltree: They had really gelled—that was a really great band. Of all the bands Tommy had, that was the best band he ever had. Those guys really played well together. Jimmy Haslip being a left-handed, upside down bass player, and Mark Craney, who was right-handed, but played drums for a left-hander, because his dad set his drums up wrong. You had a lot of left-handed stuff going on. I think [Tommy] liked that band more than all the other bands he had.

I only experienced one bad show, and that's when he got really mad at the audience. For some reason, the audience wasn't very responsive, so he kept saying, "You better fucking clap . . . *or we're out of here!*" He got a response out of them alright—I don't know if it was the one he wanted, but he got a response! That's what he was into. He was out there kicking ass every night—the same with the rest of that band. And he didn't miss a thing. If somebody screwed something up, he was right on us—especially Norma Jean Bell. Other than her, the rest of the band just kicked ass every night. Tommy was very aware of what was going on, so his shows, almost all of them were impeccable. Whether he was high or not, I have no idea—all I know is he played his ass off. I just got done working with musicians that don't get high, so I saw no difference in the way he was playing and some of these other great guitar players, like John McLaughlin and Jeff Beck. They did a lot of his tunes, but they also did a lot of improv. Sometimes, Mark and Tommy would break into Mahavishnu material [live].

Jeff Cook: I believe it was pretty shaky. The feeling I got was members were coming and going, and that they had some gigs that were great, some that were terrible, and that it was really an unsettling time for him. I know they had done some live broadcasts, and they felt pretty good about that, but there were some nights where I think the drugs got in the way. And there was some personality disputes too, within the band members.

Jimmy Haslip: I think the band sounded really good every night. Now, I think Tommy was struggling a little bit from show to show—but we were jamming hard. I know that we were keeping everything moving forward. Like I said, Mark and I were full of energy, and Norma was a very strong musician and personality. Max was also very strong and talented. It was a really burning group, ready to ROCK!

Jeff Ocheltree: That Echoplex was amazing. Half the time it didn't work—he'd be kicking it off the stage. Sometimes he'd throw the slide, and he'd throw the slide *into* the Echoplex, and it would hit the tape. He'd just get the biggest kick out of if anybody noticed that. He'd be playing away, flip the slide off, and try to hit the Echoplex—on the tape!

Max Carl: We had a number of good shows on Tommy's last tour, but the most memorable for me was at the Santa Monica Civic Center in L.A. It was a good turnout, and of course, the Columbia brass was there, as well as the L.A. glitterati—a show within a show. Brian Auger opened the night for us, blazing away on a Hammond C3 through a stack of Marshall amps. Wow! Tommy had hired Gary Hart as a management adjutant who was a good guy. He was excited that night and approached me after the gig to talk about Tommy's next album. Tommy at that point had me singing a line or two here and there in the set, and Gary took notice. He was hoping I would be singing on the new album. Tommy and I were kicking around some tunes. One of them ended up on my first Chrysalis solo record, called "Faded Satin Lady" [on 1979's 'Whistling in the Dark,' credited to Max Gronenthal]. Some time early in our friendship, I sat down with Tommy—who was cross-legged on the floor, beating out a groove with drumsticks on a stack of magazines, while I sang these lyrics [recounts the song's lyrics].

Jeff Ocheltree: I heard him do a couple of tunes that they were working on with Max on the piano and B3. I definitely knew that all the guys in that band were going to be on the next album. It was more fusion-ish. I can't compare it to 'Private Eyes' or 'Teaser'—I would say there were elements of fusion. I think he really wanted to go in that direction, because he saw what was happening with that music. And he loved playing it. 'Spectrum' was a great way for a lot of people to hear Tommy play with great fusion/jazz musicians. But what nobody understands is he was capable of doing that because he liked playing—he could play anything. I think the next record would have been very interesting. The fact that he had Norma, who played with Zappa, I think he would have gone in a similar direction as Billy and those guys at the time.

Johnnie Bolin: We had done a song called "Down in the Dungeon"—it's a neat riff, a neat song. It was kind of a reggae-type deal. He said, "I'm writing this for my new album," and that I was going to play on his new album. Lyrically, it's like "Post Toastee." He doesn't say much in the song—only one or two verses were written. It's the way he was feeling—he says, "Leave me alone, even my best friends." He might have been talking about his relationship and what his state of mind was. He knew he had to do a tour and all that, but he still had a deal, so he was already thinking about a new album.

Jimmy Haslip: He mentioned that he had been writing some music, and that he had a working title for a record that he wanted to start recording. This was the end of November/beginning of December, and he wanted to start thinking about recording possibly in January or February the following year. And he thought of possibly calling this recording 'Gotta Dance.' I think he was thinking about doing some more R n' B inspired music. Like I said, he was always looking to experiment. I think with this group of musicians, he had a shot at doing some R n' B/fusion/rock kind of stuff. It was really inspiring, and we felt things were moving right along. We were trying to help Tommy stay healthy and continue his quest.

Tommy Bolin: We start the 2nd with the Jeff Beck tour, through the south, and then the 12th, and then I do the album in January. And then we go out with Fleetwood Mac in February.

Max Carl: I had developed comedy bits and characters. Tommy had listed them on paper and taped it to the inside of his wardrobe case. Right before we would go on stage, he would look at the list and shout out a character for me to assume—Irish priest, redneck, hippie, etc. I would improvise a dialogue and launch into a one-man skit. It worked every time. Part of my value to Tommy was to make him laugh. We had a collective security blanket around Tommy on that last tour. Mark Craney was a diabetic looking for a natural cure, and we followed him into health food stores wherever we went. We had t-shirts made that said "THE BIONIC GINSENG TOUR." Tommy tried his best to get with the program, but sadly, he was distracted.

Jeff Ocheltree: There was a lot of mistaking attitude with Tommy, I found. For instance, we made it a habit of every third day of the tour to call Barry Fey up. And that son of a bitch wasn't doing anything for Tommy. He was lying to him, he was deceiving him, he was downplaying certain things. I think he was on purpose holding him back. And what Tommy would do is ask for an accounting, because the road managers he had were idiots—they didn't do very good accounting. They didn't seem very forthright. So yeah, you could see him maybe having a couple of beers and getting high on something, but most of the time, [at] the shows, he was amazing. He kicked ass almost every night.

I'll never forget being in a hotel room—I think it was Peoria, Illinois. We went to Tommy's room, and he said, "I want you to witness this phone conversation." He wrote down all the questions he was going to ask Barry, and he would hold the phone in such a way so that I could hear. What Barry would do is say, "They're good questions, but your information is not correct." And Tommy says, "How can I have information that's correct or incorrect, when I haven't got the information? You're pissing me off, and you better start answering the questions! And why would I want you to keep managing me when you're *not* managing me? You're not doing a good job and you're not telling the truth." That phone call was going to be the last time he talked to him.

Charlie Brusco: There became a time when something was going on with him, where he was getting ready to leave Barry. And he and I started talking that he wanted me to manage him. I talked to him about it, and I told him once he was out of whatever deals he had with everybody else, that I was definitely interested. There was somebody—and I can't remember who it was—at Sony at that time, that was also helping me in the situation of getting Tommy.

Barry Fey: He wanted to spend Thanksgiving with his band—at home with his parents in Sioux City. I'll never forget, I get a call, "Barry, can you wire me some money? I want to get a nice present for my mom." So [through] Western Union, I wire him some money. This was Thanksgiving, and the next week, he's going to open the tour with Jeff Beck in Miami. And people are whispering in my ear. His road manager/tour manager is Gary Hart—he had a good reputation, a solid guy—and he said, "You've got to send someone down there with Tommy. *You've got no idea*—there's so much drugs down there, and Tommy doesn't have the willpower. I said, "Who would be good to send?" He said, "Send L.C. Clayton." He was an old friend of mine, and he was the head of my security for a while. The guy is as tough as nails, and if anyone's going to fuck with Tommy, he'll take them apart. I send him down, and he's going to open up with Jeff Beck. We're talking every day.

Johnnie Bolin: The bodyguard's role was to try to keep the chaos out—the bad souls and stuff like that. Jeff Ocheltree should have been Tommy's bodyguard. He's a big guy and he's got an attitude—but he's a great guy.

Jeff Ocheltree: I took care of Tommy as best I could. It wasn't like, "Big brother's watching you." First of all, you had to be pretty tough to survive that kind of stuff that was going on all the time. If we were doing a show and the promoter wasn't being a very good promoter or some things were missing on the rider of the contract, we'd really have to fight for everything. And Tommy loved that about us crew—we would fight for respect. The reality is in those days, we were writing the script as we went along. There were no mentors saying, "Here's how you do it, kid."

L.C. Clayton: I've been with hundreds of groups—I've done Stones tours, Who tours. You name it; I've been with them. I was sort of 'a trouble shooter' for a while there—if [Barry] was having problems with anything, if people were bothering you or whatever, then I was called in. [Tommy's tour] was like no tour I'd ever been on before. There were money problems all the time. The road manager didn't even stay in the same hotel—I had to figure out where he was. Call around and find him, because he wasn't there. We went to hotels and credit cards weren't good. It was difficult time, which was strange because the album was doing pretty good. You had two people running things—Barry was running it and Bill Graham. I don't know who had more power doing what, but it was a real drag. Especially for Tommy, because he was used to having a little more leeway, and anytime he wanted something, he had to come and ask me for money.

Jeff Ocheltree: L.C. was supposed to look after him. What he was doing was stealing needles from Mark Craney—[Mark was] diabetic and was giving himself insulin shots. He would get a key to his room or whatever, and would take drugs.

L.C. Clayton: I didn't supply him with any heroin—that's not my deal. I hate the shit, to tell you the truth. Lost too many people. I had a suitcase of soapers, but [Tommy] didn't get any—that was the last resort to put him to sleep or whatever. But he didn't need that.

Phillip Polimeni: He had the pressures he was under—trying to keep musicians of his caliber in his band. Those people wanted real money, and they were running behind $10,000.00 a week in the red. In the '70s, that was a lot of money. It became a problem.

Johnnie Bolin: The way he looked at it, he had money if he wanted it. He could ask for it. But he never walked around with any money, he never spent a whole lot of money. Things were either given to him . . . he came back to Sioux City and borrowed money from me! It was like, *"But you played with Deep Purple!"* He says, "I'll pay you back, just give me the 75 bucks." And I'm like, "I really don't have it" [laughs]! That's a prime example. And Karen used to run the banking—if Tommy needed something, she'd write the check out. But he didn't get what was coming to him. He just didn't worry about that part of it. If you wanted to rent a house, you'd rent a house. If you wanted get into this limousine service with Phillip . . . that's the only real investment I'd ever heard him doing—other than possibly buying a house. Phillip had an 'in' into the limo thing anyway—actually, Phillip was even driving at one point, and he knew a couple of the drivers. Back then, it was kind of brand new to people—the limo service. That's really the only investment I knew of. The money thing—he had it, but he never had money on him.

L.C. Clayton: Like I said, the road manager, I couldn't even call him to tell him what was going on. But he knew. He was in another hotel all together—he was on the other side of town, as far as I know. And the whole time he was out there, he was never there. I called Barry every night, and Tommy would come in my room, because he couldn't call from his room. I'd sit there and talk to Barry, "I'll send you another credit card, it will be there in a couple of hours." I've been on tour with people that carried their own equipment back in the day, but there was always money. You don't go to the airport, and they tell you, "No, you can't go, because the card's no good," and you have to call fourteen other people and have them wire [money]. I can't even remember what [the road manager] looked like, because the asshole was never even there. We'd be like, "We need some food." And Barry supplied me with money. 'Cause if I didn't have any money, we wouldn't have ate. Tommy didn't even have food money. The group was so young and half of them were vegetarians—I'd get them some ginseng tea and biscuits, and they were happy as hell. It's like, "That's a meal? You guys are really strange!"

Barry Fey: [Tommy] was nice enough—he volunteered to take out an insurance policy on his life, which he did.

Robert Ferbrache: I took Tommy to the physical for that, and that would have been about [November '76]. Barry took the life insurance policy out, and it had two payees—him and his family. He had to have a physical for that life insurance policy. That's what that physical was for—that's standard operating procedure for that. You have to have a life insurance policy for that kind of thing—I'm sure that even Angus Young or whoever had life insurance policies through their manager. I assume that's pretty standard.

Barry Fey: I don't know if it's standard or not. It's hard to believe—and you can check with Chuck Morris, who was there at the time—Tommy wanted it. Because he knew . . . I can't even tell you if it's verifiable by going over old books, how much he owed the company. It was way north of $300,000.00. And Tommy wanted to take out a policy to protect us. He was a good kid—he must have known things about himself that I had no idea about. What's the statute of limitations on insurance fraud, do you know? Well, I would only be an un-indicted co-conspirator—from what I was told later, it was not Tommy's urine. He knew he couldn't pass—so that should have been another big hint to me.

Johnnie Bolin: It's like, how could he owe Barry money? If you have a record deal, the manager doesn't give you the money, the record company does. He threw some figures out. He said, "That's money that Tommy owed me." It's like, "We don't know why he would owe it to you."

Charlie Brusco: I was known very much as a hands-on manager, and I think Barry didn't really manage anybody else. And if he did, it wasn't anybody of consequence. Although Barry thought that Tommy was great—and that he had a superstar in the making—I don't think Barry knew how much went into being a manager. And he was very busy being a promoter. I don't think Tommy felt like he got the creative input that sometimes a manager gives. And Tommy was close with some of the guitar players that I had at the time. I think he felt it was time to have somebody that what they did was *manage*. I know it was really bothering him, because he felt that Barry was his friend, but he didn't think he knew how to handle record companies. Barry got him a great record deal at

Sony, but he wasn't good at when things weren't all pumped up, to be able to keep Sony interested in what was going on. And in those days, you had to.

Jeff Ocheltree: I think Tommy believed in [Barry] in the beginning, because he was a great promoter—he did a lot of big shows, he had the wherewithal to be a good manager. But like I say, we're not talking about the year 2008, we're talking about 197-something. It's not like managers were the best people around. There were good ones and there were bad ones—and mostly, bad ones. And why would attorneys want to be involved in certain musicians' dealings, when they weren't even getting all the correct information? It was a lot of work.

Tommy Bolin: Tomorrow being turkey day, I'll be able to spend turkey day with my parents. It's been three or four years.

L.C. Clayton: He wasn't clean. At Thanksgiving, he went back home—we did a concert in his hometown. For some reason, I was told to come back home—mainly because of money problems. I told Barry, "He's going to go wild at home, because people are going to give him shit free." I didn't want to leave. And he did get wild there, and went through some changes.

Johnnie Bolin: They got here—they all flew in. T.V. stations were all out there filming him coming in. Took him into town down at the Hilton, and they go, "We don't have any room for you." He's like, "What do you mean?!" He brought the whole band to my mom and dad's house—he was really pissed off. It was only for an hour or two—they didn't mind. But *he* did—that wasn't what he wanted. But once they got their rooms, it went just fine.

On Thanksgiving, we had a little jam in the kitchen—we lived about four or five blocks from where I live now. My mom would have Syrian food. There's tapes of us playing—my dad always had that tape recorder going, one of those little small ones. It would go all day—you'd forget he had it on, but it was always going. I have to try and find some of those tapes sometime. We'd get the spoons out, an acoustic guitar, and Tommy and my dad would sing. There was some drinking involved [laughs]. We'd have a whole bunch of people over for dinner.

Jeff Ocheltree: At his parents' house, what was really neat about it, he might have been getting high once in a while, but the focus wasn't on, "What's Tommy doing? Let's go find out what he's doing." Because he was there really interacting with his parents and being in Sioux City. I went there several times, the first time was really cool—his mom made us a really cool dinner. We had a lot of fun, talking about his youth, and a lot of laughing. Tommy was a very down-to-earth person. He really related to people well from Iowa.

Johnnie Bolin: We'd go running around, but there wasn't really a lot of places you could go—went down to Stereo Land, went down to the music store. I think he was home to relax and get out of the rigmarole.

George Larvick: I knew he was in bad shape. When he came back to Sioux City for that concert, I could tell he was a heroin addict, because his eyes were all rolling and really glassy. He had tracks up and down his arms pretty good—that's not from one-time use. We talked to him for quite a while about trying to come back, and he could stay with me and try to figure it out. But the issue was it would have to be totally where nobody knew he was back. The problem Tommy had was when he came back to Sioux City, there were so many people that wanted to be with him, and the guys that knew he did what he did wanted to give him more. He needed it as well, but it was hard for me to be with him because of that. It was hard for me to deal with that—I didn't want to see that happen, and tried to help him. But he said that they were trying to do their best, and were trying to work with him to try to get him down off of drugs.

Johnnie Bolin: We always played when he came back home—we had our little gig downtown at the Jet or the Ozone. Actually, the picture from [the 2004 Archives release] 'Live at the Jet Bar' is from the Ozone—the picture is at a different place. That was John Bartle and Tommy on the front.

John Bartle: When he came back, we had a band called Magic, and we were playing at the Jet Bar. [Tommy] sat in with our band. We were all experimenting with heroin. We were in this room, and we were shooting it. I'm clean and sober now. I looked around and he was on the bed, and he had swallowed his tongue and was not breathing. I had to give him mouth-to-mouth. We had to resuscitate him, and then we had to walk him around the block.

Johnnie Bolin: He seemed like he was going back to that 'avenue' again. And in Sioux City, at that time, there was a good batch—it's a small little cow town, but there's dope here. These guys that had it, they're out of most people's league. I think when he did it; he had no idea how good it was. He thought it was just going to be average shit. But yeah, he did go . . . kind of lost him there for a second. Not where we had to call paramedics or nothing, but we had to stand him up, walk him around. It was snowing out—we had to throw snowballs at him, and he came around.

George Larvick: I asked him, "How did you get to this stage?" The same thing happened to Elvis. He would pop something to go to sleep while you're traveling, then you pop two more to wake up—you can't get up. It was a see-saw battle with that, and then of course, he did a little bit of the recreational stuff, and then it turned into a little bit more than recreation, and the drug got him. He said, "You pop a downer to relax and go to sleep, and you have to pop two more to wake up. You may have to pop another one just to stay even. Then you've got to play the job and you may feel tired, so you pop another one." That goes on and on. You try another drug—like heroin—to see if it can help you, and pretty soon, you're hooked on heroin. Then that gets out of control, where you need more and more to survive and be normal. And that's the kind of thing he told me was hard to regulate.

John Bartle: He was happy that he had his own band going. He was on his way to play with Jeff Beck—he was pretty happy. I remember a couple of lines he'd say. We'd talk about the business, and he'd say, "I don't care what people say about me, as long as they keep talking." And then of course, "Live fast, die young, and leave a good looking corpse." He always said that.

Rick 'Pudge' Bolin: He was boarding the plane to do the Jeff Beck tour, I had a feeling I wouldn't see him again. I turned to him and said, "Tommy, if I don't see you again in this world, I'll see you in the next world, and don't be late." Then he hugged me and said, *"I'm never late."*

Miami/December 3rd and 4th, 1976

Glenn Hughes: He sent me and Karen—to our home in England—a postcard from Miami. It was two flamingos—Tommy was crazy about flamingos. This pink flamingo postcard, all it said was, "Come on in, the H2O is fine. See you at Christmas."

Johnnie Bolin: When he went down to Miami, the last postcard we got was, "Walking on the beach, I'm feeling healthy." He was with Valeria and it was just the two of them—she doesn't do [drugs].

Stanley Sheldon: He sent me a postcard from Miami for Christmas. He kissed it—there's an imprint of his lips from lipstick!

Johnnie Bolin: He called from Miami—he was down there for a week or something. I think he was calling every day or every other day. It was winter here—he was kind of rubbing it in, like, "Walking in the ocean, went swimming earlier. What's the weather doing back there?" He was sounding real happy.

L.C. Clayton: I came home, spent a day, and went out back [to Miami]. When I got there, I couldn't find him. I had to look all over town for him.

Jimmy Haslip: [The tour with Jeff Beck] was scheduled to be seven or eight dates, or maybe less—five or six dates. It was definitely multiple dates, and the first was to be in Miami at the Jai Alai Auditorium. We were scheduled to go up to Tampa the next day. I found that to be interesting, because I did [shows] with Harvey Mandel's band, and we did like a dozen dates opening for Jeff, from the east to west coast of Canada. So the first date in Miami, there I was again—I saw Jan Hammer, Fernando Saunders the bass player, Tony Smith the drummer, etc. They said, "You're playing with Tommy now?" It was a cool reunion, so I was looking forward to doing all these dates with these guys.

Jeff Ocheltree: I didn't see any kind of competition with Jeff Beck and Tommy. Tommy had a great sense of himself, very confident, very happy with his music—but appreciated Jeff, loved his music. Jeff is a similar kind of guy—he never really fit well with other bands. He definitely didn't fit well with the Yardbirds. He was a guy that realized, "I need to have my own music." I mean, if it wasn't for Jeff Beck, we wouldn't have had Rod Stewart and all these other characters.

Phillip Polimeni: I was in the studio—I had people that were renting the studio. And these guys loved it—these guys from Motown. So I had it booked. Now, Tommy's calling me every fucking ten minutes from Miami. He's telling me, "All I've got is alcohol and downers. Goddamn it, you better get down here with some coke! Your ticket is at the airport, you better get there right now! I don't want to fucking call you back again!" And he would hang up the phone. And then he would call me again, and say, "You didn't leave yet?!" It was *a day* of this. Finally, I told everybody, "Look, I've got to shut this studio down—I've got to go."

L.C. Clayton: It was a great show. The band was up to par and everybody was happy.

Jeff Ocheltree: The show was amazing. The soundcheck was probably the best part of the show—Beck's band was playing great and so was Tommy's band, and they played together during soundcheck. I was watching Beck do some stuff that I couldn't believe.

Max Carl: I was in awe of Jan Hammer. The first night went well and I recall being blown away with Jan's Moog synth solos. And Jeff's entrance was dramatic—he popped out unexpectedly from behind a stack of Marshall amps. The crowd *exploded.*

Phillip Polimeni: I missed the show, where they had an encore and Jeff brought him out, and they jammed together. Everybody said it was unbelievable.

Jeff Ocheltree: That night, everybody played their asses off. Tommy went on stage with Jeff—they played a little bit together. It was an incredible show.

They partied afterwards—everybody was very happy, because it was embarking on a great tour. So it was an amazing show—a lot of great playing from all the players, a lot of goodwill, good spirits. Everybody was real happy and excited.

Jimmy Haslip: It was very energetic. We were performing before an icon, so we wanted to play well and hard. Tommy played his ass off that night. We finished the show, and I was really excited. It felt good. I wanted to get back to my room and practice. I saw Tommy in the dressing room—they were drinking champagne. I guess they were celebrating the beginning of that tour—it was going to be the last leg of the tour before the year's end. We were going home for a Christmas break, then get together again—maybe in mid-January—to start rehearsals for a new record. An exciting time for us all. I think I looked at [Tommy], and told him to be careful. And then I left the dressing room area. I think I talked to Jan and Fernando in the hallway for a minute, and then I got a ride back to the hotel.

Max Carl: The night for me was quiet. I went back to my hotel room and watched T.V., falling asleep early, thinking of the promise of this tour and what was to come.

Charlie Brusco: I think I was in Pittsburgh, and he was in Miami—he called me. It might have been 12:00—he'd just gotten back to the hotel, and said he just had this great show with Beck. He said he was going to go out with a bunch of people to do something for the evening. But he didn't sound right—he sounded like either he was a little messed up or he wasn't feeling good. I remember catching something in the tone of his voice—that there was something wrong. I said, "Is everything cool?" And he goes, "Yeah, everything's great. The show was great."

Jan Hammer: After the concert, I saw him at the hotel. He was 'party hearty.' He was already buzzed. He said something along the lines of, "I'll see you tomorrow . . . *if* I see you." The impression I got is he was being very flippant about the whole thing. It just gives me chills.

L.C. Clayton: Some friends of his had shown up—I had never seen them before. They're the ones who brought 'the devil.' I brought down the rules of what was to be and what was not to be. And they broke the rules. We were in my room, and Tommy wanted to go to his room. I said, "O.K., I'll be down in a minute. None of this, none of that." Tommy wasn't clean—he didn't have enough money to do what he wanted to, but anything he could find . . . he had a problem. But the money problems didn't help none. When you're happy, you can get along with less. When you don't have money at all, then you need as much as you can possibly find.

Jeff Ocheltree: Even at the hotel room afterwards—there was a lot of good spirit, good feeling, and good camaraderie. Until he decided to take a left turn on us and get upset. We were sitting in my room, and he was sitting on the floor talking to [Karen, on the phone]. He started talking to her about marriage. And there was a lot of people in the room—Jeff Beck came in for a second. And man, [Tommy's] face just went *white*. He got off the phone and he wouldn't talk to us. We kept asking him, "What's going on?" He said, "I just asked Karen to marry me, and she said she's going to marry Glenn Hughes." That was the beginning of the end. I sat with him on the floor for a while to find out what was bothering him when he got off the phone. In fact, he never hung up the phone—he just left it laying on the floor. I noticed he was really upset, and he didn't want to talk about it.

Phillip Polimeni: I got to the hotel room, and it was a chaos thing—musicians everywhere, groupies, roadies. And there was a guy with me that had coke and heroin. They went in the bathroom. I went in there for a minute—I had some coke with Tommy. I was talking to him. But I went also with a guy who was bugging me to tell Tommy to invest in the limousine business, because Tommy was using limousines so much, he said, "He can have one of the cars for his own personal use." So I went into the room to talk about [the limousine business], and they were shooting up. At that time, needles to me were taboo. There were four people in the bathroom—they were all sharing this needle. I said, "You guys got to do this shit?" I walked out of the bathroom.

Jeff Ocheltree: There was a guy there that I happened to know gave him coke. Which is really sad—[Tommy's] whole life was being turned around. He realized he wanted to be physically healthy, more stamina. He wanted to stay away from drugs—especially coke. He didn't want to smoke pot, didn't want to drink a lot—just be healthier. And the fact that that thing jolted him, he allowed himself to be really upset about it. To the point that this guy who flew from L.A. to Miami to 'see the show,' *just happened* to be carrying cocaine and heroin with him. If we'd known that, of course we would have kicked the guy out of the room. But then again, if a guy doesn't want to be strong, then he's not going to be strong.

L.C. Clayton: Everything was good until these people showed up. The thing to this day I can't understand is with him having no money, why would these people show up with all the stuff they had? I even asked Tommy, "What's the deal?" "They're friends of mine from California." "No—friends don't come all the way from California to Miami, unless they're 'en route'." I have no idea where they came from. I had no prior knowledge of these people.

Jeff Ocheltree: It turned into 'a drug thing' for Tommy—because of the way he was feeling. I didn't see him take drugs. He disappeared for a few minutes, came back. Whatever he put in him, really screwed him up. He started laying on the floor shaking.

Phillip Polimeni: Then the next thing I know, my friend comes running out, and goes, "Your buddy's passed out on the floor! He's purple, he's dying!" I run back in there, and Tommy is purple. So we throw him into the [bathtub], I call downstairs, and the doctor says, "It sounds like you've got more than I can handle—I'm the house doctor. I would suggest you call 911." So I told one of the roadies, "Call 911!" And they said, "What are you, fucking nuts? There's so much drugs in this room we'll *all* get busted!" So they started putting ice on his genitals, took his clothes off, and were running cold water on him. And he came to—he threw up and talked a little bit. Everybody said, "Oh, thank God—he's O.K." But he was mumbling and not really making sense. He was still in a semi-coma.

L.C. Clayton: I went down to his room. I waited ten minutes, I said, "Call me in about five minutes," and he didn't call. So I went down and they had him in the tub. I was like, "What the fuck are you guys doing?" And there were syringes on the toilet seat. They just fucked up—they gave him too much of 'too good.' He was out of it—I got him out of the tub, I walked him for about an hour and a half, maybe even more than that. Got him halfway together, and they came back. I said, "Get lost!" His girlfriend was tripping.

Jeff Ocheltree: Somebody said something about drugs, and we said, "Get the ambulance on the phone, get the doctor!" We get him in a bathtub full of ice. In the meantime, I call, and [L.C.] puts a gun to my head, and says, "Nobody's coming up here—he'll lose his record contract." I said, "Record contract? *He's going to lose his life in a minute!* Forget the fucking contract!" He says, "Well, I'll just blow your head off." So he kept some of us at gunpoint. The guy answered the phone, I said, "Send an ambulance up here." They came to the door and knocked on the door. L.C.—with the gun—wouldn't let them in. And we couldn't get to the door, because he was six foot eight, and had a gun. And actually kicked one of us away from the door.

L.C. Clayton: I'm the one who said that we should call the police, [Dave] Brown's the one who said, "He's done this before." I did call downstairs and talked to the people at the desk, and told them, "I need a doctor." And [Brown] called down and told him it was O.K. He said, "It's happened before, don't worry about it."

Phillip Polimeni: The roadies put him in bed, and I said, "I'm out of here." My cousin was there—I didn't want her around that, so I said, "Let's go back to your house." So me, [another friend], and her went to her house.

Jeff Ocheltree: Then Tommy started feeling better, and we let him stay with Valeria. He was actually talking, [but] not talking really well. Mark Craney stayed there with him for a while. And then Mark called me in my room and said, "It seems like he's going to be O.K., but this isn't going down very well. I don't like the way it's going down."

L.C. Clayton: [Tommy] was saying that he was sorry that he did it, and this that and the other—"It's all good, it'll be O.K." [Valeria] was in the room with me—she was upset. He was waving like, "Take her away." He was sitting up, he said he was tired, and I said, "Get a little rest—I'll be right back." Just a couple of minutes. I wouldn't have left if he wasn't fine. There were no 'units' in the room—I checked all his shit out. [Dave Brown] was supposed to come back to the room before I left, but he didn't show up while I was there. I had puke and shit all over me—stuff all over my clothes. That's basically why I went [back to L.C.'s room]—to change my clothes. About 20 minutes or so—it couldn't have been much longer than that, I don't think. I just walked down the hall—the rooms weren't next to each other.

I walked in [to Tommy's room], and said, "How are you doing?" At first, I thought he was cool, because he was laying on his side. I thought, "Maybe he went to sleep." I went to the bathroom and came back out with some water, and said, "Here, drink this." And he was laying there with a syringe in his arm. *Somebody* came back. Me and other people that were there swept the room to make sure there was nothing else there—then we come back, and there's stuff sitting there. And he's laying there foaming at the mouth. I gave him mouth-to-mouth and whatever I could try to do, but it wasn't any good. Somebody intervened, because [Tommy] wasn't in the position to do it. And it was the wrong area—a different arm. He didn't do it, somebody did it for him. And after passing out the first time, I'm sure he wouldn't do a large enough dose to kill him. In some kind of way, it's foul play. I love Barry to death—he's like my father, and he loved Tommy—but like I said, I'd never been on a tour where there was no money.

Barry Fey: I spoke to him from Florida—but not that night. He was always 'up' for me, because he wanted to fool me.

Robert Ferbrache: One thing I know, Barry Fey made a big deal about him not knowing what was going on that night—he had no contact with anybody, blah blah blah. But that's bullshit—he knew what was going on. There's that one rumor that was like, somebody gave the order not to call an ambulance to avoid publicity. That was from Barry Fey, despite the fact he'll deny that. He did talk to them, he knew what was going on, he knew that Tommy was passed out.

Barry Fey: What could they possibly say I had to do with his death? I wouldn't hurt this kid for all the fucking tea in China. My whole family loved him. Who would say something like that? May anybody who thinks that or says that die of bone cancer.

L.C. Clayton: Not Barry's cup of tea. Barry loved him. But somebody, some kind of way . . . like I said, if you don't have any money and you're on tour, and you can't go get a cup of tea because you ain't got no money and you're the main performer—people don't come up and bring tons of fucking drugs to you. To tell you the truth, it wasn't kosher at all. I hate to say this, but I think that it was planned that it was supposed to go down that way. No, I don't want to say [who was responsible for giving Tommy the fatal dose], because I don't know. I had ideas, but y'know, one of the main people isn't around anymore. If I had known exactly who did what or whatever, they wouldn't be here today, because Tommy was good people. I liked him a lot. You spend a lot of time with somebody when they don't have nothing else to do [laughs]. Sitting in the hotel room, and they come up and tell you a half an hour later that you've got to leave because the credit cards didn't go through—you have a lot of time to talk.

Barry Fey: I always assumed it was this Phillip guy who brought the heroin from L.A., because L.C. would never hurt Tommy. Let me tell you about L.C.—he would never have hurt Tommy.

Johnnie Bolin: Unfortunately, whatever happened that night—that's a different story completely. He had a bodyguard—what did the bodyguard do? Was he just taking a nap or something? There's a lot of unanswered questions, like there is with anybody's death. But I just don't get it—it doesn't add up. Tommy wasn't happy with his management, he wasn't happy with this and that. Where was [the bodyguard] at? He was along so Tommy could make it through. He must not have been doing his job.

Reaction

Jimmy Haslip: My regimen was to practice a little bit, get some sleep, and get up the next morning—ready to rock. But I got woken up by my roadie, which was unusual. I got a knock on the door, I looked at my clock, and we were supposed to be in the lobby at 9:00am or something, and it was like 6:45. I went to look in the door, and my roadie was standing there in tears. Obviously, I knew something was wrong, but I didn't know what. I thought something was wrong with *him,* maybe. So I walked him into my room, sat him down on a chair, and I said, "What's going on?" And he could hardly talk. Then he blurted out that Tommy had passed away. I sat down—I couldn't believe it. It was a total shock.

Phillip Polimeni: In the morning, we go back to the hotel, and the first thing I get is Norma Jean Bell meeting me at the lobby, and says, "Tommy's dead." I go, *"What?!"* She goes, "Tommy's dead, and you need to get out of here—the police want to talk to you. And I go, "Why me?" She goes, "Because the roadies said you came in with some guy and he had drugs. And after you left, Tommy passed out." It was definitely a thing that to this day I'm still haunted by.

Jeff Ocheltree: I fell asleep, and three hours later, Mark Craney woke me, and said, *"He's dead."* Then the F.B.I. came—wouldn't allow us to leave, wanted to ask us all questions. "Where is L.C.? Where did he go?" "What do you mean?" "You should be asking the guy that held a gun on us." "What are you talking about? Give us a description." "What do you mean, give you a description? He's in his room!" "No he's not." He fled Miami. So that's where everybody's got all these great ideas—"Well, L.C. was hired by Barry Fey." Whatever. It doesn't make any difference.

L.C. Clayton: After Tommy died, I got everybody out of the hotel before the police even got there. The band, the light crew—*everybody* just on the road and gone. When [the police] finally got there and got their shit together, they had no one to even talk to. I got everybody in a limousine—and the limousine driver fell down and hurt himself—but I got to the airport and put them on whatever planes wherever I could possibly get them to. As quick as possible.

Max Carl: A stark shuffle of travel arrangements and a long day's flight back to L.A. found us on the street, in Mark Craney's van heading for Santa Monica from LAX. At the time, there was a group of doomsayers waging a campaign predicting a major natural disaster of biblical proportions in L.A. We stopped at a traffic signal and out the window loomed a billboard with one of their "The world is coming to an end" messages in ten-foot letters. The feeling was apocalyptic, apropos.

L.C. Clayton: I got on a plane and got back to Denver, and called Barry. Barry called me back about an hour later, and said he wanted me to talk to the Miami Police. They wanted to know what happened. They had his body, and that's all they had—and a bunch of empty rooms. There was no reason for me to stay there. My responsibility was to Tommy, but also to the group. If you're not around to be involved, then it's the best thing. That's my policy on the road.

Barry was half sobbing, because he knew nothing about it—I don't think he even knew that Tommy was gone. On the phone, he said some captain or lieutenant wanted to know if I wanted to tell him what happened. I tried to keep it as 'good' as possible. Like I said, it had to have been set up. There was no one there in the room to take the syringe out but me. So anyone else that knew anything about it would have been the one that had to do it. That's why I was waiting to see if something else came out. Y'know, you're the first reporter or anyone to talk to me other than the police. No one else has ever talked to me, and I couldn't find out why no one else has ever mentioned me.

Barry Fey: It must have been 5:30 or 6:00 in the morning—I get the call that he's gone. I said to Gary Hart, "Well, go find him!" "No, no Barry, you don't understand—*he's passed away.*" I started crying and I don't know when I stopped. I got told that he had been drinking, taking valium, shot some heroin, and did some cocaine. And not one of the things was enough to kill him, but the combination stopped his poor little heart.

Phillip Polimeni: The detective called from Miami, and he goes, "This is an obvious O.D. thing. I'm just going to tell you this—this kid had three times the possible limit of alcohol that a body could take and still be alive. He had enough gin in him to kill a horse. And then on top of that, he had barbiturates—we found Tuinals in his system. Well that's a deadly mix—barbiturates and alcohol—by itself. And then they said, "On top of that, he had cocaine and heroin. He had two fresh needle marks—that's what we're concerned about. What can you tell us about that?" I said, "I can tell you this—there was a rock n' roll show, and the room was filled with rock n' roll people, including groupies, hang-on's, and people that were selling drugs. It was total chaos. When I had my fill of it and it got uncomfortable, I left with my cousin." And I told them the address I went to. And he said, "O.K., I just needed to get a version of it. As far as I'm concerned, this is a death by O.D. accident." When he was talking to me, he said, "What is your name?" And he wrote it down as 'Tolimeni.'

L.C. Clayton: The police told me that there would be no further problems, but just don't come back to Miami. I couldn't sit there and tell the police, "Somebody stuck a needle [in Tommy's arm]." It's like, "Oh, *really?*" You just can't do that—enough stuff was going on as it was.

Johnnie Bolin: The next morning, somebody contacted my uncle, and he came over and told the family. I remember I was upstairs watching 'Bandstand,' and I heard my mom just freak out—crying hysterically. I went downstairs. So that was about noon on Saturday, and that's when I heard about it. Just changed my life. I tried to explain to my mom and dad about drugs. I said, "He didn't have a problem all his life. It wasn't like he was a junkie—it just happened." That's the most dangerous drug out there. I think also, he's down there in Miami, and it's really good. He hadn't done it in a long time, so it's *really* good now. He had no tolerance at that point. I moved down there about four months after, and I got a chance to see how people live in Miami. That stuff was right off the boat, so it's pure.

Phillip Polimeni: I can't tell you what talent this kid had—whatever demons were driving him nuts, that he had to get so far out each night that he had to drink himself to sleep and do downs . . . it wasn't really 'a heroin thing,' per se. It was more 'an alcohol and pill thing.' Of course at the end, there was heroin and coke involved. But Tommy didn't run around with heroin—he didn't have tracks when they found him. He wasn't a junkie—he was an alcoholic. He always had a martini in his hand. Tommy had 'the shakes' when he woke up—he was a legitimate alcoholic.

Mark Stein: Karen called Patty [Mark's wife] in the morning—hysterical—to tell her Tommy died. I almost fainted. We were blown away. Patty and Karen were close back then. The next day, I called up the Rainbow—the girl answered the phone crying and really depressed. She told me she had just found out the bad news. That was just an awful time.

Bobby Berge: It was late at night; I was sitting up, smoking a little doob. Then the phone rings, and I hardly even remember this guy—I don't know how he got my number, but I remember he called me from Minneapolis, and said, "Bobby, I got some bad news—Tommy died in Miami after the concert." I was in shock—I broke down and cried. It hit me hard.

Stanley Sheldon: It shocked me more than surprised me. After the shock of it, I wasn't so surprised—knowing his history. But shocked, yeah, and devastated. I remember just shutting myself up for a couple of hours—I didn't know what to think. I was still using at that point myself, and I had to play a three-night engagement at the Forum, which precluded me from attending Tommy's funeral. Which has haunted me all these years. I don't know, Peter and Dee Anthony [Peter Frampton's manager] might have let me leave, but they innuendoed that I better not. So I don't know, I didn't push it—I don't like funerals anyway. I'm sure Tommy would have forgiven me for that one, but it bothered me for a lot of years that I didn't attend his funeral.

David Coverdale: It was heartbreaking when I heard of his demise. I can't say I was shocked. There's a problem when you're elevated to that kind of 'superstar status'—you think you are immortal, and you think you can do more than mere mortals. When of course, your body has the same metabolism, chemistry, or whatever.

Jim Fox: [The James Gang] were on the road—we had moved on with a different guitarist. I got a call early in the morning from a fellow named Ron Albert, who was a principal in Criterion Recording Studio, where we had worked on 'Miami' with Tommy. Ronnie woke me up and said, "I'm afraid I'm going to be the bearer of some pretty bad news. Tommy died down here last night." That was a mind blower. I mean, I have experienced other musicians dying over the years. Like that? No. Not that suddenly and not that close. Tommy was such a kid. That's horrible. I don't even like to think about that today.

Martin Barre: Jethro Tull was never a drug orientated band and I was shocked at the discovery of his involvement in that side—he never seemed to need anything but his own energy. I've lost a few friends to drugs and will always regret that I wasn't around to help them. What a tragic loss of a great talent and a great person.

Alphonse Mouzon: I was angry, upset, sad, and hurt when Tommy died. I'm still sad and angry that he left us. Tommy had so much more to offer the world musically.

Carmine Appice: Well, it wasn't a surprise for me—I saw it coming. I thought for sure if he didn't straighten himself out, he was definitely going to be the next casualty. And he was.

Jeff Cook: It was like losing a parent or a family member. I guess we could have seen it coming, but I don't think any of us thought it was going to come soon. Because again, *all of us* were partying. Everybody thought they were ten feet tall and bulletproof. Nobody thought you could die from this shit. I also don't feel that Tommy should have died. I think that had the ambulance been called sooner or had people opted to stay with him and revive him rather than leave him alone in a room, that he probably would have lived. Don't know how much longer, but I believe he would have lived. It's always been an unfortunate truth about when you're involved in drugs and alcohol, you don't end up associating with the finest people in the world. And sometimes, things can happen like that.

Robert Ferbrache: The time I realized that there might have been a problem, [it] was too late. Everybody alongside him was doing it. I was doing it—everybody was doing drugs. Barry Fey wasn't. It was all recreational—it was for fun back then. Obviously, things have changed. Somebody could have come forward, but that's not what people did in the '70s—nobody intervened or stepped in. You could see it in the last batch of pictures that I took of him just a few days before he died. You can see it in his skin, in his face, and on his hands—there was a prolonged problem that was coming to a head there.

Jeff Ocheltree: We went to the [Jeff Beck] gig the next night—we drove the truck up. Of course, they had already heard about it. I knew Jan Hammer real well, and we all got together in the dressing room and had a really somber, upsetting few minutes to talk about it. Then they went up and played, and it wasn't the same. We listened to the gig, then we went to another town, where the Outlaws—some other friends of mine—were playing. I had a briefcase of really cool photos—of me and Tommy, and Tommy and the band—and I gave them all to the Outlaws. They loved Tommy. I remember giving them all my photos—now I wish I hadn't of done that, that was pretty lame. I was so out of my mind, I was so upset. I couldn't believe that had happened.

Dave Brown and I took the truck with all the gear and all the wardrobe cases to Denver—to Barry Fey's office. We parked the truck, went up, and saw him. And we said to him, "First of all, we're really bummed out—we're really upset. And we need money to get the truck back to California. We need money for the per diem we haven't been receiving for the last several weeks. We want our fucking per diem *now*, and we want this, this, and that." Do you know what the son of a bitch gave us, right before Christmas? He gave a hundred dollar bill a piece, didn't pay for the truck, and left us stranded—so to speak. We had to drive to Sioux City to drop off the wardrobe case, to get one of Tommy's coats out of it, so he could be buried in it. Then we had to return the truck, and we didn't have any money to pay for the truck. Then we had to figure out a way to get a ticket to fly to the funeral. *This guy did nothing.* He didn't even buy us lunch.

Karen Ulibarri: There are so many circumstances surrounding it that were too ridiculous to believe. So I don't want to say what I think, but it's still a very unanswered puzzle in my mind. I have yet to accept all the things I heard. It could have been prevented, and the people around him could have done much, much more to take care of him. To save his life. So, you can draw your own conclusions.

John Bartle: Johnnie and I had talked at length about it—there's possibilities of all sorts of things. If he did in fact die from suffocating or whatever—that's totally believable to me. Just being left alone, I can believe that. Anybody—all of us—that were in that era and done that heavy of 'experimenting' have had episodes. I mean, I can tell you [stories] about myself that are equally as scary.

Johnnie Bolin: Something went wrong there. Tommy had too many drugs in him—something was set up or something. If you ask anybody that was there, they'd be the first to tell them that something was fucked up.

Jimmy Haslip: I tend to agree that there was some sort of conspiracy theory going on. Looking at all the circumstances, I can't dismiss that. I wish I could figure out what happened that night. From all the different little tidbits of information that I gathered from various people about the events that took place after I left the dressing room, if you put these elements together, it could possibly point to some sort of odd and uncomfortable situation. And even with some of the events that happened after his passing.

I don't know that [L.C.] was doing a great job. Tommy was still partying and stuff. If somebody was sent out to really watch the guy, I think it should have been a guy that came out there to help with curbing his 'party mode.' For example, you'd think they would try to get Tommy in bed at a reasonable time, and try to keep people away from him that were bad influences. But I didn't see a lot of that happening. In fact, I saw almost the opposite—there was even *more* partying going on. So that was perplexing to me. It wasn't my place to question it, but why was this guy really hired to be out on tour? It raised questions and posed some concern, for sure.

Johnnie Bolin: You can do that with John F. Kennedy and you can do that with Marilyn Monroe. Really, the way it went down was Tommy didn't like Barry towards the end, and Barry was never really a manager—he was a promoter. He was a great promoter, but he didn't really know how to manage anybody.

Glenn Hughes: I believe that yes, it was a terrible accident. But I believe there was some foul play here. Because there was an insurance taken out on Tommy on the start of that tour. And he was being shot up—an extreme amount of opiates in Tommy's system. I don't think Tommy was deliberately killed, I just think that in hindsight, that it was a terrible way to die—seven people standing around while he died. Let me tell you this—even in my stupor, on December 3, 1976, I would have done *something*. I wouldn't have stood there, put him in the bath, and then just leave him in the bed. I'm still 30 years later thinking, "What the fuck were you people [thinking]?"

Robert Ferbrache: The only way I can equate it was when the '84 Cubs went and won the division title—they had this strong rotation of pitchers and it was incredible. '85, they had the same rotation, and on June 1st, they were in first place by six games. Then, they lost out big because four of their starting pitchers were on the D.L. When one's on the D.L., it's something, when four is on the D.L., then you have to look at management—what are they doing? That's the only equation that I can give. I thought the manager should have been a little more knowing—and he did know. He knew what was going on.

Jimmy Haslip: The saddest situation in all of this was the fact that we had just met his family several weeks prior to the Miami gig in Sioux City. His family just rolled out the red carpet for us. They were so gracious, wonderful, and hospitable. That's a wonderful memory of meeting them, and spending an evening with them. They were so happy to have us there and it was a very joyous moment in the tour. And then literally, two or three weeks later, to be back in Sioux City for Tommy's funeral . . . it was a total shock for us all.

Max Carl: There was one last trip on this tour—from sunny L.A. to icy Sioux City. Mark Craney, Jeff Cook, Jimmy Haslip, and I were pallbearers. My family was there, driving over from Nebraska. My dad burst into tears when he saw me. It was a day we'll never forget.

Johnnie Bolin: The guys in his band were the pallbearers, my cousin, and somebody else. I was in a daze—it hadn't really hit me yet. I was trying to be real strong for my mom and dad. But I think everyone didn't really know how to act—it was unbelievable. The day of the funeral was a really cold day. He's buried up on top of a hill. My family has a nice burial place on top of a hill that overlooks all of Sioux City, which is really beautiful up there. But on that day, it was pretty damn cold—lots of snow. They had to climb a hill to get up there. Kind of miserable.

Tom Stephenson: A lot of people went to the funeral. Stanley and I thought about going, but there were so many phony hangers-on.

George Larvick: It was a pretty good size church, and it was completely full—there wasn't one inch open. It was packed to the gills.

Glenn Hughes: It shook me to the core. I was 25 when he died. But having seen him in his casket, it did not deter me from seeking out more cocaine. Because an addict is an addict. Back in the early '70s, there was not a Betty Ford around, there wasn't any of that going on. Although I did prior to Tommy's death go into my first rehab—in '75—for cocaine addiction. And I could not get a grip on it. There were a number of people at the funeral that continued to get high. Not *at* the funeral, of course. Every time I used drugs after Tommy passed away, it was a really bad thing for Karen to see. She did not like the fact . . . I didn't use cocaine all the time, but I'd binge on it periodically. But it wasn't pretty—I couldn't be around her, so I'd have to leave. It was a killer to anybody's marriage, let me tell you [Glenn and Karen were married from 1977 through 1987].

Robert Ferbrache: I remember going to his funeral, and I did blow with this record exec—we were sitting in a hotel. This guy wasn't surprised at all, he said, "Tommy had a death wish—it was stamped on his forehead." And he's seen it with other people—just like that. I didn't agree with him at the time, but I know what he meant now.

Barbara Bolin: They called the doctor at the Newport Hotel [before Tommy died], where they were staying. And he said, "Rush him to General Hospital," but none of them did that. Later, when they came for the funeral, I asked them, "Why?" And the they said they didn't want to ruin his image.

L.C. Clayton: The man had a lot to give, and a long time to do it in. If he did it himself, that was on him—but he didn't do that. I tried to express that point to his mother, I couldn't say that he had nothing to do with it, but it wasn't his fault.

Johnnie Bolin: Jimi Hendrix's manager once gave a ring of Jimi's to Tommy. Tommy didn't wear rings, so Tommy gave it to Karen to hold on for him. When he passed, she brought it with her, and put it on his finger. He was buried with it.

Barry Fey: When I went down to the funeral in Sioux City, I had to do the eulogy at the gathering at the funeral, because the Catholic Church wouldn't do it. I mean, Mr. and Mrs. Bolin had been in that Church for 30 years. [The Church] thought it was a suicide or drugs—they wanted nothing to do with it. But they relented and said they'd do the service. All during the service, the priest wouldn't call him Tommy, he kept calling him 'Thomas.' It was cold and it was so unhappy. Then I did the eulogy—his mother asked me to do it, his mother and I had become very good friends. I think one of the best things—and hardest things—I ever had to do was that eulogy. I don't know where the words came from. I know it was bitterly cold, and the sun came out—the sun hadn't been out for days.

L.C. Clayton: We went to the funeral, and these fools showed up [referring to the people that brought Tommy the drugs in Miami]. I wanted to kill them, but Barry stopped me. I guess Barry knew them—I don't know how he knew them, because I'd never seen them before. But he knew them and some other people knew them. And [Tommy's] mother was there—I didn't want to upset the cart any more than that. But I left early because I was so pissed off. I don't appreciate shit like that on my watch—I don't appreciate shit like that when I'm not around.

Glenn Hughes: At the funeral, I have to tell you, I was ready to fight—I was really angry.

Barry Fey: After I delivered the eulogy, Mrs. Bolin comes up to me—crying—and says, "Barry, why wasn't Tommy ever rich?" And I had to explain to her that he would have been richer than we could have imagined, but he lived over his head, and spent so much money. And you know what she said? "You must be right, because when he was down here for Thanksgiving, I had to give him money." It broke my heart —he used the money I sent him and the money his mother gave him for drugs.

Jeff Ocheltree: At the funeral, I think we made [Barry] pay to get us beer and food, because he wasn't offering anything, yet he was there. So here's all these people—Joe Walsh, Jimmy Haslip, Mark Craney—and we're all digging in our pockets, and none of us have been paid. We didn't even care about the pay, it's just be accountable and be respectful of the situation. And the guy just didn't do that. Tommy's mother was freaking out—she was so upset, because she knew this guy wasn't going to come through, take the high road, and show integrity. I think he used Tommy and took advantage of the fact that Tommy was high sometimes.

Phillip Polimeni: There's a lot of enemies of Barry—because of how he treated Tommy. How he left him hanging so many times with bar bills and not paying musicians. And musicians walking out on sessions because of checks bouncing. These are worries that Tommy shouldn't have had to worry about. There was a manager in place—that was his job. Tommy trying to figure that out—everybody's rent, and me on top of it with my drug habit and my rent. I used to rent the studio, but Tommy wouldn't let me rent it out—he'd say, "That's my studio, and I want it whenever I need it." So I made Barry a deal, and he used to send me a weekly check. So we had that kind of arrangement. But Barry and I were not friends. There were a couple of incidents where we had words, and I told him, "What the fuck are you doing with this guy?" And he'd say, "It's none of your fucking business."

Joe Walsh: I just remember standing at the cemetery looking around at people. And it was real cold and everybody was crying . . . and I just remember standing there and people coming unglued one at a time, and I remember walking away and turning around and saluting.

Jeff Ocheltree: After the funeral, I never saw [Dave Brown] again or talked to him again. And could not figure out where he disappeared to. He was a cool guy—I liked him a lot. Tommy liked him a lot. I just find it very odd that he disappeared and haven't heard from him since.

Tom Stephenson: It's the same principle with Barry—"We've lost a great talent, and if I could have done anything, I would have." Well, you could have. You can ask Stan, you can ask Jeff, you can ask Bobby, and you can ask anybody that was really close to him, and I would say there was nobody any closer to him than the guys in Energy. *We* really know what happened, and all these other guys were just peripherally circling around—and never really knew what was going on with Tommy. Because a, he was so fucked up he wasn't coherent enough, and b, they weren't there. One of our roadies—Dave—took all his fucking guitars.

Jeff Ocheltree: When Tommy died, [Jeff and Johnnie] had to go around L.A. and look for stolen gear. We had to go [find] pieces of gear and guitars that were stolen. And we'd find guys that had it, and we knew they had it. One guy, we chased around L.A., finally caught him, dragged him over to where we were living, tied him to a chair, told him to tell us where the gear was. I told him, "This is the real deal. Here's what's going on—we're going to kick the shit out of you, and you may not even leave this house. But we *will* get the gear one way or another. So you cooperate, and I'll spare your ass. If you don't cooperate . . . " So he says, "Oh no, I'll take you to where it all is!" Well, we followed him, and it was to his parents' house. He got in the house, locked the door, and called the police. So we stood out there, because we didn't do anything wrong—we were simply catching a thief who was part of the tour. And we never did get the gear. We would hunt around, find people, and everybody would lie. It was a very strange thing—it was discouraging. It was very hurtful to see how people behave after someone dies, when it comes to money or their gear.

Mark Stein: The good thing out of it all, I remember putting a benefit together for Tommy's parents, who weren't in real good financial shape. My wife Patty and I had put together a bunch of bands to do a benefit at the Roxy in Hollywood. We recruited a lot of great talent. George Duke and his band came down, Eddie Money came down—he wasn't even famous at the time, he was recording his first album with Andy Johns down at the Record Plant— he was just a fan. Glenn Hughes was there. We had a band with me, Glenn

Hughes, and Carmine Appice. Just a whole bunch of musicians—the guitar player from Yes came down. It wasn't Steve Howe; it was one of the earlier guys [Peter Banks]. We raised a whole bunch of money for Tommy's parents which was really cool. The place was really packed. We continued helping the Bolin's over the years.

Johnnie Bolin: Tommy died in December, and I think that tribute was in January. It happened real fast—I wasn't at that. It was something real nice to do—they sent the check to my mom and dad.

Richard Bolin: We cried for a whole year, and the priest said, "Y'know, you cry and he cries, too." I stopped.

Life Insurance Policy

Johnnie Bolin: My parents never did accept Tommy's passing. At first, they were just numb for a good couple of months. Barry promised to help them sort this whole mess out financially, and he never did anything. He paid for the funeral and paid for the headstone—but nothing else. I was on the phone with him and my mom, and he said, "I'll make sure this and this happens." You get real skeptical, and then, five or six years of being absolutely broke. And of course, with anybody dying, foul play is always going to enter, no matter who it is. It was always very hard for them.

L.C. Clayton: I heard there were problems with his mother getting money. It's like, "What the fuck?" There should have been *something*. His record was selling—you've got two records and you've got no money?

Glenn Hughes: Tommy's manager did get that bloody insurance [payment]— Tommy's parents got nothing.

Johnnie Bolin: We asked Barry, and he was beating around the bush. He said, "There's money out there." We thought—at that time—he was going to help us. And he came here and gave a eulogy like you wouldn't believe—everyone was in tears. He sure fooled us, and continues to. We never got nothing, no. And then he never really helped us out after that. We got him involved in publishing, and I think through bankruptcy, he gave me Bofe Music—Tommy's publishing company. He had to get rid of some things to keep other things apparently—that's the only way I could figure out what happened there. I got a call from Tommy's accountant, and he said, "He's giving you the publishing, and there's $3,000.00 worth of checks. Do you want them?" And I'm like, "Yeah, but why would he give me the publishing?" He said, *"Just don't ask questions."* Tommy didn't have it together exactly in the legal department, but they made sure of that. They made sure it seemed like he was fucked up or he didn't sign something—they purposely made him sign something that he shouldn't have, and when he should have signed it, he didn't.

Barry Fey: He never earned any money. I don't think he ever earned on his albums—it might have [on] his first one, but the second didn't sell enough. I know he didn't recover anything on his second album. And like I said, he was spending money like he was . . . and I know, because it was my money.

Johnnie Bolin: Why would he be the beneficiary? He had Tommy sign all sorts of shit that he never should have signed. It's like those stories on VH-1's 'Behind the Music' about Grand Funk. Barry will deny it. Rolling Stone even put it in there—it didn't make any sense what happened.

Jeff Ocheltree: To not give the family the money—the insurance money—I think is disgusting. And to make up stories that Tommy owed him money—how could he be owing him money? We're out there on fucking tour! We had one of the great sound engineers take his monitor system, get in a truck, and drive away, because he hadn't been paid. Who's got the money? Tommy's not going to the box office to get the money. We had a road manager who was an asshole. We just kept saying, "Where's the money? How's this tour running along when there's no money?"

Robert Ferbrache: His family didn't get paid, because Barry said, "He owes me $250,000.00—I'll just take that insurance check." So he ended up getting both checks—the one that he had and he got the family's one, and left them out to dry. I gave a disposition to the insurance company over that—somewhere, I was on record with that. The insurance company was trying to claim that Tommy committed suicide, and they didn't want to pay on that. But they had the disposition, and then they paid on it. I know they paid on it.

Johnnie Bolin: Tommy already had a record deal somewhat—he just needed someone to contract it. I mean, you owe *the record company,* you don't owe Barry. I know, I've had record deals—you owe them the money, but they don't come after you for it. You're not billed, you're obligated to them to stay in contracts for five years. And if you don't make it, you're dropped. If you do make it, they get the money back. Tommy was already in Purple—what does he need Barry's money for? That didn't make any sense at all. He said that in magazines, too—"He owed it to me." Well, no he didn't, and we know what you did. When you're a manager for a major artist—I don't care who it is—you're going to have insurance out on them. You've got to be insured in case something happens.

Jeff Ocheltree: The insurance policy for Tommy—how did that get in Barry Fey's hands and not to his family? And why was it such a big policy and why did Barry Fey have it? The big answer is, "He's his manager." But what kind of manager doesn't see that that money goes to the family?

Barry Fey: The accountants took care of that. I know that we got $200,000.00. People have trouble believing that—it was Tommy's idea. It wasn't like I was on the phone [saying], "Tommy, do you know how much you fucking owe us?!" He knew, and he was a sensitive kid. He said, "Let's take out an insurance policy." I don't think he ever thought the $200,000.00 would be short. We were way up in the $300's. But I don't know whether Mrs. Bolin should have got some. Maybe . . . should I have given her some of it? Let's just say she's not entitled to anything legally—which I'm sure she isn't, because she would have got it. But we paid the premiums and Tommy didn't pay the premiums—he had no money to pay the premiums.

What I'm saying is, I wonder if I should have given them something. I didn't think of it. When someone's just lost a son like that, what do you say? "Here's $20,000.00?" I'm sure she would have taken it—maybe I should have done it. But I honestly did not think of it. And like I said, we were still upside down. But I should have done something maybe, and it's hard for me to say, because I don't know what I would have or should have done. But it seems to me, if you're going to be upside down, another $20,000.00 doesn't hurt. I can tell you, my feet were so straight that when they'd bend over they'd crack. If there was anything in writing for her, she would have gotten it. But I don't think so, because Tommy wanted it for us. I'm sure he would have wanted something for his parents too, but he didn't think along those lines. He was paying us back. I don't know what was in there, I just know that we got what we were supposed to get. If someone promised them, said, "Mrs. Bolin, if something happens, you'll get something," it wasn't me. And I don't know who else would have the authority to do it.

David Givens: He was young and you've got to remember, Tommy was really poorly educated about business stuff—and the world in general. I mean,

Tommy was a genius guitar player. He could be funny and pleasant, but he could do some really stupid stuff. At one point, early on when we were traveling [in Zephyr], we hung together pretty well for probably the first year. One day, we're driving home in the truck from the airport in Denver, and Tommy goes, "I just thought I'd let you guys know, I'm going on 'an ego trip' now." We're like, *"Huh?"* And of course, we're hippies—going on an ego trip is like saying, "I'm cutting my hair and I'm getting a job." He goes, "All the guitar players that are making it out there are on ego trips, so I'm going to go on one." And he meant it!

As it turned out, he really did—he turned into this arrogant, 'Tommy above all,' instead of working with the group. Even John—and John loved Tommy—when the band broke up, John stayed with us. That's the kind of stuff he would do. He was not a real thoughtful person—Karen did a lot of his analytical thinking for him, I think. Tommy really went by his gut in how he felt about people. "Y'know, Barry's a great guy to hang out with. He doesn't drink, he doesn't smoke, he doesn't chase girls." Therefore, he's a good person. Nevermind that he was hugely fat and ate constantly—but other than his appetites for money and food, he was a real clean-living kind of guy. He had been a Marine. He was a tough, smart guy. Tommy never ever confronted Barry about anything. Barry was like Tommy's godfather. I was told later on that Tommy was in deep debt to Barry when he died. Barry was an enabler for Tommy. But from Tommy's point of view, Barry was his buddy.

Barry Fey: He was like my son. I say sometimes I've got four boys—I don't know what would happen if anything ever happened to them, but Tommy was close. He wasn't as close near the end—he couldn't be. He was 'out there'—he didn't care. I don't know if he was a sad kid.

Johnnie Bolin: Well, we receive royalties now, but then we didn't. After he passed away, we assumed Barry would take of everything. We assumed we'd get money right off the bat. Well, my mom and dad didn't get a check until 1983/1984, when an attorney got a hold of them and said, "There's a bunch of money here, I found it for you." What this attorney did is he found deceased artists that had money that people didn't know had money. He said, "I charge a third." So they got a check for like 60 grand or something like that. But that was the first money they got in probably eight years—not one penny beforehand.

Barry did not help us, he just pulled the plug. Columbia, once he died, Tommy wasn't big enough to make a big deal about him, and he couldn't tour no more. But when it came back around again—CD's, 'The Ultimate' [a Tommy box set released in 1989], and magazines—he's a big deal. 'The Ultimate' kind of straightened everything out. It was like, "Who owns Tommy's publishing?" They had to get it straightened out to put 'The Ultimate' out—it helped us immensely. Then it picked up. But I'm sure I don't get 100% of what I'm supposed to get. With Purple, it was kind of like 'hush money'—"Don't ask any questions, here's some money." Once again, they're a corporation; they all make the same amount of money. Tommy wrote the whole album, but they all get credit for writing it. It doesn't make sense. I haven't talked to Barry in many, many years.

Charlie Brusco: Barry was always a big gambler and he liked to play the ponies. Basically, all the money that he made, he gambled on horse races.

Barry Fey: I retired in 1997, and in 2001, when House of Blues bought out Universal Concerts—who had bought me out in 1997—they asked me to come back. I did it for three years, but I just can't put up with the business as it is now—$400 tickets, it's ridiculous. It's all corporate bullshit. Now I'm just doing consulting work.

L.C. Clayton: They had a big thing with the insurance companies, and Barry went through changes with debtors and everything else, and they stopped him from doing shows—that kind of cooled it down. I didn't want to do much more—I'd done it long enough. I just got out of surgery here—they did four vertebrae in my back.

Johnnie Bolin: After Tommy died, I didn't play for six months—I wasn't too enthused to jump back into it. It had a bad effect on all of us. Later, I lived in New York, ended up in Minneapolis. I was playing with Richard T. Bear, this guy that was on RCA. I went down to Miami and lived there for about a year. I played with Richard for about three years. I pretty much lived in a hotel in Times Square in New York—the rest of the band went back to Miami. We went over to Germany twice, France, we went out with Black Sabbath, played with J. Geils at Cobo Hall, played some gigs with Boston, Eddie Money, and the Doobie Brothers. Then he lost his record deal around 1979.

That's when I came back to Sioux City for a month, got together with John Bartle, and we started the band D.V.C. We got a record deal with Alpha and moved to Minneapolis—had two records with those guys. That fell out about '82. There was a band out there called Dare Force—a metal band—and we did some independent records. I played with them up until Black Oak Arkansas, in '88. I quit in '94, things were not going exactly quite right. Then my girlfriend and I had my son, Bobby. I went out with Black Oak for a little bit longer, but with having a child, it was too much rigmarole, so I couldn't go out anymore. I quit for two years. Before I had Bobby, I lived in Texas with Rocky [Athas, former Black Oak guitarist], for probably half a year. We had a Tommy Bolin Tribute Band—we played a handful of dates. I rejoined Black Oak in '96, and continue to play with them to this day.

My dad continued to work and my mom continued to work. My mom had a stroke in '89 or '90, so she was in a wheelchair—half her body was paralyzed. My dad retired—he was in the packing plant. My dad died in '92, my mom died in '94. My dad went in for a gallbladder problem, and they said he had cancer. He was a strong guy—he might have been in pain for a long time and never said nothing. Once he got in the hospital, he only lived for another couple of weeks. Pudge had a child and got married. Right after Tommy died, his son Cozmoe was born—in '77. And then they moved to Dallas. He worked at a Country Club, he was a bartender. Got divorced towards the end of '80, and then moved back here, and worked different places. Pudge died in '94—it was cirrhosis of the liver.

Posthumous Projects

Johnnie Bolin: We had advertised in the paper that we were selling some of Tommy's amps. Willy Dixon [not to be confused with blues musician Willie Dixon] came up from Hastings, Nebraska, and bought an amp from my mom—he was a big fan of Tommy's. He and Pudge became really good friends—I wasn't living here then. He had a reel-to-reel—we gave him all our tapes of Tommy to sort through, and he said he would take the time to sort through all the songs and mark them. There were a good 75 tapes—at least. It was a big box of tapes that we had—some were in cases and some weren't. It was a big mess. So Willy did all that. Other people had recorded Tommy's gigs, so it wasn't like only we had tapes—there was a lot of bootleg stuff floating around.

So Willy and me started talking, and he heard through somebody about Tom Zutaut—he was doing Guns N' Roses and Mötley Crüe. So I suggested we try to get a hold of him and see if he might want to do a compilation. We got a hold of him, and he was interested. He said, "Yeah, we'll do it. Let's put it in motion." And he'd tell us what to do. We didn't know for sure if we were going to use any unreleased live stuff—he suggested for this one, to just keep it as a compilation of songs that had already been on record. Including live tracks would have taken longer, because we would have to mix it . . . but it would have actually took a lot shorter time, because it took *forever* to clear all that stuff through licensing.

I was on the road, and Willy was living in Montana, so we'd take turns going to Zutaut. We did this, we got that, and he'd say, "I should have some time in a couple of months," and it would be that long that we'd have to wait. The first actual meeting, we all went out there—I think I was playing out there—Willy came out and we met with Tom, and he said, "I'm ready to do it now." I had an anvil case full of pictures, and I left that out there with him, and we started the ball rolling. I'm happy the way it turned out [the 1989 Geffen Records two-CD box set, 'The Ultimate']. Tom wanted it to be that whoever got the record; they'd think it was something special. That's why you can't find them—we made as many for the amount of money that we had. I thought it turned out great—it was definitely a labor of love on his behalf. He said to Willy and me, "Pick the songs you want," and Tom picked his. We pretty much agreed to everything.

Simon Robinson [the head of the Deep Purple Appreciation Society] originally confronted me about doing a label thing with his record label—to issue unreleased Tommy material. So I thought about that, and somehow, Mike Drumm had found out about who I was, because he had known Tommy when Tommy lived in Boulder. So he got a hold of me, and it made more sense to do it out of the United States rather than England—it's a bigger market. He landed a deal with Rhino right off the bat, so I went with Mike Drumm. We went through all the reels, and that's how the Tommy Bolin Archives came about. Then we started selling concert recordings, t-shirts. It's been fairly profitable, and everything we've put out, it's been digitally remastered. 99% of them are masters. The whole thing behind the Archives was to prevent bootlegging. Something needed to be done.

Mike Drumm: It was really a series of events that led to the formation of the Archives. When Tom Zutaut decided to do 'The Ultimate,' people who had really been into Tommy were aware that there was a big volume of unreleased stuff out there. And there was in fact this cassette trading circuit going on, where everybody was into posturing and protecting what they had. So when 'The Ultimate' was put together, there was hope that there would be a variety of these unreleased tracks on there. And what Zutaut wanted to do was make the most commercially viable set he could. It just included the "Brother, Brother" acoustic track [a demo of the song "People, People"]. It came out, and Bob Ferbrache was in a position to go to the family and have some of this [unreleased] music all ready himself. He put together a single disc bootleg—he made it look like it was a Japanese bootleg. This is like '92/'93—it was from his frustration, from how 'The Ultimate' hadn't tapped into any of this stuff. I got a copy of it, and my first thought after hearing it was, "How do we make this legal?" And the way to make it legal was to form the Archives, and to get a hold of Johnnie. So I got a hold of Johnnie, and we went through about six months of back-and-forth, and then put the structure of the company together—with him as an owner.

At the same time, [someone] was doing this 'Fever' box set thing—he was putting out true bootlegs and profiting on them, and Johnnie wasn't getting a penny. And a lot of it was shit—it was like eighth generation, and they were trying to put out everything they possibly could. So our thing was, "How do we do it right?" So we approached Rhino Records and cut a deal with them for [1996's] 'From the Archives: Volume One,' which ended up being pretty successful—although it wasn't up to what they were hoping [sales-wise]. Maybe they wanted to sell 100,000 copies—I think over a year and a half it sold 20,000 copies. But when we set it up, we thought, "Let's start our own mail order division, and have products we can sell direct." So we got a card inserted in those first 'From the Archives: Volume One' CD's. We had a really good response—there was tremendous enthusiasm right off the bat. It set up a dynamic where we were more interested in doing direct marketing, so we did that.

Rhino didn't want to do a second CD, so we did 'From the Archives: Volume Two' through Zebra Records, which was a jazz label that has since gone out of business. And as time went on, we wanted to do what we could to really draw attention to this, so we started staging tribute concerts in Denver—that I produced. The first one [in 1996] was getting the original Energy together, and then the next year, we did the Zephyr reunion, and that's when Glenn Hughes came. I put a ton of time and energy into these things, and we packaged them up where people would get their next release. We did all this P.R. and got the local media involved, and put on two great shows. But we never did completely sell out the Bluebird—we would come close. And even though we had created these incredible/intimate experiences, at the end of the day, after all the work we put into it, they would basically break even. And part of doing it was to have it be a business where you could make money—and help promote the Archives better.

At that point, I saw the ceiling on the thing. So I said to Johnnie, "We really need to get Norm Waitt involved." [Waitt] had gone to high school with Tommy, and was one of the brothers that started Gateway Computers—and in the '90s, with the whole boom of dot com and computers, he had become a billionaire. So my idea was, "Let's try to get Norm involved and do a proper tribute." Where you get Jimmy Page, Jeff Beck, Joe Perry, and Eddie Van Halen—all the guys who bow to Tommy. What we need to do is create an event that will be national in scope, because the people we brought in [previously] were totally authentic, but none of them were really superstars in their own right. So let's put together 'the ultimate superstar event'—stage it for a national audience, shoot it for a big DVD, and get the big publicist who could get the Rolling Stone article. Really bring [Tommy's music] back.

And I could never get this to stick. Norm had formed his own record company at that point [Samson Music—a subsidiary of Gold Circle Entertainment], and Michael Shrieve, who used to be in Santana, was the head of A&R. I spoke with him, and they crunched all the numbers—"Oh no, this wouldn't be profitable." And the whole point—it's *not* about it being profitable. It's about somebody needs to be 'the sugar daddy,' like Paul Allen has been with [Experience Music] up in Seattle. So Norm in theory could have been that guy, and it just never came together. That was my vision. We had done everything we could do—and it was pretty darn good. Pretty high quality, sincere, creative, accurate, and focused. So we kept putting out CD's . . . and we needed a sugar daddy. And I couldn't get that done—nobody's been able to get that done. And then, Greg Hampton came along—he got Johnnie and they put out the 'Whips and Roses' things. There was a point where we had run out of quality materials—after putting out 20 CD's—and Greg was able to find that stuff, which breathed a little bit of extra life into it. But it was really just a continuation of what we were doing, which had already run its course. We needed to do this bigger thing—to get the larger world to get who this guy was. The fact that he died before he could go platinum.

Greg Hampton: I had become friendly with the Bolin family in the early '90s, through Johnnie and Pudge. I had been a fan of Tommy's since '75. I had gotten in contact with them, and originally, I had brought Pudge to L.A., and we tried to get an Archives sort of set-up. But from what I was told by other people, there would be licensing issues. I was involved with so many other projects; it was really hard for me to devote an adequate amount of time to really pursue the Archive concept, which subsequently, the Tommy Bolin Archives went into effect.

Johnnie and I got together and talked, and we happened [to come across] some multi-tracks that we found in a storage unit, that had been there for many years. They were outtakes from some of the many sessions that [Tommy] had recorded in Los Angeles in '74 and '75. To my ears, honestly, you can't compare. I thought it was *better* than the other performances of the released material, because it was just so untamed—it was absolutely insane. The technology today is definitely the key. Just listening to the hours and hours of all the different playing—the riffs and potential things that he could have grown into. Because there are so many different things that you heard on these sessions that were never really documented on anything that was publicly released in the '70s.

The Archives things are just bits and pieces from little rough mixes that were taken either from cassettes or half-inch, two-track, or four-track recordings. This stuff is from multi-tracks. The difference between these releases and 'Teaser' and 'Private Eyes' are just like a universe away. The best performances of his career. [An instrumental called] "Blowin' Your Cookies" certainly surpasses his playing on 'Spectrum' or 'Mind Transplant,' as far as his fusion ability. Another [instrumental] called "Cookoo." Alternate and various outtake versions, like "Wild Dogs," a version of "Teaser" that absolutely surpasses the original version on the original album by miles. There's versions of "Savannah Woman," "Marching Powder." Numerous versions of "Crazed Fandango," which are amazing. Each version [contains] completely different instrumentation and also the way they applied the whole arrangements, and had certain featured soloists within that realm of each song. There's versions of songs like "Lotus" and "People, People." I approached SPV Records about doing it, because I work with SPV on a lot of different records. They were fans, and they said, "Let's do it" [the tracks were released in 2006, as two releases— 'Whips and Roses I & II'].

Johnnie Bolin: I keep putting all this stuff out—there's demand for it, people are interested in it. For instance, Friday Music has just put out a great new Tommy compilation, [2008's] 'The Ultimate: Redux,' and they're going to be putting out more releases in the future. I'm lucky in a lot of ways—I ran into people that have helped me out.

Elliot Rubinson: [Artist] Nicholas Simmons, who's a big fan, got in touch with Johnnie, and said, "I have this friend that owns Dean Guitars, and there's never been a commemorative Tommy Bolin guitar." We all know he played Strats and some Explorer-style guitars, but Fender never did a guitar—never showed any interest in doing it. And then we started thinking, "Well, he didn't play a Dean"—Dean was barely in business when he died—but the fact of the matter is we said, "Let's take a Stratocaster, and take it up a couple of notches.

But work off the specs of his original guitar." I found a guy in Massachusetts, who owns one of Tommy's Strats from the '70s. So we decided, "Let's take measurements of the body, let's take a profile of the neck, and let's duplicate this guitar in exotic, beautiful wood on the neck. Let's do a killer graphic for a commemorative of Tommy [on the guitar's body]. Let's even take the pickups out, measure what the outputs of a '70s Stratocaster would be, and duplicate the pickups. We upgraded the hardware—we decided to use the Wilkinson tremolo, which is a lot smoother. We designed a new headstock for it, which is kinda Strat/Tele-ish. We're going to make a run of a hundred pieces of them, and if it does well, maybe we'll put out another model—a different style.

Nicholas Simmons: The idea to begin with—for Dean to make a Tommy tribute guitar—that was the main thing, just selling [Elliot] on the idea. Which wasn't too difficult to do—Elliot's one of my closest friends, for a long time. And I knew the Bolin's for a long time, although before the guitar situation happened, I'd never actually met Johnnie in person. I met his parents a couple of times, and hung out with Rick. I guess I was the right person to bring those two together. So I came up with the idea in August 2006, and approached Elliot with it. Then, the idea was to come up with what kind of guitar—I did it based on a Strat shape. Did another design that we might make that is based on the Explorer shape—since Tommy played an Ibanez Destroyer. I even have another design that is a real crazy, custom thing—it would be a collector's model, where the whole body is shaped like Tommy's image on the 'Teaser' album.

Greg Hampton: I was contacted by Theo Hartman of Hartman Electronics—he's designed a 'Tommy Bolin fuzz pedal.' It's being based around the exact copy of Tommy's pedal, which was a Sam Ash fuzz pedal—made in the late '60s/early '70s, and then discontinued. [Theo] had gotten the exact diodes, capacitors, and transistors, and compared the sound. It's amazing—if you plug your guitar into the pedal, and you listen to it going into the amp, you would think you're in the room with Tommy Bolin. It's so real it's scary! What I would do is A-B the stereo with a Tommy solo or rhythm playing—some song, like "Dealer" from 'Come Taste the Band.' It starts off with just a rhythm guitar, and I'll A-B the rhythms with that song, stop the CD player, and then we'll play the track, adjust the tones, and see how the tone settings fare with the actual record. It's identical.

Johnnie Bolin: I'm still very much involved with the Archives, and we've got a Tommy Bolin Foundation. We play tribute shows around his birthday. The Foundation is going pretty good, it's not nationwide yet. We got money for schools the last few years.

Phillip Polimeni: I sold some of [Phillip's 'Glen Holly' Tommy recordings] to Michael Drumm from the Archives [released as 2004's 'After Hours: The Glen Holly Jams Volume One']. In his thing, he says he bought the whole cache. Well, nobody in their right mind would sell everything. I sold him *some* stuff. The highlights of what is going to come out is just going to blow everybody away—it's amazing. I've got some of Tommy and Jeff Beck, Tommy and Todd Rundgren, Tommy and a couple of the Wailers, Tommy and Rick Grech. I've let Johnnie hear some of it. I've got stuff that still gives me the chills today. It still stands up. It's documenting a piece of rock history. I held onto it for thirty-some-odd years. It's not a money thing—it's a passion to show Tommy in the best light possible. I've got reel-to-reels that I had preserved over the years, and I took care of them. Tommy used to tell me, "When I die, you're going to be a fucking millionaire off my stuff!"

Greg Hampton: Warren Haynes and I are trying to co-produce this Tommy Bolin tribute together. Logistically, it's going to take quite a while, because of the fact that everyone is all over the world. Jeff Beck was influenced by Tommy—he's expressed interest. He did a tribute to Tommy on his last couple of tours—he would play "Stratus," the Billy Cobham song that Tommy was a part of. We have a wish list of guitarists that we would like to have on the tribute, playing with Tommy. We'd love to have Slash, Joe Perry, Carlos Santana. And some other guitar players that played with Tommy or were influenced by him—Vernon Reid. And also, this 26 minute instrumental, of having all these major stars of today, playing along with Tommy Bolin—trading fours. It's another thing that's never been done, to my knowledge. Each guy is going to take a three-minute pass, and is going to be 'sparring' with Tommy Bolin—like they're in the same room with him! It's going to be the original versions with guitarists playing with the actual multi-tracks that exist, as well as there will be new re-creations of some of the actual songs, with the solos kept intact, with new musicians playing the original arrangements.

Tommy

Glenn Hughes: I miss him dearly as a brother. Johnnie wouldn't mind me telling you that I call Tommy my brother—and I call Johnnie my brother, because I don't have any blood brothers. To have him taken from me was cruel. We have a very big relationship, Tommy and I. We were very close. We had a very feminine side to our manhood—I'm not gay, but I'm very much in touch with that 'European side' of my way. Tommy had that way with him as well, as does Steven Tyler and David Bowie. Tommy and I had that going on, and it was beautiful. We were very huggy and lovey about that. With Tommy, we were very open, and I miss that—I was robbed of that. I've spoken to Tommy since he passed away, I do that. And he's still very much involved with me. I talk to him all the time—I ask him questions and decisions in my life that I should do. There was a period right before I went sober in '91, where I was trying to channel him to help me quit this shit. And it was really important for me to get help from Tommy, and from John Bonham, actually.

Jeff Cook: He was the most natural musician I've ever known. He had a great ear and he could pick up things quickly. I think a testament to that is great jazz musicians were gravitating toward him. The Billy Cobham's of the world, John McLaughlin, Alphonse Mouzon—all these musicians that had tremendous technical chops realized that this guy was a very natural musician. Even Narada Michael Walden was very enamored with Tommy, Dr. John—all kinds of people were gravitating toward him. I really believed if he would have lived, he would have evolved into probably one of the premier jazz guitarists in the world.

Phillip Polimeni: Tommy was the type of guy that everybody loved. He had a personality and a heart of gold, and he was a very kind person. He was a beautiful soul. He had a talent that there just wasn't enough time for it to get out. It's so sad that one person had that much talent and it didn't get out—that he didn't become the star he should have been.

Jeff Ocheltree: The main thing I'd like him to be remembered for—he was a really good person. Second of all, he was a brilliant guitar player, who could play any genre of music. And he was well-versed in knowing about different kinds of music. If you said something about Django Reinhardt, he would be able to talk to you about Django Reinhardt. If you said something about Les Paul, he would talk for hours about Les Paul. If you talked about Chet Atkins, he'd talk about Chet Atkins. See, the thing about these guys is we didn't sit around and talk about stupid rock bands—we talked about *great musicians.* That's why the great musicians listen to great musicians. I don't think that's happening as much [today]. Like, I do a lot of work with Danny Carey of Tool, and some of the music his bands play—when he's not on tour with Tool—is Billy Cobham, Zeppelin, all kinds of fusion stuff. His influences were Billy Cobham and Lenny White. If you say "Tommy Bolin" to him, everybody in that band knows who Tommy Bolin is. But if you say "Tommy Bolin" to all these other bands of that genre of music—metal bands—they go, "Who? Deep Purple? James Gang . . . what's that?"

The difference about today and yesterday is that we listened to all kinds of things, we knew where the players came from, and the different parts of the United States where different types of playing came from. I think that's what the English thought was so odd about Americans—I talked to Tommy about this a lot. I said, "Why do you suppose Americans don't know about the music that we invented?" He said, *"Because they have their heads up their asses.* They're fed shit on the radio, and that's all they know." Unless your parents are playing for you different types of music, or you somehow get wind of it and you seek out more information about it, how are you going to know? That's the responsibility of Americans, to educate their people about their music—that *we* invented. See, that's the difference between talking to him and a guitar player of today. As much as he had the colored hair, the feathers and all that, he was actually a really down-to-earth person. It's easy to misunderstand that because of drugs or alcohol, but also, if you were going to talk about something that didn't have any kind of substance to it, he didn't have the time for it.

Mike Finnigan: The thing when I read about Tommy—that I think a lot of people miss—is what a sweet guy he was. He was just really a nice cat—warm and personable. He treated everybody well, never had an attitude. None of the 'Guitar God/my ass weighs a ton' stuff. A really sweet guy that played his ass off.

That's the biggest loss—he was barely scratching the surface of his talent. I'm sure great things were awaiting him. It's another case of chemical dependency wipes another one off the planet. When you're young, everybody's ten feet tall and bulletproof. So you don't think of there being any real consequences.

David Givens: [Recalling Candy Givens' death in 1984, as a result of being under the influence and drowning in a hot tub] As I recall, there was alcohol, Quaaludes, cocaine, and some other little pill that people used to take. She had done a whole lot of stuff. Just to put it in perspective—she had taken a year and gone to Mexico, and cleaned up her act. Ate right, lived by the beach, hung out with a rich guy, wrote a lot, stayed clean. Came back to town, and for the first week she was back, we spent a lot of time together—we were planning on starting a new band. We stayed in contact the whole time she was away—divorced or not [David and Candy divorced in 1976]. She was really doing well. She had been in Boulder about a week, before she started hanging out with her old friends. Then, after about three days of that, she was dead. She didn't have the tolerance anymore.

John Tesar: It's a shame Candy didn't live—it would have been interesting to see what she would have done.

Otis Taylor: Sometimes when I'm playing with Gary Moore, I get flashes of, "Wow, I get to play with a great guitar player again!" Kind of brings me back to thinking of Tommy.

David Coverdale: With the greatest love and respect. At the time, it was really difficult. Afterwards, I'm very honored that I had the pleasure to work with such a creative force. He was a beautiful boy. He really was—a genuinely beautiful boy.

Prairie Prince: His music stands up today. I've been listening to it a lot since 'Whips and Roses' was released. There's no telling what that guy would have done if he were to continue to play. I think he would have definitely evolved with all the music around us, but still stay true to his psychedelic roots. I think he was a brilliant musician, and a really sweet person. He seemed to be caring about the youth, and the history—past, present, and future. Hopefully, he's sending down some messages about the future right now—giving guitar players something to strive for.

Mike Drumm: I would like people to understand that they *should* bother to pay attention, because in any given era, there are very few musicians who come along, who have a supremely special gift. And that gift enables them to create music that can bring tremendous gratification and enjoyment to people. He had that gift. He was one of the top talents of that era. And anyone who is one of the top talents, you say to somebody, "Would you be interested in checking that person out?" How could you say no? Of course you should check out one of the top talents of that era, because that era was a huge piece of rock history.

I'd like for him to be remembered for what he was—an incredibly talented and gifted musician, who had the ability to touch people. On a lot of different levels. And who created connections with people through his music—that's what happened to me. People can go deeper within their own appreciation of music by gaining an appreciation for Tommy. If you get into studying his entire career, it's like a rollercoaster. You can be way up here doing this, and then you can come down here doing that. There's all these different shades of musical expression.

Tommy was getting there—he was starting to develop 'a formula' in a sense. But I think he would have strayed from it—he would have done a side project that wouldn't have been bounded by that. He was one of a kind. And on a personnel level, when I saw him in '76, that genuine nice guy was there. Even though he'd become 'a crazed rock star' and drug addict—that's before there was a Betty Ford Center. So there wasn't this other counterpoint out there—"Hey, you can go into rehab." But with all that, when I saw him again after two plus years of not seeing him, there was still this warm heart that was there.

Jim Fox: The sky was the limit for him. He could have done anything. The music speaks very loudly. I would like for as many people as possible to listen to the music he made—I think it really tells the tale. And it should be remembered what kind of a sweet guy he really was. This was a guy without a mean bone and his body. Pure musical innocence—that's all it was.

Jan Hammer: He was as unique as the others you've just mentioned [Jeff Beck, John McLaughlin, and Carlos Santana—all of whom Jan has played with]. He was on that level. It's a shame that he wasn't able to continue. Because look at for instance how Jeff grew—and is *still* growing. I played with him in England a couple of years ago on a tour, and he's just totally reinventing himself every time. It's beyond guitar now—*it's a voice.* And Tommy was like that—he could have amazed everybody to no end. I would put him in that order.

Eddie Kramer: I don't think many people know about his guitar playing, unfortunately. I think his legacy is such that it needs to be promoted. I think somebody should just do extracts from the Zephyr album—just pull out the solo section! You should definitely promote him, because he was a terrific guitar player. He's an unsung hero of the '70s, and had tremendous potential. He could have been another Stevie Ray or Clapton. He certainly had the potential to be a world-class guitar player. But it was cut short by the bloody drugs.

David Givens: Tommy was a uniquely gifted person—a musician. I've heard people say all different kinds of things about him. There's a rabid group of people who just love Tommy. And then there are other people who say, "He was just a Jimi Hendrix clone." To me, he had a unique gift. He was very musical—he spoke music as a language. He didn't have to think about it, he didn't need to go to Julliard or Berklee to learn how to do it. He was a natural and he was passionate. Tommy used to dog people for being jocks, but he was a jock-y guy himself. He was a real manly guy—surprisingly enough for the way he dressed and whatnot. But he was a real 'guy guy.' I think that showed in his playing. I wish he had lived longer. I wish Barry Fey had not fucked us. I wish that he had had the opportunity to do what he was capable of doing. A lot of people tell me that they think the stuff he did with Zephyr was the best stuff he did. Everybody has a opinion—whether that's true or not, I don't know. What I do know, when we were working as an ensemble, and we were reading each other's minds, and really tuned into the same vibe, it was tremendous. And the reaction we got from the people listening to it backs that statement up.

    We played in Detroit once—this is my favorite gig that we played out of all the Zephyr gigs, other than the stuff around Boulder when we first started. We were going into this place called the East Town Theater. We had played there once and done really well. In those days, they had three bands on the bill—we went on first the first time we played there. We expected—and were told—that the next time we went there, we would go on second. Well, there was some political bullshit, and they made us go on first. I said to the rest of them, "Let's just go play [Pharoah Sanders'] 'The Creator Has A Master Plan' for an hour." So we did—we went out and jammed for an hour. *It was brilliant.* People were still cheering 20 minutes after we were off the stage! The people wouldn't shut up. We should have learned our lesson and just done that for the rest of our career. But that gig, that was one of the few times that we were really united, that far along in our career. That was probably in early 1971. That was a moment we all pulled together and really did what we wanted to do—play for the audience. Tommy was brilliant. It's like this to me—Tommy had more success than the rest of us, but I don't think that Tommy was a better musician than John, for instance. I don't think Tommy was a better singer or performer than Candy. We all contributed to what we did as Zephyr. And we all stood on an equal basis. The fact that we made music that spoke to people, that's something to be proud of.

Barry Fey: He had the different hair colors before anybody, he was doing fusion before a lot of people. He would have been a leader. And his mother would never have had to ask, "Why isn't Tommy rich?" He would have been rich. He was a little boy. He had a good heart. See, the musicians loved Tommy, the girls loved Tommy . . . the problem is, *Tommy* didn't love Tommy. I could say he never should have gone to L.A., he should have stayed here—but there's nothing creative here, you have to go. Musicians have to be with musicians.

John Bartle: He was just a prince of a human being. His music definitely holds up. There's a certain mystique about it that captivates people. All special music is really timeless. He was a rocker at heart. He never did pay much attention to trends—he always was on the edge fashion wise and music wise. I think it will hold up for years to come.

Tom Stephenson: The writing [and] the playing holds up to anybody I've played with and ever seen. He was a prodigal player. This kid, out of the box—in his very young teens—was a great player. Here's a good analogy for you—Jeff Beck opens a lot of his shows with a song off the 'Spectrum' album,

"Stratus." That should just tell you right there. And I've had conversations with Stevie Ray [Vaughan] about this, that he absolutely loved Tommy—considered him an equal. Not, "I'm better than you." "We're all great at what we do, and Tommy's right up there with us all." It was almost verbatim. And was really saddened by his death. We were down in Memphis—that was only about two months before [Stevie Ray] died.

Joe [Walsh] was terrified of Tommy because he was so good. If you ever hear any stories, like Joe and he jammed together—bullshit. Joe wouldn't even let Barnstorm jam on stage—we'd get fined if we did, because Joe wasn't 'a jammer.' Tommy could plug into the oldest amplifier in the world, take a Silvertone guitar out of Sears-Roebuck, and make it sound like a fucking stack of Marshalls and a '56 vintage Strat. *He was that good.* And as a person, he was just a great guy. He'd treat you with the utmost respect. Never—unless it was warranted—did I hear him say a negative word about anybody. Music was his life, and if you treated him well, he treated you just the same. He was a wonderful person. An incredible player—if he was alive today, God only knows what would have come out of him. We got just 1/100th of one percent of his talent—that's what we got to hear.

Nicholas Simmons: A lot of people think he was the heir to the Hendrix throne.

Karen Ulibarri: In fact, it took me ten years to listen to his music again after he died. But I was able to be objective, and I listened to it, and I heard a musician that just blew my mind. Someone who was just so ahead of their time, and just so innovative and so talented, that I just said, "God, this guy was amazing!" And I took it for granted—I'd hear him play like that every day. God, I couldn't believe it—it was like hearing someone new and fresh for the first time. So I'm not surprised at all that his music still holds up today.

Barbara Bolin: He never bragged about himself. We really didn't know all the good things. Because . . . we'd read about them, but he was just himself, and he enjoyed himself when he came home. In fact, we all did. We still have kids come . . . ones we don't even know write letters and want to come and see us, and it's just been going on ever since he passed away.

Rick 'Pudge' Bolin: To me, Tommy was not only a brother—he inspired John and I to dedicate ourselves to music as a profession and not just a pastime. He was also one of the biggest influences in music in my life. It's hard to talk about one of your favorite guitar players when it's your brother.

Johnnie Bolin: As my brother, I loved him. He had great talent, and I miss him. I wish he could have been around—just like I do my younger brother. I think my mom and dad put in their time, but my younger brother and Tommy left way before their time. I remember him just what I got out of the 25 years. I think his music holds up real well. I listen to it, and I have other people listen to it. Even my son's friends—it's not "Smoke on the Water," they love "Post Toastee" and "Teaser"—whether it's by Tommy or Mötley Crüe.

Jeff Cook: The fact that Mötley Crüe has recorded "Teaser" four or five times says to me that the music has some merit, and some validity that younger generations of people would be interested in playing the music of Tommy.

Nikki Sixx: Tommy Bolin was an artist maybe only in line with a David Bowie. But unfortunately, he never achieved that level of success—he seemed to grow bored of his own styles before they had a chance to catch on or become vogue. He moved through musical phases quickly—jazz, fusion, rock, reggae, metal, and funk. He mixed these together frequently, as well. I never met the man and that saddens me, because I lived and breathed his music for many years, and it was—and is—a major influence on me, my music, my life. Whether his guitar was heard with the James Gang, Deep Purple, Billy Cobham, or on his solo L.P.'s, as I said, he was ahead of his time and sadly ahead of me ever meeting him.

Narada Michael Walden: Nat Weiss, who was a big helper with the Beatles, really came to his aid. And that's not small potatoes, man. I don't see anybody else walking around that Nat Weiss was going crazy for—besides John McLaughlin and Tommy Bolin. It was a very elite crowd. I knew that Tommy had to be a bad boy to be in that circle, and he was.

Joe Walsh: Tommy will always be to me a great guitar player, and a wonderful friend, and I miss him.

Mike Drumm: The James Gang—before they did their [reunion] tour about eight or nine years ago, they got together for the first time and played the Rock N' Roll Hall of Fame. Joe on stage or somewhere around those events was just going on and on about Tommy. There's radio broadcasts [with Joe] saying, "Tommy played rings around me—forget it. Couldn't even touch him."

Joe Walsh: He had brilliant technique . . . he could actually kind of play circles around me . . . but I think his music stands on its own, and I think he's just as valid today as he was back then.

Steve Vai: I was thirteen years old when a friend played me Billy Cobham's 'Spectrum' album. I was stunned. It was as though I was hearing something I had been craving. Up to that point, there was no guitar player that demonstrated such control, rock virtuosity, and sheer visceral passion. Here was an unequivocal guitar God. I couldn't understand why he wasn't on the tip of all musicians' tongues, but when stints with the James Gang, 'Bang,' etc. and finally Deep Purple came to be, the secret was out. Most people believe that a virtuoso's prime element is their speed. But to truly be considered elite, one must possess the honed qualities of technique, control, vibrato, tone, reaction, musical awareness, and perhaps the most important virtue, confidence. Tommy wielded these qualities into a fine audio elixir. And he made it sound simple. It's good to see more of his secrets being let out of the bag.

Jake E. Lee: [Badlands' song "Silver Horses" contains] a part which reminds me of Tommy Bolin—another of my heroes.

Mike Drumm: I met Vernon Reid four years ago—I was shooting the Warren Haynes Christmas Jam down in Asheville, North Carolina for Warren, and his wife was managing Living Colour, and wanted to introduce me to Vernon. So he's backstage sitting there—noodling on the guitar, looking at the floor—and I go, "Hey man, I've been president of the Tommy Bolin Archives." And he stopped cold, and looked right up to me, and was like, *"You're shitting me!"* Then he talked about how when he was fourteen or whatever, there was a fusion show in New York City, and they were playing the 'Spectrum' album, and that was *it*. What kicked Vernon Reid in the butt was Tommy Bolin.

Jimmy Haslip: I thought he was totally outrageous. He was really going for it and seemed to always strive to be a better musician. He would practice hard and frequently, listened to a lot of different music, and was very interested in pushing the musical envelope—as far as combining rock, jazz, and fusion music. I thought that it was a unique direction at the time. He was really involved with rock and blues obviously because he played with Deep Purple, the James Gang, and Zephyr. He also had an extreme interest in more the complex kind of music, which I was really into, like progressive rock. Groups like Yes, Gentle Giant, Soft Machine, U.K., Mahavishnu Orchestra, King Crimson, and Tony Williams Lifetime. In fact, we even did some dates with the Lifetime band. It was an interesting time in music for sure, and Tommy was definitely a standout as a guitarist at that time. As a musician, you felt that he was into exploring this 'exploratory genre,' and he was trying to experiment with things all the time. That was very appealing to me. I felt great about being involved with a musician that was totally open to experimenting with the music, and trying to explore a lot of different ways of expressing that music. Tommy was very inspiring to play with.

Karen Ulibarri: Tommy was a delightful, entertaining, ambitious boy-genius whose whole existence was absorbed with music. Writing, playing guitar and performing were his passions and he wanted to share that with the world. Tommy was also a recalcitrant brat, an egocentric, whose motto was, "Fuck 'em if they can't take a joke." He was also an incurable romantic, whose passion for living was lived to the fullest and in excess. But he was my first love and one never forgets their first love. I'll always cherish the memory that he was a little boy to the end.

Narada Michael Walden: Tommy I would like to be remembered as a noble and kind brother, who was a blues fanatic, and loved to pioneer—pushing on the edge of the boundary of life. And he did in his music every day. I'm just sorry that he tipped at the scale. However, all of us are here for not very long, and the mark he made is immeasurable. To all the great musicians that I know, they all speak very highly of Tommy. He'll be loved and revered forever, I'm sure. There's a sadness that comes along with it, because we want to be around for a long time. I mean, we all miss Jimi Hendrix. You think, "Damn man,

I'd love you to be around, so we could talk." I think that's the saddest part. I think he'll be remembered with love and kindness, because he was truly a noble person. It's very important to remember the good things, the kind things, and the remarkable things. Because there sure were lots of them.

John Tesar: I'll be 60 on my next birthday, and when I look back and say, "How many extraordinarily talented people did you know in your lifetime—people whose talent just overwhelms you?", you can count on one hand how many people have the capacity to sort of change culture. And Tommy's one of those people. He was *massively* talented.

Jeff Cook: Try as I might, I've tried to cultivate songwriting relationships with people since Tommy passed away, and I've never been able to find that kind of chemistry. So I realize how really special it was.

Charlie Brusco: A lot of musicians that I've been involved with have passed away. A number of them were really good friends. I don't know why, but Tommy is one that I always think about, that I still miss, and that I still go back and listen to his records. A couple of months ago, I pulled up his stuff on iTunes, and there's like three or four versions of "Alexis." It almost brought tears to my eyes. I think I remember sitting in a hotel room with him somewhere—with his legs crossed, his hair hanging down, and in a t-shirt—and he started playing that song for me. I just remember going, *"Holy shit,"* because I love that song. It was such a quick thing with him—he didn't get to finish what he started. I'd love to see young kids today pay attention to that stuff, because the stuff is so good. It deserves to be heard by a lot more people. The other thing was, Tommy was before MTV. With his looks and that whole package, if he had been during 'the MTV era,' God knows how big he would have been. But it just wasn't to be. Van Halen came right after that.

Jan Hammer: The whole package. Especially when he got his look together. He looked unique and he sounded totally, unbelievably unique. He could have been a major league icon. He was robbed of that . . . or he robbed himself of that.

L.C. Clayton: Smiling, playing music, and enjoying himself. That's where he enjoyed himself the most—playing music. At the time, with other things going on his life, that was the happiest part that he had. Getting high and shit—that's just a cover. But he enjoyed himself when he was one stage—he just lit up.

Max Carl: In the end, of course we all miss Tommy for what we had all collectively lost—no more the chance of being able to look across the stage at him, one hand on the Strat, one on the Echoplex, roaring and soaring.

Earl Johnson: I used to say that guitar players were a dime a dozen, and there were only so many great players like Beck and Page who took the guitar to different levels—'genius levels' I called them. Tommy was in that level, and a few more years would have showed that to the world.

Greg Hampton: I think a lot of great music or songs are timeless. But *his* particularly, he would meld so many genres and styles of music in one big melting pot, stir it up, and make it his own. That was to me the most inspiring and interesting part of Tommy Bolin's writing and presentation as an artist and guitar player. He was—in my opinion—better than Jimi Hendrix or really anybody else. I don't think any of these other guys can touch him—including Jeff Beck, Jimmy Page—when he was really *on*. The problem was, the live shows were so dodgy—he went back and forth because of his drug intake. It really affected that. In the studio though, you can turn the machine on and turn it off—still, it's the playing that stands out. It's not like it was any 'smoke and mirrors job,' he actually played all that stuff. It's still very fresh. I think it was way ahead of its time.

Johnnie Bolin: It's going to hold up—I think it's not going to go nowhere. It's not dated. A lot of it has to do with his playing. Technically, he was way ahead of his time. It shows when he plays on the 'Spectrum' stuff and with Alphonse Mouzon. It also shows by him playing "Savannah Woman" or "Bustin' Out for Rosey"—he doesn't have to do burning solos to know the guy had a lot of soul. His music is just 'of today.' Him being my brother has everything to do with it, but it has very little to do with what I think of his music. Just because he's related to me, doesn't mean I have to like it. But of course, I do.

Robert Ferbrache: 'Teaser' stands up like no other. That'll stand up forever—it still sounds fresh.

George Larvick: "Teaser" and "Homeward Strut"—they all have their flavor, they're not all duplicates of one kind of sound. They're all different and they're all fun to play. You can put that album on today as [with] any Van Halen album—people discover him every day. I have people call me from all over the country and want to know about Tommy. I always want to remember Tommy as the way he was—flamboyant. Tommy Bolin when I first met him—when he was twelve and a half years old—was the same Tommy Bolin at 25. Tommy's music stands up today. I mean, I've played music my entire life, and it's just as hard for me to play his music today as when he first recorded it.

Jimmy Haslip: I think he should be remembered as a visionary and an outstanding musician. A really wonderful human being. A very caring human being with a great sense of humor. An incredible musician that was willing to experiment with music—someone who had a lot to give, someone [with] interesting ideas and someone that was interested in contributing something truly innovative and special to the history of music. And leaving an important legacy—a life's lesson—for one and all to learn from.

Mark Stein: I thought he was a great guitar stylist. Definitely one of the innovative guys from his time. He left us way too soon. I think he would have gone on to become a major force in the music industry, especially from the guitar standpoint. He was definitely unique, he was smooth and silky—he could play with speed and taste. Obviously, he had a lot of problems that led to his demise. But I think under all that superficial crap, he was a very soulful guy and he was a very caring person. I just think he needed a lot of supervision at that time. If he would have had stronger supervision, it would have led him out of a lot of those unfortunate things he was involved with. He might have still been with us today. But who knows. As a person, I thought he was a really good guy. We were pretty good friends there for a while. We used to hang out a lot—I got to know him other than his 'influence' with the alcohol and the drugs. Underneath it all, he was definitely a good guy.

Carmine Appice: I think Tommy should be remembered as one of the laid back, great American guitar players. The key there is *American* guitar player, because there weren't a lot of American guitar players that went on to become guitar heroes in those days. It was mostly English—Jimmy Page, Jeff Beck, Eric Clapton, Ritchie Blackmore. Jimi Hendrix was American, but he made it in England, so he was conceived as a little bit of both. But Tommy was one of the guys that was hanging around and doing stuff, and went on to do big things as a guitar hero. I think he might be remembered as one of the American great guitar heroes.

Johnnie Bolin: I don't know where his guitar playing style came from. It's far different from anybody else's. I mean, Stevie Ray Vaughan plays great, but there's a lot of guys that kind of sound like him. I never heard a guitar player play like Tommy. He's got a different style.

Narada Michael Walden: He came along at a time when there really weren't that many rock guitar players that could understand off-meter, improvisation, and strange terrain—like seven, nine, eleven, thirteen. He wasn't like John McLaughlin, who was a pioneer of that stuff—he was bluesy and gutsy enough to pull off almost anything. And he was so respected because of working with Billy Cobham on 'Spectrum.' Tommy was really royalty. He was beloved by everyone. It's a great loss that he's not with us at this time, but his records still speak and live triumphantly. He was so far ahead of his time that nothing ever grows old.

Jeff Ocheltree: I spoke to Billy [Cobham] a lot about it. They didn't really become friends—they just didn't really communicate that much. I don't know why. Billy lived in New York, he lived in L.A. But he was proud of that record—he was blown away by Tommy's playing.

Tom Stephenson: Of course [Tommy mentioned wanting to work again with Cobham]. But again, Billy saw the drug thing. The same with Narada—they noticed a difference. You could hear it in his speech and [see it] in his face. It was like he was an empty shell. And they just said, "No, I couldn't do that." Yeah, they talked about that [Robert Plant and Tommy working together]—I know they talked about that, because I talked to Tommy about that. But it was one of those things where Tommy talked to a lot of people. But it was one step forward and five steps back because of the drugs. It was these grandiose ideas because he was so fucked up. His playing was effected by it—he wasn't the same player. He was better on a joint or nothing—on a lot of coke or heroin, you physically can't play. And that was the deal. He fucked it up.

Reggie McBride: Tommy was one of the greatest artists who had ever lived, and a hero of classic rock.

Dale Peters: He was really a great person. It's just the drugs destroyed him. And it's a shame, because he was a very nice guy, fun to be around, one of the best guitar players I've ever seen, an incredibly talented musician—and it just got all thrown away. Terrible shame. Tommy really could have been one of the great ones.

Jan Hammer: [Tommy's music] is as valuable and valid as when he first played it. Compared to all the guitar players that play by rote—they memorize a couple of blues licks, and that's it. They're not really inspired—it's just repetitive. His stuff was touched by magic—it was unreal. That totally holds up.

Jeff Cook: I would just like him to be remembered, and I'd like the music to be what people remember about it. I'd like the music to be able to stand. And one of the affirmations to me that we did write music of value and worth is that there still seems to be interest in Tommy—in both his solo career and his band careers. I think some of the songs could be covered and played. I'm hoping that musicians will continue discovering him as a player and as a writer. Because I think the writing skills that he had are vastly underrated—he was a really good composer of songs. The case could be made that the James Gang and Deep Purple's careers were somewhat faltering when Tommy joined them, and he ended up making records for them that were really high quality, solid records. So I think that's what's worth remembering about him, that he could step into any situation, and make something good out of it.

Bobby Berge: As a warm, caring, loving human being. Very outgoing, and the most easygoing guy that I've ever worked with. Of course, one of the most talented musicians—guitarist/songwriters—on the planet. But it was just so easy to work with him, because he never pressured you. He never demanded anything. He let you be you, and he would let you know if he wanted something—but he had a great way of putting it across. So it made you feel comfortable.

Robert Ferbrache: I was trying to think of an estimate how many times I saw him play, and the number 200 came up. That seemed a little much—but I know I saw him play well over 100 times. So somewhere in between there.

G. Brown: Like the best music, his stuff still resonates with people. Whenever I play [on the radio] "Savannah Woman," "Post Toastee," or any of those classics from 'Teaser' and 'Private Eyes,' I always get phone calls, and it's kind of split up—between people who knew him and love hearing it still, and people who never heard of him, but it still catches their ear. And it's always my pleasure to share the story. For those of us that lived here in Colorado, we legitimately thought he could be the next Hendrix. And he was really on his way to becoming a legend. It's sad that before he could prove it, he passed. 25 is way too young.

Johnnie Bolin: It was bad timing, too—'Private Eyes' got released in September, and he passed away in December. After that, they just kind of pulled the plug on it, until later on, when CD's came out. 'Private Eyes' is now certified gold— it ended up selling half a million records [certified in 2000]. I've got the plaque here. It sells better, because you can find it everywhere—'Teaser' is available only as an import. It's no longer 'the nice price' anymore, it's $22/$23.

Mike Drumm: Tommy was a one-man band. I always said if he had become big, he would have had a career the way Santana had it. You do the commercial record, and then you do a side project—jazz or whatever. And then all the world music stuff started coming in—there were all these directions he could have gone in. But he never got past 1976.

Mark Stein: I think he could have evolved into a real positive musical force, if the Devil didn't get a hold of him. But unfortunately, it did. God bless him.

Barry Fey: As a 16-year-old kid, walked in, picked up the guitar, and made everybody notice. Including Jerry Garcia. He said, "Look at this kid!" A big fan of Tommy's music was Jimi Hendrix—you can't get any better than that.

Jimmy Haslip: I always think of Tommy in a good light. I'll always remember Tommy as a joyous human being, and as a very talented guitarist, musician, composer, and singer. And I'll always remember him for his great sense of humor—his very personable, good-natured ways. I have a fond place for Tommy in my heart. He was the coolest!

Stanley Sheldon: As a true master for young guitar players. Generous in every way—especially musically. He just loved to give freedom to musicians in an improvisational manner. He loved to play with the most incredible musicians—that's what he got off on, because it made him play better. He liked that freedom that great players would give each other. Even when he died, we were still planning on getting back together.

Tom Stephenson: When [Tommy] went to New York to do that stuff with Cobham, *that's* the type of stuff he wanted to do—but all he really got to do was replace people. So he was 'the guy that stepped in.' Even his solo albums were not up to the standards of what Tommy really played like. I have live stuff that he played ten times better than he played on any of those records. I love a lot of those records, but he was just so drugged up and unhappy. He was such a good guy that he would give the shirt off his back to you. And people took advantage of him. After he died, he actually got more famous—which is really unfortunate.

Bobby Berge: I had heard that [Tommy] would always tell people that he loved the stuff with Energy, and had thoughts of going in that direction again. I don't know exactly what his plans were, but I remember him talking about the Energy type material.

Jeff Cook: I think one of the plans was again, to try and grow away from just being 'a rock star guitar player.' He was very interested in Indian music—not American Indian music, but Eastern Indian music. I think he was interested in experimenting with that. He was more and more drawn to jazz and that kind of music. Again, I'll say that I think if Tommy would have lived, he would have evolved into a jazz-fusion player of the highest magnitude. I always think about, "What would Tommy be like playing with Stanley Jordan, or with some of the other brilliant guitarists that have come along since Tommy's demise?" And I feel confident that he could have held his own with any of them. But that's something we'll never know.

Glenn Hughes: We talked for many hours—whether it was drug-fueled or not—about forming a new band after 'Private Eyes.' He died when he was 25. You don't get it, you don't understand when you're that young. He would say to me, "I'm going to die one day and leave a great looking corpse." But he shined brightly; and he was way ahead of his time. I believe firmly that we would have done something. But remember now, I was in the throes of my addiction, and I didn't even start my full-blown addiction yet. I was 'a baby user.' The fact of the matter is we were both addicted. If you would have had a normal Glenn and Tommy, we would have gone on to conquer the world. But we were so far gone in early-mid '70s Americana, where cocaine for me was like drinking whiskey today—it's normal. We were inured by our disease. But if we would've had a handle on our disease, we would have gone on to greatness. Tommy and I, as soon as we put our instruments on, shit happened. If you listened to any of the live stuff we did, *we were on fire*. We would have been a tremendous force. If Tommy Bolin was alive today, he may not even be playing guitar, he'd probably be playing something else. Because he was just way ahead of his time. Tommy would have been really avant-garde. Probably wouldn't have gone mainstream, he wouldn't have been like a Jeff Beck—Tommy would have been your 'Jeff Buckley' of the axe. He was a genius.

Karen Ulibarri: He was so ambitious. He wanted so badly to be heard—to say what he had to say. It's like he knew he wasn't going to have much time on this earth—he had so little time to do it. He lived and breathed music. He was just music—all around. Tommy typified music. Of anyone I know—musician or otherwise—he lived and breathed music. And that's what he was all about.

Johnnie Bolin: There's a great storyline to tell people through this book, and maybe a possible movie. I see 'La Bamba,' and I've talked to people out in L.A. A friend of mine is an actor, and I sat with him for two days for like five hours a day, and told him whatever stories I know. And he's going, "All you need are four really good stories—or five—to write a movie. And you've told us about 15!" And that's just me—there are other people's stories . . . these are just the ones *I* know as a brother. It's a real interesting tale to tell.

Discography

Albums:

Zephyr

Zephyr (1969, ABC)
"Sail On," "Sun's a Risin'," "Raindrops," "Boom-Ba-Boom/ Somebody Listen," "Cross the River," "St. James Infirmary," "Huna Buna," "Hard Chargin' Woman"

Going Back to Colorado (1971, Warner Brothers)
"Going Back to Colorado," "Miss Libertine," "Fades Softly," "Radio Song," "See My People Come Together," "Showbizzy," "Keep Me," "Take My Love," "I'll Be Right Here," "At This Very Moment"

Billy Cobham

Spectrum (1973, Atlantic)
"Quadrant 4," "Searching for the Right Door/Spectrum," "Anxiety/Taurian Matador," "Stratus," "To the Women in My Life/Le Lis," "Snoopy's Search/ Red Baron"

The James Gang

Bang (1973, ATCO)
"Standing in the Rain," "The Devil is Singing Our Song," "Must Be Love," "Alexis," "Ride the Wind," "Got No Time for Trouble," "Rather Be Alone with You (a.k.a. Song for Dale)," "From Another Time," "Mystery"

Miami (1974, ATCO)
"Cruisin' Down the Highway," "Do It," "Wildfire," "Sleepwalker," "Miami Two-Step," "Praylude," "Red Skies," "Spanish Lover," "Summer Breezes," "Head Above the Water"

Alphonse Mouzon

Mind Transplant (1974, Blue Note)

"Mind Transplant," "Snow Bound," "Carbon Dioxide," "Ascorbic Acid,"
"Happiness is Loving You," "Some of the Things People Do,"
"Golden Rainbows," "Nitroglycerine"

Moxy
Moxy (1975, Mercury)
"Fantasy," "Sail on Sail Away," "Can't You See I'm a Star," "Moon Rider,"
"Time to Move On," "Still I Wonder," "Train," "Out of the Darkness
(Into the Fire)"

Deep Purple
Come Taste the Band (1975, Warner Brothers)
"Comin' Home," "Lady Luck," "Gettin' Tighter," "Dealer," "I Need Love,"
"Drifter," "Love Child," "This Time Around/Owed to 'G'," "You Keep on
Moving"

Last Concert in Japan (1977, Warner Brothers)
"Burn," "Love Child," "You Keep on Moving," "Wild Dogs," "Lady Luck,"
"Smoke on the Water," "Soldier of Fortune," "Woman from Tokyo,"
"Highway Star"

Tommy Bolin
Teaser (1975, Nemperor)
"The Grind," "Homeward Strut," "Dreamer," "Savannah Woman," "Teaser,"
"People, People," "Marching Powder," "Wild Dogs," "Lotus"

Private Eyes (1976, Columbia)
"Bustin' Out for Rosey," "Sweet Burgundy," "Post Toastee," "Shake the
Devil," "Gypsy Soul," "Someday Will Bring Our Love Home," "Hello,
Again," "You Told Me That You Loved Me"

The Ultimate (1989, Geffen)
Disc One: "Sail On" (Zephyr), "Cross the River" (Zephyr), "See My People
Come Together" (Zephyr), "Showbizzy" (Zephyr), "Alexis" (The James
Gang), "Standing in the Rain" (The James Gang), "Spanish Lover" (The
James Gang), "Do It" (The James Gang), "Quadrant 4" (Billy Cobham),
"Train" (Moxy), "Time to Move On" (Moxy)

Disc Two: "Golden Rainbows" (Alphonse Mouzon), "Nitroglycerin" (Alphonse Mouzon), "Gettin' Tighter" (Deep Purple), "This Time Around/ Owed to 'G'" (Deep Purple), "You Keep On Moving"—live (Deep Purple), "Wild Dogs"—live (Deep Purple), "Dreamer" (Tommy Bolin), "People, People" (Tommy Bolin), "Teaser" (Tommy Bolin), "Sweet Burgundy" (Tommy Bolin), "Shake the Devil" (Tommy Bolin), "Brother, Brother" (Tommy Bolin)

From the Archives, Volume One (1996, Rhino)
"Wild Dogs" (acoustic demo), "Red Skies" (Energy—demo), "Evening Rain" (acoustic demo), "Sister Andrea" (Jeremy Steig—demo), "Heartlight" (Energy—demo), "Teaser" (acoustic demo), "You Know, You Know" (Tommy Bolin & Friends—live), "San Francisco River" (Tommy Bolin & Friends—live), "Meaning of Love" (acoustic demo), "Shake the Devil" (The Tommy Bolin Band—live), "Crazed Fandango" ('Teaser' outtake), "Jump Back" (acoustic demo), "Wild Dogs" ('Early L.A.' demo)

Whips and Roses (2006, SPV)
"Teaser," "Fandango," "Wild Dogs," "Cookoo," "Savannah Woman," "Marching Powder," "Flyin' Fingers," "Dreamer," "Just Don't Fall Down," "Blowin' Your Cookies"

Whips and Roses II (2006, SPV)
"The Grind," "Crazed Fandango," "People, People," "Homeward Strut," "Sooner or Later," "Bagitblues Deluxe," "Spacey Noodles," "Lotus," "Journey," "Bolin's Boogie," "Tommy's Got Da Blues," "Some People Call Me"

The Ultimate: Redux (2008, Friday Music)
Disc One: "Teaser" (acoustic demo, 1973), "Sister Andrea" (demo, 1971), "Cross the River" (Zephyr, live in Colorado, 1973), "Hard Chargin' Woman" (Zephyr, live in Colorado, 1973), "Red Skies" (Energy, 1972) "Heartlight" (Energy, 1972), "Hok-O-Hey" (Energy, 1972), "Got No Time for Trouble" (Energy, 1972), "Miss Christmas" (Energy, 1972), "Journey" (demo, 1973), "Alexis" (acoustic demo, 1973)

Disc Two:

"Standing in the Rain" (acoustic demo, circa 'Bang'), "Cucumber Jam" (early version), "Spanish Lover" (acoustic demo, circa 'Miami'), "Stratus" (live at Ebbet's Field, 1974), "Gettin' Tighter" (Tommy Bolin Tribute, Denver, 1997), "Homeward Strut" (live at Ebbet's Field, 1974), "Teaser" (live with Tommy Bolin Band), "Wild Dogs" (early L.A. demo version), "Dreamer" (early L.A. demo version)

Disc Three:

"People, People" (live with Tommy Bolin Band at Ebbet's Field, 1976), "Lotus" (live with Tommy Bolin Band at Ebbet's Field, 1976), "Savannah Woman" (demo), "Crazed Fandango" ('Teaser' outtake, 1975), "Sweet Burgundy" (acoustic demo from 'Naked II'), "Shake the Devil" (live in Albany, 1976), "Someday Will Bring Our Love Home" (acoustic demo from 'Naked I'), "You Told Me That You Loved Me" (live in Albany, 1976), "Post Toastee" (electric guitar demo from 'Naked I'), "Post Toastee" (live in Albany, 1976), "Slow Driver" (acoustic version from 'Naked I')

[Note: The Tommy Bolin Archives website has a large selection of Tommy Bolin CD's—containing rare and live material— for sale on their site]

Websites:

Tommy Bolin Archives—www.tbolin.com

Official Tommy Bolin Site—www.tommybolin.biz

Tommy Bolin Myspace—www.myspace.com/tommybolinbiz

Official Tommy Bolin Myspace—www.myspace.com/tommybolin

The Bolin Foundation—www.tommybolin.org

Friday Music—www.fridaymusic.com

Dean Guitars—www.deanguitars.com

Hartman Electronics—www.hartmanelectronicstore.com

Deep Purple Appreciation Society—www.deep-purple.net

Acknowledgments

I would like to thank everyone who helped with the creation of this book, especially Johnnie Bolin, Damian Phelan, Greg Hampton, John Herdt, Mike Drumm, Tamy Thomas Morgan, Simon Robinson, and Andrea Troiano.

Also, everyone that I interviewed—thank you for offering your Tommy memories and stories. And thanks to all the photographers who sent in great photos—Jamie Bateman, Johnnie Bolin, Ken Bowe, Robert Ferbrache, Richard Galbraith, David Givens, Wyndham Hannaway, Tamy Thomas Morgan, Marvin Rinnig, Jim Summaria, and Sean Vennett—it was much appreciated. And thanks to Linda Krieg for helping design the book, Lloyd J. Jassin for publishing advice, and Dave 'The Wolf' Kay for supplying some crucial help in the photocopy department.

And lastly, I would like to thank my patient wife Mary and all my friends and family, and I would absolutely like to offer a warm thanks to 'Big Michael' Prisciandaro.

Source Notes

Early Years/Iowa

Richard Bolin: "I told him . . . gave that up." (*"The Music Link's Tommy Bolin: The Ultimate Documentary"*)

Tommy Bolin: "I used to . . . wanted to do." ("Tommy Bolin Interview," Lowell Cauffiel, *Guitar Player*, March 1977)

Richard Bolin: "I took [Tommy] . . . best at something." (*"The Music Link's Tommy Bolin: The Ultimate Documentary"*)

Tommy Bolin: "I actually started . . . for two years." ("Tommy Bolin Interview," Lowell Cauffiel, *Guitar Player*, March 1977)

Tommy Bolin: "Then I went . . . like a piano." ("Tommy Bolin Interview," Lowell Cauffiel, *Guitar Player*, March 1977)

Tommy Bolin: "I started off . . . wasn't it, either." ("Tommy Bolin Interview," Lowell Cauffiel, *Guitar Player*, March 1977)

Richard Bolin: "He'd practice and . . . up with one." ("The Tommy Bolin Radio Special," reprinted in *'The Ultimate' box set booklet*)

Tommy Bolin: "It was a . . . every other year?" ("Why I Joined Deep Purple," Jeff Burger, *Creem*, November 1975)

Tommy Bolin: "Well, Django Reinhardt . . . were pretty basic." ("Tommy Bolin Interview," Lowell Cauffiel, *Guitar Player*, March 1977)

Tommy Bolin: "A lot of . . . step by step." ("Tommy Bolin Interview," Lowell Cauffiel, *Guitar Player*, March 1977)

Tommy Bolin: "My first joint . . . what it was." ("Footloose & Lawless: The Tommy Bolin Interview," Scott Cohen, *Circus*, November 10, 1976)

Tommy Bolin: "When you come . . . kids, and everything." ("Footloose & Lawless: The Tommy Bolin Interview," Scott Cohen, *Circus*, November 10, 1976)

Tommy Bolin: "The first time . . . I thought, *"No."*" ("Footloose & Lawless: The Tommy Bolin Interview," Scott Cohen, *Circus*, November 10, 1976)

Colorado

Tommy Bolin: "The turning point . . . having long hair." ("Road Trippin': The Deep Purple Mark IV Tour," Geoff Barton, *Classic Rock*, October 2003)

Barbara Bolin: "One day, [the . . . way it is." (*"The Music Link's Tommy Bolin: The Ultimate Documentary"*)

Tommy Bolin: "I got kicked . . . good bass player." ("Footloose & Lawless: The Tommy Bolin Interview," Scott Cohen, *Circus*, November 10, 1976)

Tommy Bolin: "After they kicked . . . a band there." ("Footloose & Lawless: The Tommy Bolin Interview," Scott Cohen, *Circus*, November 10, 1976)

Barbara Bolin: "I went and . . . faith in him." ("The Tommy Bolin Radio Special," reprinted in *'The Ultimate' box set booklet*)

Tommy Bolin: "One night, someone . . . bailed me out." ("Footloose & Lawless: The Tommy Bolin Interview," Scott Cohen, *Circus*, November 10, 1976)

Tommy Bolin: "I was doing . . . a little poodle." ("Footloose & Lawless: The Tommy Bolin Interview," Scott Cohen, *Circus*, November 10, 1976)

Tommy Bolin: "I've got arrested . . . over my ears." ("Footloose & Lawless: The Tommy Bolin Interview," Scott Cohen, *Circus*, November 10, 1976)

Zephyr

Tommy Bolin: "Uh, the group . . . I was fifteen." ("Radio interview on KMNS in Sioux City, Iowa," November 24, 1976)

Tommy Bolin: "We were like . . . psychedelic blues band." ("Road Trippin': The Deep Purple Mark IV Tour," Geoff Barton, *Classic Rock*, October 2003)

Karen Ulibarri: "Sure there was . . . any given situation." (*"The Music Link's Tommy Bolin: The Ultimate Documentary"*)

Zephyr II

Karen Ulibarri: "They were different . . . as recording was." (*"The Music Link's Tommy Bolin: The Ultimate Documentary"*)

Karen Ulibarri: "It turned sour . . . to go on." (*"The Music Link's Tommy Bolin: The Ultimate Documentary"*)

Legendary 4-Nikators/Jeremy Steig

Tommy Bolin: "So I left . . . kind of stuff." ("Road Trippin': The Deep Purple Mark IV Tour," Geoff Barton, *Classic Rock*, October 2003)

Tommy Bolin: "The way I . . . and Jan Hammer." ("Tommy Bolin Interview," Lowell Cauffiel, *Guitar Player*, March 1977)

Energy

Tommy Bolin: "I learned a . . . a beautiful player." ("Tommy Bolin Interview," Lowell Cauffiel, *Guitar Player*, March 1977)

Billy Cobham/Legendary 4-Nikators

Tommy Bolin: "It was really . . . me a lot." ("Tommy Bolin Interview," author unknown, *Melody Maker*, June 28, 1975)

Barbara Bolin: "Somebody like Billy . . . as he was." ("The Tommy Bolin Radio Special," reprinted in *'The Ultimate' box set booklet*)

Karen Ulibarri: "Quite honestly, it . . . was just brilliant." (*"The Music Link's Tommy Bolin: The Ultimate Documentary"*)

Tommy Bolin: "Cobham called me . . . every player has." ("Tommy Bolin Interview," Lowell Cauffiel, *Guitar Player*, March 1977)

Tommy Bolin: "The sessions with . . . before each take." ("Purple's Tommy Bolin: 'We're A Real Family Now!'," Dan Nooger, *Circus*, December 1975)

Karen Ulibarri: "I cannot believe . . . just blown away." (*"The Music Link's Tommy Bolin: The Ultimate Documentary"*)

Tommy Bolin: "'Spectrum' to me . . . thing with horns." ("Tommy Bolin Interview," author unknown, *Melody Maker*, June 28, 1975)

The James Gang

Tommy Bolin: "What the hell . . . instead of starving." ("Purple's Tommy Bolin: 'We're A Real Family Now!'," Dan Nooger, *Circus*, December 1975)

Karen Ulibarri: "To go from . . . James Gang albums." (*"The Music Link's Tommy Bolin: The Ultimate Documentary"*)

Tom Dowd: "Tommy was an . . . of his instrument." (*'The Ultimate' box set booklet*)

Tommy Bolin: "They were tight . . . explore other places." ("Why I Joined Deep Purple," Jeff Burger, *Creem*, November 1975)

Tommy Bolin: "I called my . . . say about that." ("Bolin Quits James Gang: Hopes to Rekindle Energy," Luce Endz, *Colorado Times*, September 1974)

Alphonse Mouzon/Los Angeles

Tommy Bolin: "I also did . . . minute too long." ("Tommy Bolin Interview," author unknown, *Melody Maker*, June 28, 1975)

Tommy Bolin: "I think the . . . a lead player." ("Tommy Bolin Interview," author unknown, *Melody Maker*, June 28, 1975)

Tommy Bolin: "I'd like to . . . writing a thing." ("Bolin Quits James Gang: Hopes to Rekindle Energy," Luce Endz, *Colorado Times*, September 1974)

Tommy Bolin: "I don't know . . . New Orleans stuff." ("Tommy Bolin Interview," author unknown, *Melody Maker*, June 28, 1975)

Tommy Bolin: "I want the . . . to see us." ("Bolin Quits James Gang: Hopes to Rekindle Energy," Luce Endz, *Colorado Times*, September 1974)

Moxy/'Teaser'/Deep Purple

Tommy Bolin: "When Purple first . . . much Deep Purple." ("Why I Joined Deep Purple," Jeff Burger, *Creem*, November 1975)

Tommy Bolin: "I was very . . . ever been better." ("Road Trippin': The Deep Purple Mark IV Tour," Geoff Barton, *Classic Rock*, October 2003)

Karen Ulibarri: "I think it . . . money and ran." (*"The Music Link's Tommy Bolin: The Ultimate Documentary"*)

Tommy Bolin: "It's an ideal . . . a new band." ("Deep Purple Roaring with Bolin in Blackmore Chair," Steve Case, *Billboard*, 1975)

Ritchie Blackmore: "Tommy Bolin is . . . with them, 'Stormbringer.'" ("Road Trippin': The Deep Purple Mark IV Tour," Geoff Barton, *Classic Rock*, October 2003)

Ritchie Blackmore: "I just didn't . . . brash, demanding band." ("Road Trippin': The Deep Purple Mark IV Tour," Geoff Barton, *Classic Rock*, October 2003)

Tommy Bolin: "I consider myself . . . players each time." ("Why I Joined Deep Purple," Jeff Burger, *Creem*, November 1975)

Tommy Bolin: "I really love . . . and "Wild Dogs."" ("Interview with 7HO radio, Melbourne, Australia," interviewer unknown, November 26, 1975)

Tommy Bolin: "I think I . . . 3rd in Munich." ("Tommy Bolin Interview," author unknown, *Melody Maker*, June 28, 1975)

Tommy Bolin: "I love that . . . do the lyrics." ("Interview with 7HO radio, Melbourne, Australia," interviewer unknown, November 26, 1975)

Tommy Bolin: "Jon and Glenn . . . my half 'Win.'" ("Life Without Ritchie," Dave Thompson, *Goldmine*, October 9, 1998)

Tommy Bolin: "I think they're . . . Highly. Very highly." ("Road Trippin': The Deep Purple Mark IV Tour," Geoff Barton, *Classic Rock*, October 2003)

Tommy Bolin: "Nothing's going to stop me now." ("Purple's Tommy Bolin: 'We're A Real Family Now!'," Dan Nooger, *Circus*, December 1975)

Deep Purple II

Karen Ulibarri: "He always had . . . just engulfed him." (*"The Music Link's Tommy Bolin: The Ultimate Documentary"*)

Tommy Bolin: "It's about junk . . . when you don't." ("Purple's Tommy Bolin: 'We're A Real Family Now!'," Dan Nooger, *Circus*, December 1975)

Tommy Bolin: "That was the . . . watching everybody swim." ("Radio interview on KMNS in Sioux City, Iowa," November 24, 1976)

Tommy Bolin: "For a first . . . each other out." ("Deep Purple Roaring with Bolin in Blackmore Chair," Steve Case, *Billboard*, 1975)

Tommy Bolin: "He fell down . . . could hardly play." (Untitled, David Rensin, *Rolling Stone*, February 26, 1976)

Tommy Bolin: "If someone yells . . . to the audience." ("Purple's Tommy Bolin: 'We're A Real Family Now!'," Dan Nooger, *Circus*, December 1975)

Karen Ulibarri: "Again, it was . . . it after that." (*"The Music Link's Tommy Bolin: The Ultimate Documentary"*)

Solo Tour/'Private Eyes'

Karen Ulibarri: "Well that was . . . pressures were phenomenal." (*"The Music Link's Tommy Bolin: The Ultimate Documentary"*)

Bill Graham: "Dear Tommy: Sorry . . . You're a winner." (*'The Ultimate'* box set booklet)

Tommy Bolin: "Well, I went . . . it all up." ("Radio interview on KMNS in Sioux City, Iowa," November 24, 1976)

Tommy Bolin: "Well, it gets . . . speaks for itself." ("Radio interview on KMNS in Sioux City, Iowa," November 24, 1976)

'Private Eyes' Tour II

Tommy Bolin: "We start the . . . Mac in February." ("Radio interview on KMNS in Sioux City, Iowa," November 24, 1976)

Tommy Bolin: "Tomorrow being turkey . . . or four years." ("Radio interview on KMNS in Sioux City, Iowa," November 24, 1976)

Rick 'Pudge' Bolin: "He was boarding . . . *'I'm never late.'*" (*'The Ultimate'* box set booklet)

Reaction

Karen Ulibarri: "There are so . . . your own conclusions." (*"The Music Link's Tommy Bolin: The Ultimate Documentary"*)

Joe Walsh: "I just remember . . . around and saluting." ("The Tommy Bolin Radio Special," reprinted in *'The Ultimate'* box set booklet)

Richard Bolin: "We cried for . . . too." I stopped." (*"The Music Link's Tommy Bolin: The Ultimate Documentary"*)

Tommy

Karen Ulibarri: "In fact, it . . . holds up today." (*"The Music Link's Tommy Bolin: The Ultimate Documentary"*)

Barbara Bolin: "He never bragged . . . he passed away." ("The Tommy Bolin Radio Special," reprinted in *'The Ultimate'* box set booklet)

Rick 'Pudge' Bolin: "To me, Tommy . . . it's your brother." (*'The Ultimate'* box set booklet)

Nikki Sixx: "Tommy Bolin was . . . ever meeting him." (*'The Ultimate'* box set booklet)

Joe Walsh: "Tommy will always . . . I miss him." ("The Tommy Bolin Radio Special," reprinted in *'The Ultimate'* box set booklet)

Steve Vai: "I was thirteen . . . of the bag." (*"The Ultimate: Redux" CD booklet*)

Jake E. Lee: "[Badlands' song "Silver . . . of my heroes." ("The Two Jakes," Alan Paul, *Guitar World*, September 1991)

Karen Ulibarri: "Tommy was a . . . to the end." (*'The Ultimate'* box set booklet)

Karen Ulibarri: "He was so . . . was all about." (*"The Music Link's Tommy Bolin: The Ultimate Documentary"*)

Printed in Great Britain
by Amazon

19848243R00153